For DAYMS where I learned to love theatre and the people
who make it. To The Olympia, where I learned good theatre.
To the IDGTF which completed my theatrical identity. To
the audiences who share that love, and whose support makes
theatre possible, and to you, I dedicate this book.

First published by The International Dublin Gay Theatre Festival Ltd on May 1st 2013 in a limited edition of 500 copies of which this book is number: 368

Oscar (sits in the nursery and speaks to Bridget, the Nanny) "the best way to make children, Bridget, is to make them happy". He sings to his two sons, Cyril and Vivian and is joined by Constance:

Chorus:
So tonight you'll be 'The Happy Prince' , and you will be his friend,
'The Swallow' who, helps children to, our story's happy end,
And tomorrow in our story, the roles will be reversed,
So by Swallow's flight or Happy Prince, I know I'm truly blessed

Verse 1:
The little swallow flew through the darkened lanes, and he saw little children hungry and in pain,
Living in blackened streets, shabbily clad, poor little children, hungry and sad,
Under the arch of a bridge were two boys, shivering, how their tummies, rumbled with noise,
"We're hungry", they cried, arms together in fear, shouted, the Watchman "You can not stay here"

Chorus

Verse 2:
The little swallow told what he saw to the Prince, the Happy Prince was so distressed, "It doesn't make sense.
I am covered in gold, take it off, leaf by leaf, give it to my poor and put an end to their grief"
The little swallow did what was asked by the Prince, the children in this distant land, have been happy ever since,
Riches ly within a heart that is free, the Prince loved little children, who sleep now peacefully.

Chorus:
So tonight, you've been a Happy Prince, and you have been his friend
The Swallow who, helped children to, our story's happy end
And tomorrow in our story, the roles will be reversed,
So by swallow's flight or Happy Prince, I know I'm truly blessed
By my sons now sleeping peacefully, I know I'm truly blessed

Written and composed by Brian Merriman for 'A Chelsea Affair' 17/5/2000
Music arranged by David Wray.

Acknowledgement

The International Dublin Gay Theatre Festival was founded in Dublin, Ireland in 2004, on the 150th anniversary of the birth in the city of Oscar Wilde. The event was the brainchild of Brian Merriman, theatre producer and director, writer, singer, actor. By 2013 had surpassed its 2000th performance. The IDGTF is the biggest and acknowledged by many, as the best international gay theatre event in the world. Here is a first-hand account of what influenced its evolution and its emergence in Dublin and how it progressed in its first eventful decade.

"I encountered so many generous volunteers who shared the ambition to consolidate the identity of gay people in the arts and culture of a nation, where they share citizenship. I met so many creative artists, wordsmiths, performers, technicians, analysts and promoters, some who have inspired anecdotes here and many who contributed to the raising the standard of this fringe event on the Irish theatre calendar.

My recollections are as emotional and partisan as anyone who looks from the inside out. Therefore may not always be accurate or shared, as sometimes when I hear other recollections I comment 'Did I really do that, or is that how it happened?'. This book will definitely be more an account of my perspective than actual fact, because I am too close to it. If anyone is offended by this, then please accept my apologies. One does not attempt to record over 2,000 performances, countless incidents (many unpublishable!) and dramas, and claim to be correct or at times even fair, especially when they were personalised. I acknowledge my considerable flaws, but in creating a record, no one should think ill of anyone mentioned in this memorial of a hectic, emotional, decade of trying to define what is gay culture and where and how gay theatre emerges as a valid artform?

Be kind in your reading, as I have tried to be kind in my memories, that will do some justice to the subjects of the commentary. I am grateful to the Festival for its support in publishing this book, with the resources that have matched the development of the event over the past ten years! My sincere thanks to everyone, mentioned and omitted, who played a positive role in reaching this decade of gay theatre.

It is clear, I have a clear transformative ambition for the Festival that is not matched in anyway by its capacity. However, you must actually begin a conversation in order to engage, listen and be heard. In exploring this unique Festival's first decade, this book traces the developments of a small theatrical event, which hoped to assert a visibility and value for gay arts and artists, in the broader theatrical community and in wider society. Its success will be determined by its impact on others and should not be adjudicated from afar by those who made no contribution to its evolution, as so often befalls theatre and advocacy". The dramatization begins with a prologue, and develops into two acts with an interval and an epilogue as follows.

chapter 1

Identity and Society

There were hard hours on our journey and often we sailed against the wind

Senator Edward Kennedy, Democratic Convention 1980.

In this book and in the title of the International Dublin Gay Theatre Festival, about which I write, I use the word 'gay' inclusively. I decided from the beginning that good theatre required truth. Truth has a name and the self-labelling by gay people, by taking the word for 'happiness' and 'fun' and imposing it on a love that was constructed to be lonely, depraved and isolated, was in itself a radical act of defiance. Similar achievements are noted in the fight for Black and ethnic minority rights, where they took back the insults and remade them into badges of honour.

When I was a young journalist in the 'Waterford News & Star' in 1979, I had to do the historical media column '50 years ago this week' and spotted a 1950s New Year's Eve dinner dance advertisement that encouraged the good Waterfordians to 'Go Gay at Dooley's Hotel this New Year! I don't think it quite turned out like that!

The Festival would celebrate the rainbow, but would not hide behind its code. It would equally not initialise the identity – no LGBTQI – which only the more radical elements of the 'community' understand anyway. Many advocates differ on language, while the core issues slip away – ours was to be a simple one - we were 'gay', inclusive, and that was that!

I made several attempts to discover who I was, to relate myself to my surroundings, to fit in and belong. Born in a society that gave me no accurate reference points, by virtue of its laws, and dominant religion, all of which were reflected in the limited media available in Ireland of the 1960s – it was a voyage of discovery and contradiction. I had my 'life book' written at an early age, and gradually I realised it was not to be as planned, by an idealistic, conformist, youngster.

By the time I recognised myself, I knew further work had to be done, to catch up on my own wasted life opportunities in this time consuming search. The added challenges of 'you never told me' failed to take into account, it was difficult to find out in the first instance, in an invisible society. It is difficult to accept oneself, especially in an atmosphere of insistence of shame and encouragement of concealment, perpetuated everywhere, despite its many victims. It is often easier to confront these challenges by tackling broader issues through work, other than personal ones, through courage. In an effort to place myself, I decided to try to examine those societal negatives, endured by all gay people, deliberately, legally constructed, especially from 1885 to 1993. This was a reluctant and challenging journey of exploration into a doubtful dawn, where the light of change, was only beginning to glimmer, in a narrow minded Ireland.

I truly admire the pioneers who came to that realisation, far earlier than I did, in America, through 'Stonewall', and in Ireland, with the search for human rights through the hostile Courts. Those achievements are frequently forgotten, because they are not taught. Ireland's faults as a State and it's failings of equal citizenship, are not on the school curriculum. We are not good at being honest, and are much more comfortable with invented sentimentality.

Ireland stood convicted of a violation of human rights in the David Norris case in 1988. This was added to a litany of societal failures by the new Republic, which let down gay people, children, the Magdalen women, single mothers, minority religions, people with disabilities, Travellers and many other minorities, who were second class citizens of a 'republican' society, that still yearns for what it calls 'traditional values'. Violating human rights is not a 'traditional value' that any society should romanticise or seek to return. Violation of human rights ensures only one thing – the maintenance of unearned privilege at the cost of an equal, inclusive society.

It is important to remember. It is difficult to remember now, what you had never recognised, accepted or been taught in the past. If you can't remember, then it is important to research and learn.

Gay people were not born into their own culture. That has been deliberately erased and eradicated. It still is the case in many countries. The emerging gay identity in a young person, must first find its own reference points to know they fit in. Too often, their first port of call is the negative, constructed stereotype or the commercially exploitative, gay ghetto that thrives in the anonymity of larger cities, offering a fake welcome to the young rural gay, taking his or her unaccompanied, tentative steps towards harsh, self-realisation.

In Ireland, generations of kids never had the journey into adolescence explained to them – the 'facts of life' - but life somehow stumbled on. This 'secrecy' meant that those who were responsible to instruct you, adults, could create shame or curious mystery. In secrets, 'dark things' can happen to children, especially when the trusted parents absolve themselves of the responsibility of enlightenment and vest that in the religious. It was deliberate. I was so fortunate that my family were particularly well placed in my local community not to have been exposed to any such danger. Ireland in emerging from British control in 1922, walked directly into the control of the only other form of organised 'government' that existed, that of the Roman Catholic Church, replacing British aristocracy with its Papal princes and local dignitaries.

I had a good, but equally 'ignorant' childhood, like most young Irish Catholics of the 1960s and before. Catholic adults did know something about sexuality, but it could not be spoken about in many homes. Women were to be burdened by the responsibility to manage it, as men were 'incapable' of responsibility or control. "Its 99% the woman's fault" declared my shorthand and typing teacher to my journalism class in 1978. Her devotion to Padre Pio, was an even more discussed topic, in a State funded third level institution, than sexual rights, interspersed with a mantra that held women entirely responsible for sexual outcomes! That culture of secrecy and embarrassment offers the perfect shield to those who would do harm to the vulnerable and innocent in earlier years. Society was complicit in consigning human love 'into the shadows', where no one can really see what is going on. It was a plan that destroyed the capacity of many Irish people, straight and gay, to live loving lives in the twentieth century.

Today, gay and other different people stand upon the generous legacy of those who allowed their lives to be invaded by law, church and media, so that ours could remain somewhat private and free. The treatment of the Cloney family in Fethard-on-Sea, teacher, Eileen Flynn in New Ross, The Magee case, David Norris, The X case, Lydia Foy, and Katherine Zappone and Anne Louise Gilligan from my childhood to middle age, are testimony to the Irish voyeuristic nature, which must be the first thing satisfied, in the pursuit of justice.

Edmund Lynch's film documentary 'Did Anyone Notice Us?' of LGBT life in the 1980s shows a TV journalist ask a gay man 'was he sick'? Programmes like this also denied me of any reference point. I was young and healthy, so I knew he could not be me! Just like today, society continues to insist on people who were assigned the incorrect gender identity at birth, now must get a 'diagnosis' of having a 'disorder' to absolve the imperfections of our birth registration system. This is society's way of excusing its own blindness or flaws. Because of the actions of others, in assigning (innocently) what they thought was the correct gender at birth, and of course its regulation, it means original assigned gender identity remains immovable, without extreme personal sacrifice, courage and effort. The issue is a societal one, that can only be remedied by the insistence of some form of 'self-confessed deviance' like a gender identity disorder? The confusion of gender identity with sexual orientation has also added to the insecurity of emerging young gay teenagers, as it does with the confusion of same sex attraction with adult-child exploitation.

I knew my own gender. I like it. It suits me. I am secure in it, but found myself in a battle with societal norms, which demeaned my gender if I was gay, and devalued my masculinity, by virtue of the 'feminine' or 'butch' stereotype constructed to justify lesser treatment of gay men and women. Even in theatre, gay artists would often be referred to as the 'boys' a term particularly used for male dancers. Boys are not men. Gay artists were not men – boys have a subjective status to men.

There are no 'facts of life' books that explain this. There is nothing to use as reference points for gay adolescents? During my time as Vice President of the National Youth Council of Ireland in the early 1980s, we wanted to include very basic sex education information in a Guide for students and young people. This was bitterly fought internally at the time, and indeed in the State grant application process to publish the book. Coincidentally SpunOut.ie faces a similar challenge in satisfying partial State funding thirty years later after its advice on threesomes irked the very conservative parliamentarian Michelle Mulherin from Fine Gael.

The 'controllers' of young people in the 1980s – youth organisations, many with a religious ethos, deliberately kept young people ignorant of one of the most dominant pressures in their lives. When you keep youth ignorant, you empower the adult who pretends to hold the knowledge and teasingly offers enlightenment. This had disastrous consequences for some young people in Ireland. The notion that religion and sexuality were co-located is nonsense. The expression of sexuality was excluded from religious ministry. Sexuality is now being prized above all other religious teachings and is driving people needlessly away from the Institutions that dominated their childhood and moral formation.

Today especially, though not exclusively in rural Ireland, too many straight parents still abandon their gay kids to struggle on alone. Their search for identity completeness, which every adolescent encounters, as they seek to establish the safe parameters of their future adulthood and independence, is the first and cruel cut of the family ties. Some parents totally fail their gay kids. Many more do not.

When I completed my disconnected, dark and emotionally tortuous journey of self-realisation in the 1980s, further confused by my genuine love and admiration for women, I became angry. It remains a righteous anger. I was mainly angry with myself. I, who challenged political fidelity and religious teaching from an early age, had automatically accepted internally, the negative construction imposed on, who I was to be. With it, I had accepted the real intent of punitive law and bigoted religious instruction. Such law imprisoned few physically, because psychologically it captures many more, beyond the few who were caught and publically shamed and imprisoned. Repressive law cements and underpins ignorance and dominance. It sends a bullying message by constructing a 'shame' that doesn't actually exist.

There can be no shame in consensual adult love. It's what humans have a capacity to do well and sets us apart in this world, apparently. In that negative shameful construction, religion and politics are collaboratively one.

Theatre is a powerful educational tool in society when such grave untruths and mischief abound. The construction of real characters and diverse lives, enriches the scope of ideas to create new and relevant plays. How could we as gay people, shake our chapter of life's book out onto the table, to advance this enlightenment, needed at the beginning of the twenty first century? That was the first challenge of a Gay Theatre Festival in an emerging modern Ireland. The opportunity was to come through an economic depression, the exposure of a morally corrupt and criminal church and the implosion of the politics of favour to think anew about old 'values'. At difficult times like this, the opportunity to worry about other peoples' lives diminishes and people concentrate on their own real needs and challenges, wishing others well in their personal struggles.

The skill and courage of the early gay rights advocates is exceptional, in teaching, changing the perception and broadening the inclusivity of citizenship. Their achievement goes way beyond the subject of their initial advocacy – it challenges 'norms' on behalf of all who are excluded.

Much credit in Ireland is deservedly centred around the Festival's first patron, the magnanimous David Norris. He is the first to point out, his was a public face of a small but wider group, who built and won the battle with him. Their openness helped to build a better society that could include more people in a decent pluralist democracy. A pluralist society is the right and expectation of any citizen of a civilised democracy. Those David Norris upset along his way, waited a long time for him in the 'long grass' and repaid him in his ill-fated 2011 Presidential campaign, for teaching Ireland to honestly acknowledge and respect the diversity of sexuality. Of course David is a Protestant and got some space to be heard as some Catholics didn't expect a member of the Church of Ireland to have any morality in the first instance! How wrong he has proved them all. His generosity of spirit in supporting us and all LGBT works is as fresh and sincere today as when he set out on his journey of liberty decades ago. He was the first to support us in our ambitious work and we are truly grateful.

The International Dublin Gay Theatre Festival was not an event designed for a minority, it was for our society. We were to be out and open. 'Don't attend because it is gay theatre, attend because it is good theatre' was an initial catchphrase. Most of our pioneering volunteers were not theatrical, but they too saw the potential for using theatre as an artform to educate, assert, pluralise and enjoy. At times, they struggled with my positioning of the event in mainstream theatres, rather than in gay venues, for launches etc. I insisted on the primacy of its theatrical identity. Here was a sector known for its gay artists, but still rarely credited the art with the complete identity of the artist. That was the first port of call. We must be fully recognised in the sector we are known in, in order for all our stories to be liberated through drama, music, comedy and dance. I did also bring theatre directly to the gay venues in the programming scheduled each year and that was right, but the context was first and foremost, to be visible in mainstream theatre and engage society in what I continually would promote as, an intercultural dialogue.

It is interesting to note the difficulty in getting some bigger theatres to allow us to launch the event, and often at a rental cost, we could ill afford. However, it was one of the many areas where perseverance paid off and Andrews Lane Theatre, The Gate Theatre and The Gaiety Theatre kindly opened their doors to us over the years.

We also pushed the link between theatre, the Irish identity and Oscar Wilde. The Boston College, in the home of Oscar Wilde was always 'booked out' no matter how long or flexible our notice of our intended launch date was in advance? This was not to be a unique experience.

The Mansion House, and its successive occupants, demonstrated a sincere welcome and an acknowledgement of our citizenship, which made us proud to be making our artistic contribution in Dublin City. It is symbolic with its association with the first Dail (Irish Parliament) and all its ambitions for a republic of equals, a theme I was to use to our advantage some years later. In our tenth anniversary year, the Dublin City Gallery which houses the studio of renowned gay artist Francis Bacon, welcomed our launch to its beautiful premises and hosted our first lunchtime performances there. This was another proud connection and link for the Festival to the wider Irish gay artistic legacy that reaches out to so many.

Some of those who 'allowed us' our gay identity, then worked to ensure we could not graduate to a valid 'theatre' identity, as we are still 'on the margins'. This is despite our work for new writing, building new audiences and creating employment in the arts in Ireland – allegedly a shared agenda in the Irish arts world? Things are not apparently shared, if it impinges on established ownership and control. This struggle to claim our own portion of the art-form and to share our perspective on theatrical citizenship was to be the inspiration of much co-operation and some opposition, throughout our first decade.

I, through a slow process of 'self-recognition', knew other people who could contribute a lot to a broader artistic debate. Debate can not begin in isolation. I had identified that LGBTI identity was a story source that could infuse the arts, long considered, a bit too generously, to be a home for gay people. It was a home, provided they remained behind the scenes or strictly behaved themselves when the neighbours called! This time, I thought we could become the scenes – scenes of a new truth in Irish and international theatre.

It was time for 'reference points' to be more visible in the arts. It was time to tell our truth openly and dialogue with mainstream society. I did not have a monopoly on this truth, so it would need many artists to make this a viable ambition. So the 'Dublin Gay Theatre Festival' (honoured to be among many far more excellent advocacy campaigns, projects, events and services) was born in 2004. It was time to turn the lights on full – but would the stage be bare?

Thus we began a theatrical activity, which I hoped would inspire playwrights, actors, academics and audience. The absence of resources was laughable and remains so a decade later. The incomplete nature of our own definition was embryonic in 2004. It had to start somewhere and the irony of doing so in the last country in Western Europe to decriminalise same sex relationships in 1993, was not lost on me. But to Irish society's credit, once the 'controllers' were exposed as a sham, Ireland quickly liberated itself from its hypocritical sexual shackles and many included gay people in the progress of a modern Ireland.

What was gay theatre? To some it was 'what's your problem – you are all legal now?' It was apparently a 'problem' to want to be seen and heard in your own society? To others it was 'Theatre is gay anyway - we all know that'. To some gay artists it was "I don't want you or need you to out me". "I don't want to be known as a gay artist". And to other gay artists it was a distinct "This is my domain (or I wish I had thought of that!)". To us it was a collaborate effort to scope out our place in theatre and our place in the achievement of the arts in culture and in building a more progressive society.

My definition of gay theatre was to include 'works by a gay author, or that have a gay character, theme or relevance, such as feminism, masculinity or gender identity'. It was broad and included all artforms, that could be presented in a theatre, drama, comedy, dance, music, opera, drag, play readings and academic arts discussion. It must include the stories of LGBTQI citizens worldwide, so that we can trace and establish our common gay culture.

In the hectic early days of innovation, it initially slipped my notice that I had founded this in an anniversary year – that of the 150th anniversary of the birth in Dublin of Oscar Wilde. My first introduction to him, in a serious way, had been in the centenary of his death in 2000, when I played him in the world premiere of 'A Chelsea Affair'.

This world premiere musical play ran for a month in Dublin in 2000 written by Steve Gavin and Gerry Gallivan, who collaborated with others. Its first draft was a bit like 'The Importance of being Oscar' by Micheal Mac Liammoir in 1960 - everything central to the plot remained unwritten and indeed in the first draft, I don't think Oscar and 'Bosie' his destructive young lover, ever met indoors! However, with a lot of work, re-writes which I actively contributed, and a generous investment by Gavin, the musical premiered in the THEatre space off Henry Street in the summer of 2000.

I managed to persuade Adele King to play Lady Wilde and accordingly wrote up the role of this pivotal Wexford woman and mother. Gay men may do a lot of things people disapprove of, but often the only approval that matters is that of one's mother. King's talents are often confined to the created persona of 'Twink' – that pays the bills! She is truly a gifted, passionate and intelligent actress, of whom far too little has been seen, as the lure of more popular commercial entertainment, sustained a career in a sector that does few favours for women. Neil Watkins was emerging in theatre at the time and made a perfect, blonde, handsome arrogant, young 'Bosie', and Mark Pollard, a loyal friend in 'Robbie Ross'.

It was a stellar cast for a production with modest resources that ran for a month. The late Gerry Colgan of the 'Irish Times', a critic always generous enough to allow the play performed dominate his reviews, was positive in his reception. He even liked the song I wrote for the piece 'The Happy Prince'. The only time I had heard of Wilde as a child was when I found a book of his short stories and my father commented 'there could be nothing wrong with a man who wrote stories like that'. I hadn't a clue what was 'wrong' with him in the first place, of course. But I remembered the description well.

The research required in the re-writing of the show, spurred an interest in me about the man whose gift for language, ultimately resulted in giving society a language at last, in which it could discuss or refer to, gay life and take it out of the shadows. The language was dark and shameful, but at least it was a language. I collect early edition Wilde' books and I found inscribed in pencil on the fly leaf of a 1905 edition of 'De Profundis', dated that year 'if I return again, may my sperm not be that of an Englishman' by one owner. In fact, the custodians of these early editions and Robbie Ross, his first serious lover, are largely the reason the works survive.

Robbie Ross was laughed at when he pressed his literary executorship of Wilde's estate after his death. He was given it unopposed as it was felt the legacy of such a shameful man, was worthless. A smug society soon realised the potential of turning a profit, as Wilde's plays continued to be produced, without an author's credit, so the chattering classes could laugh in comfort at his sharp and critical witticisms, while ignoring the author and his fate at the hands of their laws.

I always hear his voice in 'Lady Bracknell'. Bracknell was the name of the family home of Bosie's (his lover Lord Alfred Douglas) mother, the rather courageous Lady Queensbury. I imagine Wilde 'well oiled' at the end of a dinner party and getting camper by the minute, intoxicated with the attention of the gathering and 'firing on all cylinders' to the hilarity of the room, (unkindly imitating Lady Queensbury). I've seen gay people do that, I think I do it, hopefully to the entertainment of those gathered. In fact, humour and wit was an essential, if one was to be tolerated in society and has remained a prerequisite for social acceptance to this day.

Gate Theatre founder, Englishman, Micheal Mac Liammoir also adopted a bit of this larger than life persona of Wilde, as many an actor has imitated since. It implies class and intellect and the pace of conversational delivery emphasises that point, as does the deliberate broadening of vowels. So from Wilde's cruel, public fate, we at least had the acknowledgement, that the gay circumstance exists, as it was 'proven' in Court.

Wilde was condemned as much by his own vanity and his nationality, than by his behaviour, in a very deviant Victorian society. In a typically Irish fashion, he committed the only sin there is – he was caught.

Bosie's father, Lord Queensbury, some claim, had failed to 'out' the Jewish, Prime Minister, Lord Ropesberry near the end of the 19th century. He was apparently having an affair with his parliamentary secretary, the Viscount Drumlanrig (Queensbury's son) and it all ended, when the latter blew his head off in a solo hunting 'accident', having been forced to announce his engagement. Not having learned the lesson of the loss of a son through suicide, Queensbury then pursued self-justification, by finally finding his victim in the vanity of Wilde. It remains a wonderful contradiction of course, that Bosie who was present in Court during the three trials, was never charged or sentenced along with Wilde. He later married and did serve time for libel - his bitter tongue finally leading to his societal downfall.

Wilde's circumstance gave us the language, that could be spoken or whispered, that kept our sexuality visible. The image of a lonely, fallen from grace, characterisation of all ostracised gays, (contradicted by Vincent O Sullivan's memoirs which record Wilde as having many a good time in Paris after his release) emanates from Wilde's imprisonment and later desolate writings. That became a vivid image of gay life and an inevitable outcome for generations of excluded gay men and women.

Gate Theatre co-founder Micheal Mac Liammoir may have repaid the racial 'debt', by coming to Ireland as an Englishman and creating the visibility through myth, impossible for any Irishman to do, in a clergy ridden country of the mid 20th century. Everyone knew, despite the translation of his name into Irish, that he was English and once again the Irish had a low expectation of morality from anyone who was not born of the catholic green sod.

Mac Liammoir, like many another gay artist may have found it easier to be himself in another society rather than in the one he was born. Mac Liammoir gave us the language of the term 'partner' – one he used in print and in media to describe Hilton Edwards, the accomplished director with whom he shared his love and home in Harcourt Terrace, Dublin. They had met as young men on the stage of the Athenaeum Theatre in Enniscorthy, Co Wexford, where I later directed and was proudly told this fact by a pioneered pinned father of a large local family! It is funny how we can often be who we really are in another country, not our own. That must change in a modern Ireland, and many had been working hard, outside the theatre, for a long time to achieve that essential inclusiveness. This is a fitting context for a decade of new opportunity in identity led theatre.

chapter 2

I Am What I Am

One transvestite…One plain homosexual

Harvey Fierstein, librettist, 'La Cage Aux Folles'

In 1993, the year of decriminalisation, my musical company (Dublin Area Youth Musical Society, established in 1984) was radically staging the Irish premiere of 'La Cage Aux Folles' in Dublin. 'La Cage' is a hilarious, warm, gay, French farce, later denuded of romance and finesse in the US movie remake 'The Birdcage'. There were many challenges in presenting this transvestite gay musical in Dublin and Waterford 1993 and the 'trans' roles were not the only challenges in a society reluctant to do anything in front of the neighbours! In autumn 1992, I had decided to produce this show on the mainstream stage, at a time when a most begrudging public debate was happening to decriminalise homosexuality, as demanded by the success of the Norris Case, five years earlier.

Sexual and gender diversity were not our only challenges in a conservative Ireland. We had battled with some success, with a 'constitutional crusade' in the 1980s, to finally separate Church and State, allowing the State to have its own identity and its own rights for citizens, without influence of a dominant, out of touch, creed.

'La Cage' had other diversity challenges. We required a black actor for the crucial comedy role of 'Jacob' the talentless butler/maid. We could not find a black person in the city in 1993. I eventually retraced and found a straight, black, bass guitarist I had known a decade previously and thanks to David Murphy, the production could authentically progress! 'La Cage' had been a huge hit in the USA, but its UK production coincided with the AIDS holocaust and the show was not so successful there, in a time when people were dying – especially in theatre.

In staging this Irish premiere, I was also 'coming out' on stage myself and that had not been part of the plan, as this was not how I perceived my own identity at all. We had fully cast the show with the exception of the leading role of the 'transvestite homosexual' the effeminate 'Albin' aka 'Zaza' the acclaimed drag star of a Riviera nightclub, 'La Cage Aux Folles'. We did have some cast leave in rehearsal, as one actor (gay) approached me saying "There is a mistake here, Francis the stage manager is dating 'Hannah from Hamburg', but you have a guy playing 'Hannah'." I replied "Yes, they are all gay!" We didn't see him again! 'Hannah' too, now a very prominent gay impresario, 'hurt' his back days before we opened in a glare of publicity, and had to be replaced. It wasn't easy for people to do this show, especially two months after decriminalisation!

We offered the leading part of 'Zaza', who sings the anthem 'I Am What I Am' to seven accomplished and gay actors. Despite this being the gift of a role, no one would do it. I did have an approach from abroad, when the actor's greatest claim to fame was that he could fit into the original shoes from the first production! I was unable to establish any other qualifications, though he was of Irish descent.

We were some weeks into rehearsals, as the dancing by 'Les Cagelles', while gender changing, is quite a skill. We had a vanity issue here too only resolved by the female dancers stuffing themselves to equal the flaunted prowess of the males!

One evening I reported that the seventh actor turned down the leading role. Cast member, director/actor Tom Singleton, who was playing 'Georges' the partner, said he and his wife had a suggestion – me. I said no, immediately. Tom pressed the point and I told him 'I do not want to be the worst thing in my own production'. His reply, gravely delivered was, 'If you don't do it, we do not have a show'. I had things to think about that were not previously on my agenda. With the greatest trepidation and the promise of Tom's additional directorial eye, I had to agree to play a role I never saw myself playing, when I began producing it, in January 1993.

One of the big challenges was the multi gender identity element of the role – there were 13 gender changes in the two acts. I felt I could do the comedy element and sing it. I struggled hugely, having overcome the negative feminine stereotype, to now present myself in public in this very effeminate role, at a time when I still was not comfortable with the perception of my own masculinity, as a gay man. Tom was correct, we had no choice and I laboured on.

Rebecca Smith, my good acting friend, gave me a video of a 'Donohue' TV talk show from the US, featuring a 'drag queen' special edition. Mid way during the show, this woman appeared and gave an interview. She had two doctorates, was dressed in a tailored business suit and was hugely impressive. She was a transgender, intelligent, plausible and real. At last I had a hook I could connect with.

We were mid-way through the rehearsals and Tom would always take notes for me while I was on stage – another disincentive for any director to take on the role. He didn't say anything one night. I was wearing a denim shirt, jeans and boots. At the end of the shared notes session, he remarked, had I noticed he hadn't said anything about me yet? I asked for a view. 'I'm not saying anything, I don't know what you have been doing, but tonight 'She' arrived'! 'Don't over analyse, just keep on going' was his sound advice. We were two weeks to opening night!

Yes 'Zaza' had arrived. I was to do a promo in 'The George' bar one evening and the costume, which I had never worn or seen before, was late arriving in the venue. It was also another first, as I was singing live, to a live accompaniment by Anne O Neill. The fabulous silver costume and lavish headdress arrived and costumier Maria Blaney dressed me upstairs in the pub and Alison Murphy created my make-up. 'Now how do you feel?' beamed Maria. "For the first time in my life, I have this incredible urge to play Gaelic Football for Dublin" was my despondent reply. I was struggling, having accepted my own identity, it was now being redefined in public, in a role that wasn't me – but 'mud would stick' was the depressing thought of the reluctant actor.

As I nervously made my way down the stairs of the packed 'George', singing live, I was very grateful to the audience, who sang along with me 'I Am What I Am'. I was so nervous walking down a staircase, in heels, to sit on a free standing ashtray with a plank on the top, that I lip read the audience to try to remember the next line! I doubt if 'The George' crowd would know the words today, but they were word and note perfect that summer night in 1993.

I went on to get standing ovations for this performance and to win awards. I even played it in my own home town of Waterford at the International Festival of Light Opera there, which was very stressful for me. I got dressed a half an hour early and walked my dressing room discussing with myself what I was about to do, in my home town. I eventually decided that all I could do was to make sure 'Zaza' was played to the full. I did it. I got a standing ovation and it took me over two hours to cross the street from the Theatre Royal to the Ballroom in the

Tower Hotel, such was the response to the role and the need for people to tell me their own stories. It is amazing how, when a man dons a dress, he becomes less threatening! It was amazing how many people had stories to tell and trusted this 'gender neutral' character of great integrity and strength.

I saw first-hand the power of theatre to change hearts and minds and I refer to some of these stories elsewhere. I had met through Kevin Smith, a friend, the transvestite community in Dublin while researching my role. They dressed and went to 'The George' on a Thursday night. I invited them to see the show. When we got to the Olympia Theatre for another run in July 1994, 'The Evening Press' newspaper's social diarist named the male transvestite community, who had attended the show dressed, some with their wives, in her national newspaper column the following day.

Some years later I was queuing for a ticket in the West End and noticed composer Jerry Herman beside me, I was able to inform him that we had staged 'La Cage' in Dublin! It was all quite a radical act to stage this work in the year of decriminalisation and later to get it on in The Olympia Theatre, thanks to Gerry Sinnott in July 1994. Gerry, never one to miss a marketing opportunity, tag lined it 'the controversial show' – it wasn't, but it worked and got standing ovations and full houses, every night.

I would never get over 'Zaza' and the things the role forced me to consider, explore and present in a most public way, in a hostile society. She also gave me a language and a context to continue to explore sexuality in theatre in the years to come, as well as the award for 'Best Male' performance at the Waterford Festival, disproving the myth that 'all directors are failed actors!'' 'Zaza' remained in some demand for years after, but only ever made an appearance, if the proceeds were going to HIV charities or gay causes.

One notable appearance was in the Irish Film Institute at a celebration of the 100th edition of Gay Community News in the distinguished company of 'Agnes Bernelle' and 'The Nualas'! That night my hairdresser failed to show due to a date mix-up. I sent the stage manager out to find a replacement. He came back and said he couldn't find any. I told him 'the place was packed with hairdressers!' I got dressed again and within minutes had a choice of the best in the country, proving the 'gay stereotype' does have its uses! Gary Kavanagh got an old wig of mine, a canister of spray gel and put it on a gas cylinder and minutes later created a wig acceptable to 'Zaza'.

At this stage I was out and proud in the theatre, but I would either now be type cast, having previously played romantic and comedy leads, as gay theatre, with the notable exception of works by the like of Loughlin Deegan at the Project Arts Centre or Gerry Stembridge's 'The Gay Detective', was still almost invisible in the mainstream. It is true that I did not get many other roles after playing the award winning 'Zaza'.

Memories influence and live with me as one night from the stage, I saw three young people in the front row – A girl and two boys. As 'La Cage' progressed, the two young lads moved together in a public place and held hands. Another older man approached me for an autograph after a show and as I wrote whispered 'myself and my friend never thought we would live to see our lives being portrayed so beautifully on an Irish stage and being appreciated by so many'. The nun who painted 'Zaza's' portrait for the show left the convent sometime later and the girls in a boarding school that attended applauded me after as I headed towards the green room. I stopped, surprised that adolescent girls would connect to 'her' and asked did they like her? – they responded 'we love her'! Theatre really can change hearts and minds and liberate. I hold that close in the days when things don't go so well.

It was not until 2004, that the perfect coincidence in a city and a theatre community, that often exploits the Wilde association, but rarely celebrates the author in the completeness of his identity, could be further evolved. A 'Wilde' play still sustains many summer tourist seasons in the Abbey and Gate Theatres in Dublin! Isn't that gay theatre? So where is he in Dublin? Where is his gay identity, other than the statue in Merrion Square, that looks a lot like Peter O'Toole playing Jacques Brel! Wilde remained in the shadows in his native country for much of the century after his death.

The great gay actor Micheal Mac Liammoir, had to raise funds privately in 1954 to get a plaque on Oscar's birthplace on Westland Row, in the centenary of his birth. No State funding was forthcoming then. He was courageous, as were his benefactors, to do this irst very public act. Mac Liammoir did a lot for and about Wilde, during his theatrical career. He was brave to do so in a hostile Ireland. He was playing the 'Importance of Being Oscar' (where the trials happen during the interval) in the Gaiety Theatre, three blocks away from 27 Upper Pembroke Street, Dublin 2, where I was born in 1961. I wonder was his onstage projection audible those few blocks away on that night? Was that my inspiration?

I love coincidence and indeed hijack it, like many Irish people, who always struggle to find an association, no matter how tenuous, in order to call you 'friend'. Indeed, I established later that Wilde had a penchant of calling his characters after friends. I knew my Grandfather, John Merriman (a Protestant) was friendly with the Elgee's in Wexford, where I grew up. Jane Elgee, Oscar's mother, became Lady Jane Wilde and her salons in 1, Merrion Square were a social must in the mid nineteenth century. She also held strong nationalistic views and published nationalistic writings under the name 'Speranza'. As a result of her son's imprisonment, and hence the loss of his financial support, this extraordinary outspoken and visible woman, rests in an unmarked grave.

In the 'Importance of being Earnest', one of the two butlers is 'Merriman' the other 'Lane' (after his publisher). 'Merriman' was later played on screen by renowned Wexford character actor Sandy Welsh. My Grandfather in the 1920s, used the names of Wilde's family in the names of his own children, including my Uncle being given the names of his sons, Cyril and Vyvyan and my Aunt, the name of Constance (his wife), for reasons I can not now discover, 60 years after his death.

In the placing of the Festival in this extraordinary Irish legacy and among many other matters, I attempted to hijack a part of the Wilde / Edwards / Mac Liammoir legacy (and later Eva Gore Booth) for the Festival's pedigree, to encourage people to recognise the contribution of gay theatre to Irish theatre and to encourage us all to feel that 'I must be Talking to my Friends' (the title of another of Mac Liammoir's one man shows) as we set out on our unique theatrical project in 2004.

chapter 3

Early Influences in Theatre

> What shall I have my son a stager now? An engle for players, a gull, a rook, a shot clog to make suppers and be laughed at?

Ben Johnson's character 'Ovid Senior' in 'The Poemaster' (1601) exclaims when he learns his son wants to write for the theatre.

In writing this piece, the most difficult element was to write about the theatre, as this is the most personal element of the story. Theatre has been in my blood since the earliest time. In a TV- less environment in a small country town like Wexford, one relied on imagination and a safe and intimate community to fill many a summer's day. The fact that there was an age gap between myself and my older brothers, meant that entertainment was often self-created and always romantic in its outlook. I dreamed and then lived it out in our first theatre 'down the lane' a shed behind Waterloo Road in Wexford town. There, many a summer play was devised and enacted with our own scripts and a conscripted audience, including my Grand Aunt May Corish who sat on barrels and home-made benches to applaud our (costumed!) efforts.

I began performing, not in a theatrical family, but in a family where music and the spoken word were valued. I remember the lay-out of the dining table: two older brothers on one side, my Mother and younger sister on the other and invariably myself at the far end from my imposing father. He was tall, handsome, had a wonderful timbre to his speaking voice and a great presence. Unusually for that time he both encouraged free discussion in a 'political' family, where one was never certain of his own party affiliations. I eventually wormed it out of him on the eve of his 80th birthday!

At a young age, especially when asserting myself from the number 3 position in the family, his counsel often boomed down the table, going no further than 'articulate Brian'. So I did. Later of course, I would have to justify my opinion in fierce debate, whose tone and passion would often reduce my baby sister to tears, as she could not yet distinguish robust debate from personalised argument. A fate I still fall foul of today, in my presentation.

I first came to attention as a skinny, blue eyed, boy soprano with a considerable vocal range. This meant that from my first entry into school in the Presentation Convent, Wexford, which had on its staff a soprano who had sung in La Scala, Milan, Mother Gabriel, that singing was acceptable. I remember being taken out of junior class quite frequently and 'touring' the school to sing. We had a boys' kindergarten and a girls' secondary school. I would find myself standing on the teacher's chair and belting out the current National Song Contest winner to applause and a significant boost to my treasure chest of sweets.

I played the 'Angel Gabriel' in the nativity play and vertigo took hold as I was terrified to stand on the baby chairs! I have never had a head for heights. I graduated rapidly to play the title role, in first class, of 'The Demon King" complete with real cow horns stitched into my red cap, and parodying 'The Pirate King' from the 'Pirates of Penzance' in my pursuit of 'Maid Marion'. I did not like being the 'baddie' to Rhuban Nolan's heroic 'Robin Hood' – even if I did get the big numbers! The 'Pirate King' was to be a part I returned to many times!

 I was also 'a hit' with the nuns – a fact exploited by my brothers when, in the late 1960s, nuns were let out of the convent for the first time, to go to suitable films like 'The Sound of Music'. My brothers would spot them in the cinema and I would be dispatched, not to return, without seriously good sweets, like chocolate, which I did.

As a boy soprano, I also learned of the power of performance to bring on emotion. I was quite shy and the performance gave me the introduction I needed, to mix in company. I was never shy singing. I earned my first 'fee' as a singer with my rendition of the American Folk Song 'Aura Lee', to the tune of 'Love Me Tender', earning me a silver US dollar and later, a broadcasting fee on the RTE radio series 'The Young Entertainers'. By aged 9, I would 'top the bill' at concerts in Wexford, accompanied by pianist, Bernie Morris. I probably featured through the charitable work of my grandparents and certainly influenced by my Godmother, Betty Murphy who played the glamorous 'Principal Boy' part in the local pantomime, in Dun Mhuire, to packed houses.

At aged 10, Brother Redmond in the Christian Brothers, Wexford, asked me to consider a music scholarship for St Finian's in Mullingar a boarding school, but I didn't want to leave home. I, like my brothers, also represented Wexford in Fleadh Ceoil's, singing ballads in Irish and English. People flocked to music events in a town famous for its opera festival. My father as Borough Accountant, was treasurer of the Light Opera Society and the Wexford Opera Festival at times. I heard my first opera in dress rehearsal, from the box in the Theatre Royal. It was all in pink and I ate colour co-ordinated pink nougat throughout. I was solely intent of leaving the biggest pile of sweet wrappers after me on the ledge, which I did – but something rubbed off, including being in awe of the packed houses!

That too was a lesson. There is no such thing as an amateur audience. In order for theatre to be viable and accessible, it needs people to attend and pay in, that in itself does shape the work presented. I have seen many an audience at an amateur production, especially in musically starved Ireland, become the audience at a professional production and needing to be similarly impressed. My association with amateur theatre as a young man was a proud one. There were no stage schools or grants to go to the UK, so this was 'my university'. This time companies in Dublin and indeed from the UK, would head to the Waterford International Festival of Light Opera. They would enthrall us with 'West End' performances and productions on that unique tiny Georgian stage, which seemed to accommodate any scale of production. They were great learning opportunities and inspired me in wanting to tell the story my way.

The late renowned Irish actor Cyril Cusack, used to question the need for a director at all. The director is the storyteller. There are many ways to tell a story and many are valid, but confusing, if all are told at once. In theatre, the storyteller presents a clear interpretation of the author's creativity.

I once said 'the best authors are dead authors' which of course is nothing but a directorial vanity and an inner envy of the skill of the writer. How quickly I would contradict that in my later work in the Festival promoting new writing.

I liked more directorial freedom, but like the actor, our real creative task is to interpret and present the author's intent. Within that, especially in a good script, directors have lots of room and inspiration for creativity. Just listen to what the writer, or composer, is saying through their work. Our best assistance in times of low inspiration, is to listen to the author, for a well written piece will guide you, if you can hear what the author is communicating. This was my benchmark when I was landed with a sudden 'promotion', in the first ever staged production, in the National Concert Hall in Dublin in 1984.

The College of Music production of 'L'Incoronazione di Poppea' by Monteverdi, which later toured Cork and Limerick, lost its director and ended up giving me a crash course in company management and stage management as I was suddenly elevated to direct my peers.

Truthfully there is a separate book in that production, including the Principal of the College of Music insisting on the removal, or added clothing to the pre-pubescent crotch of Carravagio's 'Cupid' on the poster – it was 1984 and Ireland was in a flux trying to deal with contraception, divorce and abortion and failing! Even 'Cupid' could not be naked to Irish eyes, as the State struggled to shake of church suffocation. I was itching to tell my stories and opportunities for young people to direct were non-existent, especially for an unconnected person. So I gave life to my guiding philosophy, if the opportunity does not exist – create it!

I had established amongst my friends at the College of Music in Dublin, a performance group in July 1984. I had been appearing in musical societies throughout the city in leading juvenile roles, from operetta through to modern musicals. I had just finished playing 'Lieutenant Joe Cable' in 'South Pacific' in Drimnagh MS with the incredible Anne Shumate in her signature role as 'Nellie' and Philip Byrne as Emile. Astonishingly, the College of Music which had a wonderful harvest of singers had no vehicle for them to perform, except in recitals etc. The compulsory choir was a chore. At 23, I had just bought a house in the smog free suburbs of Dublin West, in a landscape of unfinished housing estates and I needed something (cheap) to do. On the last day of College term, sitting in 'Peter's Pub' on South William Street, I decided to set up a performance group with Vivian Coates (who later became an accomplished opera director), Mezzo Soprano, Sara Mc Guinness and Johnny Magee on committee. It was my first venture out in the big city and as usual, I just went ahead!

I had had my exposure to the dynamic of what created audience and indeed apprenticeship for musical theatre in Ireland – the Association of Irish Musical Societies. More political than Fianna Fail, this entity did boast vibrant regions and 57 companies in the greater Dublin area alone in the early 1980s. It also attracted some good directors who knew their craft well and a huge diversity of musical productions which epitomised the clash between operetta and modernising musical theatre. Competition was cut-throat and behaviour mimicked the reported 'goings on' in Hollywood at times!

We thought of a name for this new group and AIMS and the DART (Dublin Area Rapid Transport) were the two big things going on in Dublin at the time, so on a once off basis, I set up DAYMS – the Dublin Amateur Youth Musical Society – fatally without 'permission'. It was a response to our College having no performance vehicles and also to the tradition of young people having to 'inherit' a role in performance groups like DGOS and the R&R!

This was the era of 'Grease', 'Saturday Night Fever' and 'Fame' – we, the young people, had our musicals, all we needed was a stage. Had I a copy of John M Crum's book 'Where The Boys Are' on musical theatre and gay culture then, it all would have fitted into placed a lot earlier than it did and been my pleasant guide to self-realisation! This book traces beautifully the special connection between gay men and musical theatre, and how it helped them express themselves in a society that insisted on existence only in the shadows.

My own belief was that I didn't need to ask permission, if I was willing to do, and if I was, I should do. That was the key to my approach to theatre. I saw it as a right of citizenship - others see it as a privilege, to be dispersed to or by the 'chosen'. It never occurred to me to ask permission or from whom this permission should be sought?

We, young people had the capacity to do theatre, so why not do it, especially as we would accept the responsibility for our success or failure? Five weeks later, my madcap, modernised production of 'HMS Pinafore' went on stage in the John Player Theatre, in that most rare of occurrences – a heat-wave in late August 1984. This theatre allowed smoking, as it was in a cigarette factory, (yards from where I would establish the Festival 20 years later). The late manager, Tom O Reilly was a genial host for ambitious young people and a charming advocate for Players cigarettes!

I modernised HMS, which had been my first musical with Edmund Rice Society in Waterford, as a 16 year old dancer in 1977, produced by Clonmel's theatre advocate, Mary Cummins and choreographed by Geraldine Molumby. This time there was 'no holds barred' in the production, which was a riotous hit, with mad cap, Marxian comedy and very fine singing. We were protected and fortunate to have on our side an AIMS stalwart, Alice Hughes – the 'adult' of the group, who acted as Stage Manager and mentor. On opening night we finished painting the set at 7.45 pm. We hadn't time to brace the upper deck, so when our elegant female chorus walked up the stairs singing, they were alerted by a painted sign on the flimsy cabin roof 'Do Not Step'. They had to make a sharp turn to find secure footing on the back ramp and many carried a bright stripe of wet paint as an additional band on their flowing robes!

I intended DAYMS and directing, to be a once off event. I enjoyed performing and was lucky to be in demand for shows from Tommy Ebbs, Kevin Hough and at times, John Allen. The late director, Frank Gormley was a generous mentor and I spent many a lunchtime discussion learning from him.

However, with no 'permission', some adult wagons circled and some in the AIMS hierarchy took huge umbrage to young people doing it their own way. 'HMS' had 'broken even', raised some hackles and attempts were made to stop us progressing. That incentivised me to assert our right as young people to perform and to maintain the company. That's what a 'no' does to me.

One of the first lessons learned was how stigmatising the word 'amateur' was in the title. Firstly, there was no indigenous professional musical theatre sector in Ireland. Many of our singers were on their way professionally, like Paul Monaghan, Sara Mc Guinness and Marie Kelly and in two years, I had to bow to pressure to amend the 'A' from 'Amateur' to 'Area' (just like the DART!). That was enough to appease the critics and open more doors for us. Within two years of some in the 'adult world' telling us we needed their consent to perform, DAYMS swept the board at the annual AIMS competition of over 80 productions, replacing the winning platform's average age, from the mid 40s to the early (if even) 20's, overnight. I was never to be forgiven!

I was the youngest director in the business and could not keep up with the amount of work offered. I set about travelling the highways and byways of Ireland, working in rural theatres, bringing a bit of musical theatre magic and fierce independence in casting and interpretation with me, wherever I went! This was breaking the mould of committee casting and role inheritance, long the practice of established musical groups! I learned a lot working with professionals and amateurs alike. I dedicated two decades to this work, which was my university in a time when none existed and to travel abroad was beyond my independent resources. After over 300 productions over 20 years in Ireland, Northern Ireland, England, Wales and the Isle of Man with professional and amateur companies with professional leads, by 2004, I needed a new challenge.

It was a link with musicals that prompted the space to establish the Festival in 2004. I had been working fulltime in theatre at home and in the UK from 1988. Once fulltime, I knew opportunities might decline so I opened up my market to the UK, where I enjoyed some success, especially in getting my work on in great theatres.

I began to get truly tired of 'living out of suitcases' and considered a return to Dublin would put an end to my hectic career. Directing was a much more fluid freelancing job than acting, where you could be engaged for a year's run! Directors were engaged for a week or a month, here and there. My production books were always prepared well in advance, so I spent a week directing, they noted and rehearsed and then I later returned with the next layers of the production. Very efficient, with me balancing up to five productions in Ireland (North and South), England, Wales and the Isle of Man at a time, liaising with professional casts, crews and theatres.

I had enough travel by 1993 and felt my options would shrink on my return home. I was wrong. My career as a director moved rapidly and unexpectedly, with a happy association with Gerry Sinnott of the Olympia. Later I would discover that Gerry's sister had been a school-friend of my mother.

I spent ten very challenging and fulfilling years on projects in my favourite performance space, under the somewhat rundown proscenium arch, of the 'Grand Old Lady' of Dame Street – the Olympia Theatre. Gerry was a decent and honourable producer and I learned a lot from him. Years later, I was honoured to be the only director present at the celebration dinner marking 60 years of employment in the Olympia of Maureen Grant. Previously Maureen had honoured me with including my photograph on her wall of stars in 'Maureen's Bar'. It is good to connect with everyone who makes a theatre what it is – and Maureen, the Front of House, Box Office and Stage technical staff, of the Olympia were as important to me, as those in power, or with theatrical talents. Many a time in hectic 'get-ins', Maureen's bar was emptied for me at short break times and the tin with ham sandwiches and fruit cake, with the kettle boiling, was produced – my haven from the insanity of technical ambition, in a 'get in' always eventually achieved by the great in-house crew, led by the knowledgeable and legendary, John Brogan.

The lack of 'permission' has been a flaw in my approach to most things theatrical. It does not indicate any lack of respect. Quite the contrary, but once the idea hits, nothing stops me! I can not wait for a 'committee' to analyse what I propose, when the muse is thumping with my adrenalin. Inspiration must be acted upon immediately. There's lots of time for study after the muse deserts or rests. Many saw that in me and would lure me into a production with the assurance, that the show was too big to be produced, or cast, or it would not broadly appeal – hence DAYMS inevitably did 'Irish premieres' over its 25 year history.

I loved something new, especially if I had never seen it. I was not one of those 're-producers' that dominated the musical society circuit and The Royal Variety show on TV fed many 'Tops of the Town' shows, as did ideas from those who could afford note-taking trips to the West End! I created what I saw on the page, including the European premiere of 'Zorba', or the 'Hired Man', 'A Chorus Line', 'The Most Happy Fella', 'West Side Story', 'Into The Woods', 'Christopher Columbus', 'La Cage Aux Folles', 'Godspell', 'Pageant', 'Anything Goes', etc. I had to work for a living most of the year and DAYMS was my creative outlet and labour of love. It has made a generous contribution to professional theatre as an incubator of emerging talent over the years. It was a partnership with Michelle Kavanagh, secretary with such integrity, for seventeen years and hugely talented people onstage and off, many who went on to earn a living in the sector in many facets of the industry.

Theatre is not controlled by those lucky enough to be gifted a talent. As titled benefactors diminished in the latter centuries, the State replaced them with Administrators and indeed enabling networks. There are some truly gifted people working in these enabling bodies. They see potential, open doors, encourage, defend, and enable art to thrive, in a resource challenged environment. There are others who for varying reasons, like an impossible budget restriction, or they are graded too low in the pecking order to influence, they are frustrated artists in their own right, or they are tired and bored, who do not enable art and in my case, theatre. To these few, a new idea is a headache.

An inflexible framework of arts administration ensures nothing of value can happen, unless it is crafted in the same way as all other events or works 'designed by committee'. The 'Committee' has designed its own framework which is often based on an academic justification and then art must be squeezed into this structure, to be supported. You must discuss, explore, get a study grant, curry favour, chatter, as the spontaneity of the original passion is drained, by the endless encirclement of bureaucracy. But my small contribution had always been 'rights' and opportunity centred. My impatience with restriction has probably cost the Festival dearly. But if you are lucky to get an idea, you must act upon it immediately.

The right to speak, innovate, create, perform and be listened to, even by an audience of one, was mine and mine to share, if I was prepared to work at it. In reply, people will say you have the right, but not with 'my' money! Fair enough, but I never relied on grants for my theatre and still survived, though not at a level that would impress those, whose greater claim to fame is the art they supress, rather than enable. Good theatre is choked by excessive control, which in itself is a form of censorship of the liberating art-form.

It is rather daft to try to impose a structure on creativity, though administrative structure has necessary transparency requirements of good governance. A transparent public service must be structured. I have met the substantial sector of the arts whose work will only been seen if it is grant-aided. They will not take a risk or invest in their own work. For work to be grant-aided, it must fulfil a policy that often was not in the mind of the creative author. Art is squeezed into abstract frameworks to fit a policy imposed on a sector (regardless of the consultation process) in a 3-5 year strategic management plan. Therefore access, not art, becomes the real currency and once you are inside, your role is to 'prevent' others from accessing the cake, in order to preserve your own slice. This is not a healthy, innovative or creative structure.

So much of the Irish arts funding is previously 'ring fenced', that there is little room for the new dynamic that will sustain it. So much is guided by the need to protect the small existing jobs funding for decent, hard-working people. That is much more identifiable in an arts structure, than the opportunity for art and that is administratively understandable.

The word 'cutting edge' can hardly apply to most current Irish art-forms these days, as the recession is defying previous ones, by proving difficult for arts and attendances.

Previously, and in no small way due to a surge in amateur activity, the arts were a cheap form of past-time. Theatre was much better priced and better value, than the corporate box vanity for chart topping performers, on a one night stand, in a luxurious surrounding. This form of theatre as a community activity, fuelled interest in performance, in learning and created a supply of audience and artists that inspired teaching, writing, production and entry into the profession. In an era of 'instant celebrity', where your tragic life-story, youth and good looks, your desperation to be in the media, and your construction into an instant media format, replaces talent, creativity, hard work and skill, has shrunk the influx of talent into the arts sector at all levels. This generous trading of participation for training that fuelled generations of worthy, artistic endeavour is no more.

I had rarely ventured into the realm of amateur musical after the early 1990s. I had achieved more than I thought I would, having won every major international competition in the country, countless 'best shows', 'best director' and including 'best actor' awards. In fact at one stage, I had won back-to-back, five major international festivals in a row, AIMS (twice), Waterford (twice) and the Northern Ireland Festival. Later, when it was announced another Dublin group had won an award in a festival, the cry from 'the Gods' was 'We beat him", rather than of celebration for their own individual achievement. It was time to move on. I left this competitive and increasingly personalised environment in the early 1990s. Many kindly tried to woo me back and in 2003, I was tempted to do a production of 'Sweeney Todd' in the theatre where I came of age – the Theatre Royal Waterford. It was clear from the outset, that I had a very particular interpretation of this great work that I wanted to pursue. Indeed as a director of musical theatre, I ensured that the direction carried through in all elements of the work. Musicals are not all slight dramas where the drama stops when the orchestra plays. Plausible characterisation must be infused in all elements of the performance. The gift of music is that it can often emote and inspire a response, in a much shorter time, when words alone prove less adequate. I like marrying all these artistic elements into a complete performance.

I directed my singers as my actors (and many to award winning acclaim). I had been fortunate to study under Daphne M Clifford, formerly of Trinidad and Tobago Opera, and though her own singing career was long over, her capacity to huskily impart interpretation of language was astonishingly enlightening. I and my colleagues were assigned to her, because not a lot was expected of us at the College of Music, which streamed its talent to particular well established teachers. Daphne upset that cart when her students frequently punched above their weight. When directing consumed any time or preparation to continue my 8 year studies in the College of Music, I would reassure her that, whereas she had not produced a great singer, she had imparted her magic of interpretation to a director who now understood singing and song. I am eternally indebted to her intelligence and patience!

I 'interfered' with the metronome led interpretation of musical theatre. My characters were formed and delivered their entire performance and as a director I equipped them to seamlessly build on the context of the drama that inspired the song. Some Musical directors worked with me in this approach and I learned so much from their vastly superior skills and musicianship, including Gearoid Grant and Colman Pearce, most distinguished musicians and conductors and many others in Britain. It became a hallmark of my approach to my theatre. The contact with them considerably advanced my capacity to encourage interpretation of music that played to the performer's strength and respected the genius of the author. The Festival project was to allow me to further this love of words and music as I explored new writing and voices from great talents throughout the world.

chapter 4

Criminals in a Changing Ireland

Not everyone will stand up and speak, so I speak on their behalf

Ugandan LGBT Activist, Kasha Nabagesera, Dublin, April 2013

In 1993, Ireland became the last western European country to decriminalise 'homosexuality'. 2004 was a time when memory is recent and opportunities to invent strategies to undo over a century of repression, are slowly emerging. The gay legal circumstance is an interesting one. It is one of those rare times when a crime ceased to be a crime and 'criminals' had their status as citizens restored, without apology. There are few precedents for such a new dispensation in other areas of law. Criminal records however were not erased or the damage of the shame of such illegality.

What changed in society's response post 1993? By Dec 14th 2001 a Garda spokesman confirmed to the 'Evening Herald' that "a large number of gay men are attacked and robbed every year. However victims are often afraid to report their attackers", proving the imperative for something more than decriminalisation, to assert their cultural context, a decade later.

Law was still not an instant friend to the decriminalised community. As no apology was being offered by the State that had constructed a crime, punishment and a diagnosis of mental illness, affirmation and understanding was needed. It was not to be immediately assisted. Change must provide for the newly liberated not to be 'tolerated' by a 'guilty' heterosexist society, but to be respected for their equal citizenship. Tolerance is a truly minimalistic benchmark on which to base a life, any life. Respect illuminates and enriches shared citizenship. The drab alternative needed the colour of truthful theatre and we had our stories to tell a rapidly changing Ireland. I wanted to see had we, the Irish and the gay artists, the courage to tell the stories and was the time right to do so?

Irish society decided, after over a century of oppression, that love is no

29

longer illegal, nor a 'destabilising threat'. The Labour party had included decriminalisation in its manifesto in 1992, when it made history by coalescing with the populist conservative, Fianna Fail party. How quickly changes have occurred can be measured with the latter's claiming credit for decriminalisation in the recent past, though it was non-existent in their manifestoes since the human rights defeat of 1988. It just fell to Fianna Fail's uncomfortable lot, as they held the Justice portfolio in that coalition government, to fulfil the Labour election policy, rectifying a negative human rights finding against Ireland in the Norris case in 1988. To the credit of all parties, it was eventually erased from the criminal statute books, despite negative efforts to raise a different age of consent for gay people, which was defeated.

You can not forget history by simply erasing the crime. History is a strong force of influence in Ireland and in any community. In such a context, society has to unlearn constructed shame and respond effectively to such change. Criminalisation had erased lesbians and gays from public view for over a century. Decriminalisation erased us from the statute book. We are continually erased. The Gay Theatre Festival was poised, amongst many other advocacy and rights based activities, to try to make its own contribution to restoring that visible citizenship.

When we seek role models from history, historians rely on the 'lack of evidence' surviving today to affirm sexuality in the past. That is not good enough. No truth can emerge in such constructed circumstances. When you remove the possibility of proof, the onus is on historians to prove heterosexuality! Step up George Frederick Handel, Padraig Pearse, Roger Casement, Eva Gore Booth et al, who made a considerable political and artistic contribution to Ireland, married and not. Many, we will never confirm and celebrate as a result of this historical invisibility. I will discuss some of these heroes later and we celebrate many of them in the Festival's honorary awards system, annually.

The Trade Union movement made the first protective moves to protect gay workers in the 1980s. Nothing positive or pro-active immediately replaced decriminalisation in 1993, leaving a vacuum of understanding and inclusion. Despite efforts to further stigmatise the newly liberated, the Parliament did positively agree to an equal age of consent for gays and heterosexuals, at least that protected children, at last. With an age of consent came the clarity of adult consent – a serious casualty of the harm done by criminalisation.

Equality is personal. You really only understand it, if you experience it yourself. Thanks to the meeting of two mothers, many people credit Phil Moore of Parents Enquiry and Justice Minister, Maire Geoghegan Quinn for advancing change. Apparently the two women talked about parenthood. The Minister's lively student son had been the subject of invasive tabloid headlines. Mrs Moore pointed out how Mothers understand their sons. However she added, only one of these mothers called the other's son a 'criminal'. When it's personal, it is easier to see unfairness. This analogy is credited as achieving this first vital measure of equality. Once convinced, Maire Geoghan Quinn made her own contribution to respect for all too, by ensuring an equal age of consent in law.

I have long held, it is only when you make inequality personal, can many people finally see the light. Privilege is not an illuminator of the condition of others. Theatre is an illuminator.

More equal rights, acknowledging the status of LGBT people, were passed by Parliament, introduced by the Labour Party Minister for Equality, Mervyn Taylor TD, in the late 1990s. Equality legislation now protected LGBT people (and other minorities) from discrimination on grounds of their sexual orientation or gender identity in employment, or when they avail of goods, facilities, services, accommodation and education in Ireland – real and important progress. The inclusion in multi-ground legislation was effective in achieving equality. Minority grounds now also being protected, like religion, did not want LGBT rights, but when presented in the context of rights for all, it lowered the decibels of opposition. Be careful what you campaign against, it might rebound on you!

Human rights are not something that by right, should be in the gift of any one group or individual. Human rights only truly exist in your own capacity to recognise them in another, and to defend those rights. Anything less is a 'degree' of human rights. A failure of that test demeans those who present themselves as democrats, in societies who do not implement full equality of rights. Human rights are a struggle to achieve the consent of the privileged for inclusion of more people in a participative society.

chapter 5

The International Gay Cultural Context

I thought there would be ten of us – there were thousands

Doric Wilson, gay playwright and Stonewall participant, on journeying to the first gay pride march in NYC in 1970.

The Stonewall Inn was the small (mafia run) bar in the (Greenwich) Village, in New York where LGBT people socialised. The Stonewall riots in New York in 1969, against police harassment, are credited as the beginning of the public struggle for gay rights. There had been previous attempts to repress the spectrum of human love in law, but this one boiled over onto the streets. Too often, of course, police are blamed, or held responsible, for the laws they have to implement. That is a debate for another time. But such zealous bullying acts by individual police, certainly leave an on-going legacy, when repressive laws are finally changed. Knowledge and trust in any community is vital for law, order and good policing. If there had been effective community policing in 1969, then perhaps the riots would not have happened that night? The anti-gay laws in the USA were draconian. More gay people lost their livelihood under McCarthyism, than did 'communists'.

The first gay rights society in the 1940s, the 'Mattichines Society' was founded by four brave men, including the inspiring radical Harry Hay, on a mountain top, as the men could not be seen socialising, together. The story of this group of four men, was wonderfully presented in the 2011 Festival with the premiere of 'The Temprementals' attended by former members of the group who travelled from the USA, unbeknown to us, to mark the premiere. I had been given the book 'Radically Gay' by Harry Hay, by Cory Thorell, technician who worked on the USA production of 'Nijinsky' in the Project in 2008, so I knew a little of the history, long overshadowed later by the Harvey Milk advocacy and murder. I was thrilled to see such a fine piece of drama illuminate these real life characters through theatre, in our Festival. A perfect fit. Another work should be undertaken sometime about the impact and vulnerability of women, who were condemned to the shadows, created by such laws where women were invisible, and we try to explore this in our Festival programming

In the 1960s USA, many forms of same sex association, including sharing a hotel room, were banned in the 'land of the free'. New York byelaws stated that men could not dance closer than 3 feet together – even in crowded nightclubs! People had to wear clothing 'appropriate' to their gender – adjudicated by the police. Even in gay dominated professions, marriage was compulsory for advancement – meaning that director, Vincente Minelli had to turn down approaches to lead the new advocacy group, fearing for his career. There are countless stories where women were imprisoned in marriage, to create an acceptable 'closet' for a gay worker – but at what cost to the woman and who cared?

By June 1969, the New York police, who were very zealous at the Mayor's behest, in implementing these intrusive laws, in a city notorious for serious crime, simply did not know their community and pushed them too far. A price was paid in righteous anger. Edmund Burke's words on 'evil thriving when good men stand by' were about to be tested and affirmed by the dispossessed gays that made up this bohemian community. The 'residents' of the Village, came from all corners of the US, long evicted by families or hostile local environments which made their love impossible. They were determined to hold onto the only 'home' and 'family' they had left. Micheal Lynch's wonderful autobiographical cabaret of his life 'Living On The Real' (Festival, 2010) captures in song and story, the spirit of the Village and its many characters.

Mayor Lindsay with his eyes firmly on re-election, launched a crackdown on the gay community. Stonewall a mafia/mob run bar, had already been raided the previous Tuesday. Emotionally, the temperature was high. Judy Garland the vulnerable screen icon had been married, amongst others, to the gay Vincente Minelli, died tragically in June 1969. Her funeral took place in New York on June 27th (though weirdly her actual burial, a year later). The gay community – widely known as 'Friends of Dorothy', were also emotionally charged that night by this grief and Lindsay's relentless bullying. Someone in the police department decided it was time to raid the gays again. They bullied their way into a grieving and angry community, but this time the gays fought back. They rioted for four days and the ultimate machismo of the NYPD never recovered, from having been held at bay by, drag queens, perceived effeminate men, women and transgendered people.

It is important to link the work now being done at this Festival with pioneers. One great link the Festival has is with a pioneering US gay Playwright, Doric Wilson. Wilson died in 2011. He was the founder of one of the first ever gay theatre companies, TOSOS – 'The Other Side of Silence' whose descendants had graced the programme of our Festivals. Wilson was in Stonewall, and was a marcher in the first gay pride parade, as his memories are movingly recorded in the television documentary 'Stonewall'. Wilson invited me to join the Honorary Board of TOSOS, in the company of great gay artists and supporters, in recognition of our work in gay theatre. In 2011, weeks after his passing, we renamed our prestigious award, the 'Doric Wilson Intercultural Dialogue Award'. It is presented to the play that 'teaches' mainstream society the most about our identity and culture each year.

Clearly in Europe, there remains an east-west LGBT divide. Our eastern European partners in the EU have many serious challenges in working under repressive anti-gay laws, despite the guarantee of rights for all EU citizens, required by membership of the Union. From the Baltics to the Balkans, LGBT people struggle for any public expression of their citizenship. The European Parliament and Commission needs to be more vigilant in monitoring compliance with EU equality laws amongst member states. It is clear LGBT citizens do not have equal rights in all EU member states. If there are sanctions for taxation, or environment, farming and grant aid violations, why not sanctions when citizens are being openly discriminated against, contrary to the Treaties and Directives?

I was present at the Budapest Pride in 2007 when the Neo Nazis rioted. The police there were excellent, but the fear was real on the streets. The rioters explained to us that they were using Pride to attack the Government, as they shouted 'drown the gays in the Danube'. We exited safely 'stage left' as the tear gas canisters exploded. It proved to me, that scratch the surface in Europe and the rights based culture is fragile.

Further afield in Russia, you will be imprisoned in St Petersburg if your 'promote' gay culture and they have banned the Pride parade in Moscow for the next 100 years! It is astonishing when the St Petersburg ban came into effect, Heineken had a TV ad featuring an enticing train journey to St Petersburg, which they never amended and continued to broadcast, despite calls to desist in promoting this discriminating city. Commerce also needs a moral compass –

one well claimed when they need the 'pink pound, dollar or euro' and explored somewhat in a later chapter about our 2009 Festival. In Iran, gay people's options for survival include culturally enforced gender reassignment versus execution, poverty and prostitution, as the death penalty also prevails in 4 other countries, that Ireland and the EU does business with.

Countries with huge air traffic business with Ireland have laws where gay people are executed. No 'warning' is issued officially to Irish citizens who fly out of Dublin to stop-over in these well-known air traffic hubs. When gay people land there, even in transit in these countries, all travellers are subject to the local law and could risk execution. Is commerce still more important than human life in Ireland? How can the (iconic) Eurovision song contest, long condemned as a 'gay fest' by the Iranian Government, even contemplate a safe return to Russia in future years, as Mr Putin's over-zealous machismo, seems preoccupied by anti-gay laws? Men who proclaim their machismo so much, have long been considered like the ladies 'who doth protest too much'. Think how preoccupied you are with subjects that do not affect you personally? Both Putin and Benedict XVI were obsessed with their notions of gay people.

Too many countries still carry harsh prison sentences for love and companionship. Roger was still a prisoner in Cameroon and had served one year in September 2012, for sending a simple text to a man "I'm very much in love w/u". Over 100,000 people signed an appeal to the President appealing to prevent him serving two more years for his crime.

Brave politicians raise these human rights violations, but it is in Europe that real progress could be made, if they address the internal EU LGBT rights abuses first. Historically, in Nazi Germany, if possible, the most harshly treated were the gay prisoners of the Holocaust, a fact recognised by international Jewry. They had harder labour and poorer food rations. In the French novel 'Ciel' one young boy had to not flinch as his young lover was eaten alive by Alsation dogs, otherwise he too would have suffered the same fate. Worse still, gay prisoners were sent by the liberating Allies, from the concentration camps back to prison, to serve out their sentences for their convicted crimes. There is no apology for this. The Nazi 'anti-gay' law remained in force in Germany until the 1970s. That remains in memory today. The Italian production of 'The Night Faeries' dealt magnificently with this subject in 2009, breathtakingly staged in Outhouse – the gay community centre theatre space in Capel Street, which I helped to design and I think to inspire. 'The Night Faeries' was played in English with a passion and empathy that often left the audience without a breath.

My own short play which premiered in the Festival called 'Seventy', dealt with this issue and how the message that there are different 'statuses' of human beings, propagated in Nazi Germany, still influence today. The infamous 'anti-gay' Christmas message by Joseph Ratzinger as Pope Benedict XVI, likening our existence, as a greater danger to the world than the destruction of the rain forest, clearly demonstrated that values instilled in children 70 years ago can be remodelled and delivered again 70 years later. The fact that so many gay priests, under their vow of obedience, read this hatred to their diminishing flocks, ranges from hypocrisy to barbarism. There is no requirement to read the messages of 'Mein Kampf' in the place of the Gospel or 'good news' in Church today, no matter what your vow of obedience requires. The vocation should have primacy.

In recession, people who have benefitted from boom, often seek someone to blame for their financial losses. People are not good at accepting blame or responsibility, especially in troubled times. When money sources falter, institutions wobble and lazy, bland politics is the norm, then society is rife for takeover by extremes who wish to preserve advantage for the few. Rights hard won, can be easily lost, once society still seeks 'someone' to blame for its own economic and moral weaknesses. Josef Ratzinger's papal message is fodder for those who seek to find 'the new Jews' in times of political and economic collapse. It is anything but Christian. Unfortunately his successor also was caught up on the requirement to demean, during Ratzinger's papacy.

The Arab world and Africa are not much better for gay people than their colonial masters were in the times of slavery. In Malawi, a same sex couple who got 'engaged' were sentenced to 14 years hard labour – 7 times the sentence designed to kill Oscar Wilde, two centuries earlier. There was a worldwide outcry. Wexford actress, Sarah Robinson alerted me to a big music festival in Malawi organised from London. I wrote to the organisers one evening and alerted them to this imprisonment and its consequences for any gay artists, audience and entourages that might wish to perform or attend this international event. I also documented the dreadful invasive 'examinations' the couple underwent by a salacious, crude police force. The following morning, I got a response to say the promoters were meeting the Malawian High Commissioner at 11am to raise their 'serious concerns' about this matter. World leaders descended on the Malawian President and Government and finally, the couple were released, though the story has not had such a happy ending, as the discrimination prevails in that and many other African countries.

In Uganda, the slightly built, fiercely brave, David Kato was murdered and then condemned by priests at his 'christian' funeral for being an activist for human rights. Theatre producer David Cecil faced two years in prison in Uganda in September 2012, for producing a play of the plight of gay people there, called 'The River and the Mountain' also that month. He was deported in 2013. In 2012, though criminal, in a breathtaking act of courage, a gay pride parade was held in Uganda.

Colonialists taught their successors very well, in how to embrace bigotry in laws and religion. When you liberate an oppressed people and finally give them a voice, very often the only language and conduct they know, is that of their oppressor and they assert their own privilege in that exploitative way.

Africa stands as a continent which is still colonial. Many countries now make colonies of their own people – minorities. Some liberated Africans assumed all the prejudices and inequality of power of the regimes they shook off, only to colonise groups of their own people, replacing racial apartheid with sexual apartheid. What freedom is that? There are very few Mandela's. Even Mandela's legacy of equality is under threat from his unworthy successor, Jacob Zuma. Zuma has said, if he thought someone was gay he would shoot them, and says so from the lofty morality of being a polygamist!

In many countries, only the skin colour of the oppressor was replaced. Our success in getting a Zimbabwean gay play 'Loupe', to Ireland during this time, for our only Winter Festival proved financially very costly, but worthwhile in 2009. It had originally been scheduled for the May Festival but did not show up. Then they got stranded in Paris for the winter programme costing us a lot to get them to Dublin on time without luggage. Our volunteers had 30 minutes at 5.30pm to prop and costume that night's performance and they did it in style. The contribution of the 'Artscape New Writing Programme', 'Phizzical Theatre' and the 'Rust Co-operative', from South Africa has been immense in linking common culture and telling unique stories that resonate. It is clear in South Africa that the coalition for an equal society, created by Mandela, still has many diverse supporters and this is reflected in their challenging works of theatre which enrich our annual programme.

Prejudice has many friends as it endorses privileged status, craved for by some, who still feel inferior, despite their wealth and position. They feel better if others are worse off. Establishing Dublin as a centre that could respond to this global imbalance of LGBTQI expression was a daunting challenge. To do it without resources was almost impossible, but as in many an LGBT rights battles, it is from pure determination to present the information that educates change, that inspires the small to take on the mighty. In 21st century Ireland, there was a lot more space to speak, more ears to hear new voices, and more generosity to enable and facilitate new theatre than existed elsewhere. That was an opportunity to be grasped and developed in 2004.

chapter 6

Gay Ireland

Long has submission played a traitor's
parts, Oh human soul, no patience any
more

Eva Gore Booth

Another inspiring moment for the foundation of the Festival was a wonderful
photography exhibition of Pride in 'The Front Lounge', Dublin in 2003. I
attended and when I saw the images, I put my head in my hands. A friend
impatiently said 'What's wrong now'? I said 'look, ten years on, we are all still
in masks'. It was true. Everyone in the photos had their identity concealed by
wonderful colour, make-up, wigs and garb – an essential part of gay identity
and celebration, but only a part – where were the real faces in a decade of
decriminalisation? This became a central theme also of my Master's thesis –
visibility post decriminalisation. My studies at the Equality Studies Centre in
UCD were another major influencing component in the founding of the Theatre
Festival.

The tenth anniversary of decriminalisation saw the 2003 killing of young Brian
Mulvaney in Dublin - the tragic murder of a young man who was perceived to
be gay – he wasn't. What a horrendous price for a young man, his family and
community to pay, for a construct, that still insists - some are more equal, or
better, than others. That case was solved, the killer Brian Willoughby, had a
series of previous violent form against men he thought, were gay. He had knifed
a man on College Green, inflicted dozens of cuts in an unprovoked attack on
Baggot Street, stuck a broken bottle in the face of a student on the Number 15
bus, assault etc. In 2003, a proper life sentence was delivered by the Courts, as
was the sentencing of his 15 year old accomplice. More recently, the Frank Mc
Cann murder, saw the same police station involved in the unsolved 1980s murder
of RTE designer Charles Self case, conduct themselves in an entirely different

manner and this time the perpetrator was apprehended and incarcerated. 'Verity Alicia Mavenawitz', an Irish author dealt movingly with light sentencing for gay murders and their impact on family and friends, in her play 'The Drowning Room', which later transferred to the Andrews Lane Theatre in 2005. It was a significant work in that it showed the difference in playing in our Festival or the mainstream. Gay characters, despite their victimhood in a play can still be funny and Festival audiences laughed appropriately. In the Andrew's Lane production this moving piece was met in almost empathetic silence. This phenomenon was later to be observed in other transfers from the Festival to the mainstream.

Identity is important. Community is diverse - therefore theatre must reflect this, to be truthful art. For centuries Ireland was a geographically and economically isolated nation. In 21st century Ireland, we have over 180 different nationalities living here. The second language spoken in Ireland is no longer Irish – it is Polish. We introduced divorce for the first time in 1996 by a 0.5% majority in a national referendum. There are now new families. Our population is ageing and ageing well. We have been rich, we have less now. The new language of those who refuse to engage with the struggle for equality, has created 'Diversity' as a tag that is more acceptable for discourse amongst the advantaged. Management consultants frequently choke on the concept of equality, in a sector that is constructed for profit, made by one at the expense and labour of another. In 1998 The Employment Equality Act was the first serious piece of legislation to recognise the economic citizenship of LGBT people in Ireland.

Diversity is not an adequate description or valuation of such change in the recognition of the unique identity of each individual. The term diversity can never replace identity. People who may represent diversity in a multi-cultural society are not different, they are distinct.

Any attempt to impose or limit a definition on who is an 'Irish' person is today is full of risk. Services and activities that rely on a traditional or limited definition are exclusionary and flawed. When the definition is unspoken in the workplace, it is impossible to measure, assess and act upon. Any attempt to split society into two groups – those we recognise as 'like us' and those who are 'different' is equally flawed and inadequate. The challenge for a modern democracy is not to make a 'one size fits all' workplace or public service, but to recognise and respect valid cultural difference and respond respectfully and efficiently to that opportunity, to fully understand our complete identities. This ethos also needs to permeate publically funded artistic policy. Real change happens when change is understood by leaders and senior management. You serve people, not categories or labels.

The history of the Festival's relationship with the publically funded arts administrative sector is interesting and is worthy of examination in a later chapter. The battle for identity was the core issue in my resistance and eventual victory, at a price, to the corporate swamping of the Festival by a rainbow covered vodka brand, which I will also discuss later. Identity, hard won, is not for sale - it is for sharing as our happy engagement with alcohol brands demonstrates in 2013, thanks to the tenacity of Jen Butler our talented fundraiser!

As discussed, gay men in particular have been constructed as feminine or effeminate. Gay women are often portrayed solely as 'butch', which is not the case. Historically it is clear that the camp guys had nowhere to hide in a hostile society and therefore with incredible courage, lived their lives as the only visible gays. My short play 'Tumbling Down' features such characters in the 1980's Ireland. Indeed, among the first known gay characters to win Broadway acclaim were 'Albin/Zaza', 'Georges', 'Jacob' and 'Les Cagelles' (gender defying dancers) in 'La Cage Aux Folles' as discussed previously. Gay men were not real men – they failed the test in some way.

Hilton Edwards and Micheal Mac Liammoir, co-founders of Dublin's Gate Theatre, were strong in their presentation of historical, Shakespearian and romantic characters for decades in theatre and yet they were known as 'The Boys'. Boys don't run theatre companies, avoid, bankruptcy, persuade investors, employ artists, and establish and sustain a national theatre at The Gate, in Dublin as wonderfully told in Christopher Fitzsimon's biography of the same name demonstrates. But 'boys', the talented gay young men drawn to the escapism of theatre in a hostile society, knew no matter what your status or achievement, a gay artist could never be a man, but remained a 'boy' forever.

The embracing of respect can remain fragile in a historically constructed 'macho' environment. Machismo is fake and insecure. How 'macho' was Cory Aquino when she stood in front of moving tanks to democratise her country? How macho was the slightly built Ghandi or is Aung San Suu Kyi? Strength comes from knowledge, action and courage. Strength comes from the absence of fear. Perceived difference breeds fear. Policy, politics, law and services are challenged, when they may only be designed to respond to a society, populated by those who 'look like' or 'behave like' the mainstream. Such narrowness of recognition fails the diverse community of pluralist societies. It leaves people unprotected, excluded and vulnerable to crime. It creates an environment where the criminal thrives on any minority's reluctance to report crime, in the absence of a respectful and safe environment. Pro-active equality and diversity engagement and implementation, counterbalances the criminal opportunity. It informs society that though privilege and power exists, so do such things as rights. Democracy must underpin rights – the benchmark of a pluralist society.

In 2006, President Mary Mc Aleese could not officially open our fifth Festival, but she did generously offer to send us a message of support. It was extraordinary in its focus and celebration. She informed us that the IDGTF was helping to 'complete the cultural map of Ireland'. That is an important message to those who seek to confine our work to their own narrow focus of what being gay, or gay theatre is. This was wonderfully demonstrated in Peter Crawley's tantrum like 'review' in the 'Irish Times' which set out what gay theatre was and then failed us. The problem was none of what was set out reflected any of our own published definitions and ambitions. By the completion of our personal identity in theatre, we are making our skill set available to our State and community, in an open dialogue centred on truthful identity.

As mentioned, some gay artists do not appreciate this intercultural dialogue initiated by the Festival's programmes. Some still demonstrate how effective the constructed shame of the past is and indeed indicate a fear or nervousness, that once perceived gay, it will negatively affect future casting opportunities? Do you need to be a plumber to convincingly act the role?

We decided that, rather than just seeking to blend in, to the flawed sterility of sameness, we needed to challenge a society, built on concealment, as a prerequisite for a 'good' life. Laws have changed, but the discussion is on-going. There is always more work to be done when we strive to serve all our communities well in a democracy. There is always more work to be done when we strive to include all our communities in society's mirror - the arts. We were 150 years behind and Ireland has caught up a lot since 1993. How much does changing a negative attitude cost? Nothing.

The real skill is to see and understand the past legally constructed difference. By 2003, the new Equality Authority and later the NESF, recommended that training be made available to all legal and judicial people on LGB issues, including the police. The somewhat lazy approach of 'one size fits all' services, attempts to consign different identities, to the 'all encompassing' but opaque label of being 'different'. It is a flawed premise. The first thing we owe all our people is their identity, and people have the right to name themselves.

So where was the 'training' opportunity for the arts or wider society? Here, the construct of theatre is truly liberating. Artists are free to present and communicate. Audiences must be left undisturbed to take from such discourse what they wish. Hence my personal dislike of post-performance discussions, which tend to impose a particular interpretation on an audience, which may not yet have digested the layers of the presented piece. Imposing an opportunity for interpretation can deny the development of an individual one, following consideration of the inspiration of the performance from each unique, liberating perspective.

Attitudes change more rapidly when there is information available – that's why so much effort is made to silence the transmission of knowledge. The voices of those being discussed are heard and with leadership from the top, more are included. Attitudes that have been embedded in culture for decades, will not be changed in any meaningful way overnight. They will not be changed by holding a conference, tolerating a small diversity project, setting up a committee, while concealing the 'old ways' at the core. They need a bigger dialogue on equal terms of shared citizenship and participation, to be fully embraced and understood. Accessible theatre can provide that forum or opportunity for society.

In so many ways, theatre created a 'safe haven' for gay people, on stage or behind the scenes, but there was a price. Few, if any of these artists, have a true, recorded, acknowledged history of identity. Their achievements remain recorded in the achievements of others, or flawed in some way for the incompleteness or concealment of true identity. One challenge for the Festival was to discover and acknowledge this achievement of the past, while situating our ethos in new voices for the future. In that, we are probably the biggest and most branded event that celebrates Oscar Wilde, in a country that has long exploited and benefitted from its association with him. From the start, I put on record at our academic seminar, that I'm not sure I would have liked him. Some speculate it is because we would have both struggled for the attention of the crowd! He was excessive in his habits and was like many successful theatre practitioners who constantly reinvent themselves, in order to survive, in an often unforgiving and trend vulnerable industry.

Many artists eventually begin to perpetuate the myths they create. None more brilliantly than a man who modelled himself on the reported presentation of Wilde, Micheal Mac Liammoir. I never met him, but I have been intrigued by young Albert Wellmore, who like so many other gay men, found space for his own identity in another place. It still happens today. Mac Liammoir was a stunningly handsome young man. His biographical notes about being born in Cork are pure fiction, but one admirably pursued in his acquisition of the Irish language to back it up. In that effort, he contributed handsomely to writing and theatre in the Irish language. It was easier in some way for these men to invent themselves in Ireland, rather than in England, though they maintained their connections there in the theatre and in attracting supports from the British Council. In 2013, as part of a series of theatre discussions, director Michael Scott will host a discussion with Alan Amsby ('Mr Pussy') who carved out a successful drag career in Ireland in the 1970s as we in turn exported Cork born 'Danny La Rue' to do the same in the UK. It is easier to be different in another country where your difference, like Wilde, is firstly defined by your ethnic origin.

chapter 7

Ireland's Stonewall

Naming the bridge after
Mr Flynn would go some way to
teaching people about the inequality that
existed before their time, while serving as a
reminder to those who lived through it

Councillor Damian O Farrell, 2013

In Ireland, we had our own 'Stonewall' year in 1982, arising from the cherishing
of hypocritical Victorian laws in our new Republic, culminating in a breakdown
in community policing and judicial response. Generations of gay citizens of the
new Republic were consigned to a legally constructed ghetto, as the oppressive
British 1861 'Offences Against the Person Act' and the subsequent 'Criminal Law
(Amendment) Act' of 1885, were embraced in the laws of the new Republic,
that promised to be one of equals. It is impossible to estimate how many lives
remained unfulfilled, concealed and shameful, in the 20th century, in the new
Irish Republic of equals, as a result of such stigma. We have seen the stigma
imposed on 'Magdalen penitents', institutionalised children, their single mothers,
adopted children, ex-clergy, and people of different faiths and abilities. It was the
same for gay people, but they had to contend with adult criminality.

In the 1960s, this began to be challenged, timidly in the voyeuristic, hostile,
environment of criminality. Ghettoes were run by mafia and criminals.
Imposed or self-exclusion from family and community, necessitated by identity
recognition, fed prostitution and poverty as the Combat Poverty Agency
reported in the 1980s. Lack of knowledge of sexuality, paucity of services and
transparency in accessing healthcare, fuelled the indiscriminate transfer of HIV.
Lack of validation of same sex love and the absence of any structure to define
and validate it, led to loss of opportunity for partnership, commitment and

indeed, loss of life, through the option of isolation and suicide.

Legal erasement can not instantly sooth or replace that embedded culture of isolated exclusion and stigma – explanation and exposition can. It is a slow and revealing process. It is a challenge for any form of theatre to take this on. It is a challenge for any society to work to overcome that inherited stigma. If it fails, the culture of concealment, will continue to be a breeding place for crime, exploitation, exclusion, isolation and lost opportunity.

Emigration was not purely economically driven, as gay family members were driven away for being different or left, for having no reference points from which to begin or pursue happiness. I met an older couple on holidays in a piano bar. I was asked to sing 'Danny Boy' for this man's birthday. He was Irish and had lived with his partner in the UK, as he had left his family in Cavan, because he was gay. He was now in a wheelchair recovering from a stroke. He was a small framed man and his partner a large burly Englishman. He wept at the song and the fact that he would soon be returning to Cavan after 49 years in exile. His grand nephews and nieces had looked him up and invited them both home, to meet the extended family in the new Ireland. These instances and causes of exile, remain in recent memory. The 1980s were a long overdue time of social change in Ireland and it was a bitter battle.

In January 1982, a very talented designer in our national broadcaster RTE, was found dead in his home - murdered. His name was Charles Self. The Garda (police) response was to round up 1,500 known gay men and build a data bank of fingerprints and photographs. They were asked who they slept with and for their partners' names. It was a pogrom. This action traumatised and destroyed many lives and of course failed to ever result in a charge or conviction for the Charles Self murder. A militant group, (note people looking for equal rights are often militants) the Dublin Lesbian and Gay Men's collective was established as a result and mounted a defence campaign against Garda harassment. Like Stonewall, in an emotionally charged community, they had had enough.

In 1982, lesbians and gays were forced by law to socialise underground, having no opportunity if needed, of seeking protection from the Gardai. No one in the gay community, at that time, ever gave their real name when socialising, even to friends. It was too dangerous. If you knew the community, you might have also surmised, Charles Self was possibly in the company of a stranger, or someone not necessarily gay or closeted, who set upon and exploited gay men to threaten them, with the blackmail that such repressive laws guarantee. Anti-gay laws are always a 'blackmailer's' charter. Identity concealment in any community, only creates crime and criminals. An older friend of mine recounted that on his first entry into Bartley Dunnes' bar (site of 'Break for the Border') he was approached and given a name, not his own and today I still hear some older men call him by that given name. The use of feminine names, usually with some loose association to your male name was also protection from blackmail. When the blackmailer reported to the Gardai that he was in the bad company of 'Stella and Bridie' it was a challenge to figure out who these men were!

The zealousness of the Gardai, in using this tragedy as an excuse to harass a community, already living in fear, not only of discovery, but now of their lives, is a negative cultural legacy that still challenges good LGBT community policing today in Ireland. And for 12 more years, those laws remained in force. After 30 years, it is time the cold case of Charles Self's murder was solved. In the meantime, men retreated from the gay bars and like the Mattichines, socialised privately. I believe if you bought a six pack of beer at closing time and visibly held it on the street outside Bartley Dunne's, a crowded car might pull up and offer you a lift up the Dublin mountains, to a mobile home or to a basement in Mountjoy Square, where an all-night party would be held, out of sight. That was the not unhappy social life of many a young country lad, who knew he could never go home with any of his social circle to rural Ireland.

It was another episode in the compulsory secret gay life many people lived in the cities. If they still maintained social contact with the families and friends whose moral outlook excluded them, from their own locality, they invented a story to tell at home. One was that if you met someone from your locality in a gay bar, you could recognise them at home saying, you went to the same church for mass on a Sunday! Many others never went home again. My life in musical theatre removed any necessity to live such a different life away from home, as I had found a new home in the theatre and that could be shared, talked about proudly and truthfully, on return visits to Waterford.

That year too, I was Vice president of the National Youth Council of Ireland in charge of Youth Affairs, a position I held for three years. The Taoiseach, Garret FitzGerald, was hugely inspirational and interested in young people. He had come to lead Fine Gael in 1977 and one of his first initiatives was to establish Young Fine Gael. He urged young people to visit their member of parliament and say 'Garret sent me'. That's exactly what I did when I crossed the bridge in Waterford at 16, unbeknown to my Labour loyal maternal family and told Eddie Collins TD, that 'Garret sent me'. I became constituency youth chairman and chaired the Waterford City branch, but gave it up when I pursued my career in journalism. I could share Fitzgerald's social democratic vision to liberate Ireland as an independent pluralist nation, rather than one controlled by a State within a State – the Catholic Church. I was civically active. Later, I became the youngest ever person to be nominated to a State body, when at 22, I was appointed a director of the Youth Employment Agency, with an unprecedented budget of £94 million pounds. It was a steep and valuable learning curve in a most vibrant, challenging and exciting time – an emerging new Ireland in the 1980s.

That year too, we were advancing youth participation in democracy. We set up the National Youth Congress, which held the first Irish Youth parliament (later Dail na nOg). As Chairman, I had a key input into the programme of the weekend, which had delegates from all youth organisations in the country. Garret was our guest speaker and did not need to be persuaded about the need for youth work funding, he wanted our views on youth policy and participation. At the dinner that night, when I complained that taxes were too high, he calculated my tax return for me on a napkin to prove his point to the admonishment of his highly regarded wife, Joan. With the support of NYCI policy officer, Tom Costello and our committee, we drew up a list of workshops relevant for young people including education, homelessness, young people and the law, and incredibly, sexuality. The media and some catholic groups went mad, when I invited Anne Connolly of the Well Women Centre and David Norris to address the workshop. The Church, including SPUC (Society for the Protection of Unborn) and the sons of Mine Bean Ui Chribin, protested outside the Hotel Victor, the conference venue. When they met David on his way in, he replied he was representing the 'North Great George's Street Preservation Society' – to their bewilderment. It was my first time meeting him.

My own organisation (where I worked) the Catholic Youth Council, also felt the heat of controversy, mainly from Auxiliary Bishop Brendan Comiskey. He spoke to me by phone at the hotel and fudged around about my participation in a workshop called 'sexual freedom'. It was 1982. I asked 'why did he think young catholics could not, or had nothing to contribute to this debate?'. He agreed we did have a relevant and informed view and that it should be expressed – a volte face on his original demand that no young catholic should attend. I told my boss this later and he in astonishment, showed me a letter from the Bishop, which appeared to be less interested in our young souls, as he wrote, 'there will be many a fence to be mended before the next diocesan collection comes around'. Comiskey later resigned in disgrace about the handling of child sexual abuse.

I was roundly condemned in an editorial of the 'Irish Catholic', of course, before the workshop was even held. Catholics commentators have been blessed with remarkable foresight. Celibates know everything about relationships, critics know even more about topics and people they have never encountered. I stuck to my guns and insisted that young people be allowed to discuss sexuality in the early 1980s. The compromise in a debate that hit the headlines, resulted in a unfortunate couple from 'Marriage Encounter' being sent in to 'balance' the panel with Norris and Connolly. The nice couple were so far out of their depth, but they probably learned a thing or two. The event went ahead as planned – a triumph in the face of opposition.

When I got into the workshop on 'sexual freedom' – it was packed. There were 12 workshops on youth issues on the programme, but this was the only one full of journalists. I noted a particularly radical woman journalist who had been in college with me, was there. I enquired 'why this workshop and not any of the others dealing with other vital youth issues? 'My editor wants blood Brian' was the reply. It seems every radical can be bought by economic necessity. I insisted that the young participants be allowed to speak freely and that they could not be named by the preying media. This was respected.

The workshop went ahead and was at a level that only honest young people can manage. Then a 20 year old young man from the Church of Ireland Youth Council announced he was gay, even his friends beside him did not know. It was the very first time I had ever heard such an admission in public or ever encountered such honesty. I didn't know who I was myself at that stage! Considering the law and the hostile public environment in the room, it was astonishing. I never got his name. I have never forgotten him and what he taught us all that day. Ireland never respected honesty in the 1980s – he taught me to respect it and he challenged me.

I made the front page of various media and lived through the catholic 'outrage'. We had broken a mould. It was a good training. Our 'Dail na nOg' went ahead too. Over a dozen members of parliament formed the 'Government side' and though I was to act as Speaker of the House, I was persuaded instead to become the 'Leader of the Opposition' at the last minute. We debated the legal status of young people in education, before the law and sexuality. It was a conflicting time in politics. Change being led by Garret, when politics engaged with young people. I'm not sure how much policy change we achieved then, but we were all invited to run for the real Dail! Impossible of course, for anyone gay at that time.

Later that year, Declan Flynn, an Aer Rianta worker, was walking in Fairview Park. He was set upon, chased by a gang of youths, robbed of £4 and was beaten to death. This time the culprits were caught and brought before the Courts. In 1983 they got suspended sentences and were immediately released. Those convicted and freed held a "victory march" in Fairview Park. But later, the Courts took a much more serious view of a crime perpetrated by some of the gang. They got custodial sentences for stealing a car.

Equally disturbing, a news story contained in the Irish Queer Archive, recounts the experiences of a man who went to a Garda station complaining about queer-bashing, months before the Flynn killing and "he was jeered and laughed out of the station". After the killers' victory march, a group of gay 'criminals' then decided to bravely protest. They were joined by good citizens, trade unions and civil society groups, and held an historic 'gay rights' march to Fairview Park in Dublin in 1983. They were out in public and photographed, but they were creating change. In hindsight, this march has been designated as the first gay pride parade - a protest on the judgement that was seen to encourage and condone attacks on anyone, thought to be gay. It was a time when Ireland howled at the denial of rights for people north of the border on the basis of religion, and here they stood accused of doing a similar thing, equally in the name of religion, to their own citizens.

In 1988, while still a 'criminal', David Norris ran for and was finally elected to the Irish Senate and was the first gay person ever elected to a national parliament in the world. He took the Irish Government and its 'anti-gay' laws through the Courts and onto the European Court of Human Rights, represented by our soon to be, first female President, Mary Robinson. He won.

Ireland often rightly accused the UK of serious breaches of human rights and drew international attention to this. It now stood convicted itself on the European stage. It took it five more years to merely erase the offending paragraph of the original Victorian law – ironically long discarded by the British themselves. Culture and prejudice are difficult to move forward. In 1990, while still 'criminals', then President Mary Robinson, in one of her first acts, hosted a reception for lesbian and gay people in her official residence. In 1990, only those who could be photographed attended. In the 1990s there were five known 'gay' saunas in Dublin and only two bars! The ghetto thrived - underground.

chapter 8

Religion and Identity

Nuns fret not at their convent's narrow
room: but surely there is no reason why
we should all be shut up in cells

Eva Gore Booth

History has been a painful lesson for this generation. Ireland had hidden too
many secrets in its past with grave consequences, especially for vulnerable
groups and children. The discovery of this has traumatised Ireland and its decent
people. The complicity of a Church controlled people, with the institutionalising
of so many people whose main flaw was poverty or difference, has contributed
to the Irish attitude of 'if I don't see it, it doesn't exist'. This has prevented us as
a society from dealing with the serious abuses that happened in the towns and
villages of Ireland, under the cruel guise of penitence, salvation and vocation.
The effects, like all bullying, went way beyond the group specifically targeted by
this brutal form of social control.

Even the construct of outlawing all forms of 'same sex' adult relationships,
created the space for no age of consent, with dire consequences, for very young
emerging gay people, in this shadowy ghetto, constructed by religion and
State. So many of the original brave 'outers' of child clerical sexual abuse are
themselves now gay adults, including Andrew Madden and Colm O' Gorman.
Did the created and deliberate isolation of their emerging childhood sexuality,
by Church and State, not provide a rich pasture for the destroyers of youth and
innocence? The abuser found many a refuge in the only place, which prohibited
recognition or discussion of real, rather than theoretical, sexuality. No wonder
it was an identified 'home' of so many abusers, where the environment of
silence ensured that it could not be addressed by those, who had been refused
the permission to acknowledge their own sexuality. For any cleric to do so,
was to call into question their own vocation. Silence bred the crime. Power

and the requirement to protect the institution above all morality, enabled such abuse to thrive, as every door was closed and every voice of dissent silenced. The recruitment of children from their own schools to join religious orders, sometimes before puberty, was another appalling act of child violence, which would not be tolerated today. I can remember such recruitment be initiated in my classroom by the Christian Brothers when I was 9 years old, and seeing teenage 'novices' in my new school from De La Salle, Faithlegg, some years later.

In the Priest was vested, exclusively, the concept of forgiveness of sin. In fact, he could forgive what he had constructed. Parents did not talk about sex in Ireland. We were to learn it sporadically in the 'Christian' context of school, more likely in the sniggers of the schoolyard. Teaching of sexuality, if it happened at all, was in religion class, by someone who by their own admission, only knew the theory and not the practice. Was the 'priest' not the designated person for the confused child to turn to, in his emerging sexuality, especially in the boarding schools or small communities? Many an innocent parent, raised in the same system, believed so and even referred their children to that reliable source. Many a priest, brother or nun honoured that responsibility, usually through the briefest of conversations!

Many times, in the pre-ordained guilty confines of the darkened confessional, it was arranged for the child to enter, unsupervised by parents, who left them to have their sexuality interrogated, without any safeguard as to the bona fides of the individual enquirer under the requirement of telling the truth. The clerical collar was an accepted badge of integrity. All that was 'normal' in Ireland – the church constructed it that way. The faithful trusted and followed.

When society hides the most normal things like sexuality, the consequences are dreadful, as Andrew Madden's book 'Altar Boy' illustrates clearly. Love was shameful in that holy environment. The cloak of shame concealed the very things we should, as a society, have protected our emerging adults from - exploitation. The cloak was constructed by some of those later discovered to have been its most serious violators. Complicity reigned between masterful Church and subservient State where the 'sin' was created and concealed, so that the real 'sin' could be in darkness and wreak havoc on the innocent. And in all this, gay adult sexuality is abusively presented, on a par with exploitation of the innocent, especially by those who lived in same sex institutions. The more lies you create, the more distractions emerge to prevent us all from seeing what is really going on and intended. Being gay is not a lifestyle choice, celibacy is.

I constructed a short theatre piece from Andrew Madden's book 'Altar Boy' at our first Gala Concert, in Liberty Hall Theatre in 2004, linking his story of his relationship with his friend Daniel to that of the song by Elton John. I had known Andrew for many years, but did not know his story. When the Catholic Archbishop of Dublin faced the cameras and assured us he had never compensated anyone for clerical abuse, Andrew courageously appeared on TV news with details of his own Diocesan compensation for his treatment by Fr. Ivan Payne. The Vatican response was to identify that Archbishop as having all the qualities suitable for promotion to Cardinal – the first in a century from the Dublin Diocese. There could be no more definite or strong signal as the battle lines of denial were clearly drawn. The mightiest institution would now take on in public, the voices of the grown children, as had been long silenced through oaths, obedience, concealment and threat. One began to see life as we knew it, changing in Catholic Ireland. The satisfactory, complete response to the child victims is still awaited as that Church values holding onto its financial assets, ahead of the obligation to offer full redress to the victims, by whose courageous insistence, the truth painfully emerged.

Andrew, years later, introduced our play on the child abuse survival story from South Africa 'The Tricky Part' on the opening night in 2009. In an abuse exhausted Ireland, it played to undeservedly poor houses, despite the excellence of the work. The Irish are worn out from the malicious repression of adult consensual sexuality that poisoned life in the twentieth century, which created a cloak to conceal the destruction of the positive emergence of sexuality in our children, as they journeyed through adolescence.

Of course, it also was constructed to deliberately confuse adult consensual sex, with those who cruelly destroy innocence amongst the young, which still today disallows any discussion about the constant sexualisation of children, equally abandoned, in a commercially exploitative media and profitable youth pop industry. I used to be in awe at the moral template of an industry that required the young 19-23 year old guys in our boy bands, who starred in my productions at the Olympia, to embrace and kiss and accept loud demonstrations of love, from girls all below the age of consent in Ireland – but that industry thrives at home and abroad. These young girls would often spend six weeks in the side lane of the Olympia to get a glimpse of their adult idols in winter. The practice continues without adult supervision today. It also denied these attractive young men from giving positive role model guidance, by ever appearing in public with a girlfriend or a boyfriend of their own age – as it was bad for business!

In many other countries where repressive laws may have eased, there is still residual stigma and the culture of religious oppression – the 'a la carte' type that selects from a list of biblical 'abominations' what is currently right and what is wrong. In the Christian religion, happily, Jesus Christ is not recorded anywhere, as having said anything at all, about gay people, during his time on earth. Few Christians know that – why should they, as the opposite is preached at them so often? Some interpretations add and only give Jesus's actual teachings, equal value, to the teachings of men quoted in the Bible, as to how gay people should be treated.

When profit, rather than prophet, becomes a significant driver, understandably an institution that accumulated vast wealth, power and estates, did not want to have to accommodate partners, regardless of sexuality and children, who might need to be provided for, as a cleric's family. Secondly, the power to order clergy to move from parish to parish would be seriously compromised, if families had to be considered. So, when power is to be challenged, put in a new rule to prevent that and the institution and its wealth will survive.

Being gay is, according to the selected passages that make up the modern bible, an 'abomination' fully equal to eating a full Irish breakfast or enjoying a Dublin bay prawn cocktail, according to the often quoted, Leviticus. Here the selected teachings of man, are equated to that of the Son of God, by his church on earth. The insistence is man-made. That is taught. It is believed. It is cultural in communities.

Religion has been hugely abusive in the treatment of difference. It sets itself up as superior and the source of forgiveness of the created sin. The sins of the Christian religion are set out in the Ten Commandments. 'Thou shalt not be gay' is not one of them. In fact the Bible should be a source of joy to gay people. It is the only book where they can be assured, that Jesus is not quoted as saying anything at all negative about gay people. God sent his only son on earth to address countless problems, it is reassuring to note, gays were not one of those.

However, this all changed later when it was decided in the fourth century to combine the 'best bits' of the 12 Gospels recorded into one book. No witnesses of Jesus survived to interfere with the judgement of men. Still, they could not find any reportage of gay people being condemned by him. So they decided to broaden Christianity into 'Leviticism' – whatever that is? Current teaching of 'a la carte' Catholicism is roundly condemned by fundamentalists, but it is they who invented the practice, particularly around Leviticus. This bad tempered guy didn't like lots of things and unlike Jesus, roundly judged and condemned his fellow 'man' at every opportunity, ensuring doom and damnations for a future Irish nation of pork and shellfish eating Catholics. Leviticus's list of abominations is only as abominable as selling your daughters into slavery, but if you have surplus sons – fire ahead! That is the only context of 'sin' in the Bible ascribed to gay people directly. That is the only one of the 'a la carte selection' held onto dearly by men, who claim to speak on behalf of God! Many of these men are bearded – in fact, if we are to believe all the images of Jesus, including the one on the Turin shroud, then Jesus himself is a Levitican abomination, because of his tidy beard – 'for the Bible tells us so' – and it promotes and prints that blasphemy?!

It is in this sorry ignorant context, that many decent people were condemned and lived miserable lives of shame, isolation and detachment. In fact, the Church really didn't get its act together on condemning same sex relations until the time of St Thomas Acquinas in the 13th century. Many decent Irish people later enslaved themselves to a hypocritical and loveless Church who created the sin, in order to have power over the sinner, in granting or withholding, forgiveness. Being in the church was a 'good gig' in the Irish social hierarchy, especially when it overthrew the British aristocracy. In a society like Ireland, that did not have its native aristocracy, it meant it could still have had few 'Princes' bedecked in regalia, as they were all anointed churchmen. My own short play 'A Gentleman Caller' now published in a new US anthology on being 'Queer and Celtic' in the 21st century, speculates about the older single people, bachelors or 'spinsters' who were the free labour of the Church, with the occasional reward of nodded inclusiveness.

The concept of a Gospel of Love is central to Terrence Mc Nally's play 'Corpus Christi' which went much, much further in including everyone, within the reach of the Christian message. It went much further in that Mc Nally's play is a warm and beautiful construction of a loving God. It gained its controversy only in the perverted minds of those who never read the play. Instead their description of this fine theatrical work is not a reflection of what is in the work, but what is in the mind of those who are allegedly the purer followers of a loving God. They created the perversion, blasphemy and promiscuity – not the spiritual and kindly, Mc Nally

My religious education began in earnest when I left home for College in 1978. I add into this mix, the misguided misfortune of my parents following a colleague's advice and placing a very young 17 year old into a University residence run by Opus Dei – which deserves another book! I then went on to work with some excellent people in the Catholic Youth Council and saw the Church's politics, hypocrisy, sexuality, financial and property greed, at first hand. Truly my religious education was complete. This too is possibly the subject of another book!

In the meantime, I had an ambitious life plan mapped out with all the knowledge that a 17 year old boy from the country can muster up. It changed somewhat when I went to study journalism in the College of Commerce, Rathmines, Dublin with an enquiring and challenging class. At graduation, I needed a job and talked my way into the Catholic Youth Council as editor of their youth service newspaper. My capacity to draw on my country upbringing gave me a much more effective conservative vocabulary, than my more liberated city colleagues and got me a job at a time of deep recession. It was a great opportunity and grounded me in many good causes.

While there, I had done my first major production as a director, amongst my peers in SYMCO in Stillorgan in 1983. As their leading man (the first ever 'Danny' in 'Grease' in Ireland) the follow-up to that sell-out show was a dilemma, for this pioneering youth musical company. I was invited to direct 'something' and I chose Stephen Schwartz's 'Godspell'. I had survived incarceration as a student in 'Nullamore University Residence', run by the cult of Opus Dei, and working for the Catholic Youth Council, I was hugely disillusioned at what I saw internally in the Church despite the many good people I encountered there. Then my youngest Uncle died suddenly and was buried on the 25th anniversary of his ordination. I had been told that my Grandfather even had to buy him his mattress to sleep on, when he joined the Order and as such, passed 'out of our family' and into this community, which were to be his 'new family'. There were hundreds of priests available and in attendance for the last rites and rituals in public. No one could get him the medical attention he needed as he declined in private. That shook all final sense of religious community I ever had. The 'gay community' too would fail the solidarity test in later years.

I poured my youthful interpretation of my faith and this traumatic personal experience into an expression of his ministry to young people and to non-believers in 'Godspell' in Dublin. The resultant holistic interpretation was roundly condemned from the altar in Kilmacud, before anyone had seen it (of course). On the final Saturday night of the award winning run, the parish priest and three nuns arrived to vet the 'heracy'. During the finale, I saw one nun in tears. They clerical party left without a word. The priest issued another round condemnation from the altar the following day, to those who had criticised the production. The Priest was reported as saying that, even though every theological 't' might not have been crossed, no one could fail to be moved by the deep 'Christianity' in the show! But the damage had been done and we lost money. You need permission to speak in Irish theatre, a point I would encounter again, in later years. The Church's enviable capacity to condemn first and enquire later, has seen it through many a catastrophe over the years. I was learning the hard way.

But, on my first mainstream directorial outing, the show gained two national nominations from the Association of Irish Musical Societies (AIMS). Later in 1987, when people were paying much more attention to my work in theatre, I did a new production of 'Godspell' with my own company DAYMS (Dublin Area Youth Musical Society). This time it won a truckload of AIMS awards including Best Show, (adding to our unpopularity!), it won the Waterford International Festival of Light Opera, and the distinguished arts critic, John Finnegan (Evening Herald) named it as the 'Musical Production of the Year' (ahead of professional work) in his New Year's accolades, reviewing the year in Irish Theatre. A considerable and unrepeated feat by any young director.

I later directed it again, with a group of young people from South Armagh and Dublin, in the tormented border community of Sheelagh, which was hugely transformative, thanks to the inspiring leadership of a man who lived his vocation, Fr. Donal Sweeney. 'Godspell's fluid structure is a director's creative delight and I took full advantage of this artistic freedom. I then brought the communication techniques into the workplace and directed the staff of First Active Building Society from Deputy General Manager to bank assistant, in an amazing workplace endeavour, starring Seamus Flavin and other professionals, that filled and thrilled the Tivoli Theatre in Dublin.

It was inevitable that religion should emerge in the Festival's programming. I like the Christian story – untarnished. Terrence Mc Nally had clearly seen and believed the merit of the message and its nasty deconstruction by man. People should have a set of guiding principles of love, to lead a good life and the core messages of many religions uphold that.

Mc Nally set his play in Corpus Christi, Texas and Jesus was gay. Jesus just completed his identity by being gay – all the rest of his characteristics were visible in abundance in the writing and the playing. Judas too was like Jesus – gay, two male apostles get married to each other and the 108 Productions' (USA) interpretation had a range of roles with 'The Apostles' being played wonderfully by men and women of all ages. In fact, later I found out that film stars Juliet Mills and Maxwell Caulfield had attended the Festival, as their daughter, grand-daughter of Sir John Mills, was in the cast of this show!

The big 'danger' with religious shows is that actors start believing they are 'God' and become engulfed in that emotion of belief, that a good 'God' inspires. I had been exposed to some of these charismatic groups previously in CYC. The emotional connection can become the centre of the production and was a very strong undercurrent in this company's work. This doesn't do full service to Mc Nally's real talent for deconstructing the nastiness of the human interpretation of Jesus's message and for his skill in liberating the purity of the 'love thy neighbour' message as it shines through. 'Corpus Christi' wonderfully connects gay people back to the religion to which they are entitled to, as a result of their cultural upbringing. I knew it was time that an Irish audience was given that opportunity to reconnect themselves with religion and 'Corpus Christi' was the perfect vehicle. It sold out. You still can not present religion without permission in Ireland and some media had just a little fun stirring up 'controversy' in a jaundiced Ireland.

We had 'two-and-a-half' protestors one night. I say a half, as one was distinctly uncomfortably reluctant and barely held his hand made poster above waist level! They felt duty bound, as it had received media attention, to object. Extremists are always available to condemn something they have neither seen or read. 'I would not want to see it if Jesus was gay' said one – well it does depend then on your own definition of 'gay'. I saw it and I saw the audience, who were transformed by being reconnected to a religion, that had most hypocritically condemned and evicted them. The audience was clearly moved as Mc Nally's Christian message hit a long neglected, but ever fertile, spiritual ground.

Religion is close to the skin of any Irish person. I was proud as our audience eloquently engaged with the 'protestors' as did I, outside Smock Alley Theatre. I approached them and gave them my word that, if they could quote a single line of condemnation, issued by Jesus Christ about gay people from the Bible or the unused Gospels, I would personally close the production down immediately. They were perplexed. One offered a paraphrase of adultery and I duly pointed him in the direction of 'The Abbey' as I thought their current offering may have an adulterous plot! Not a word could be quoted, because none exists.

The only time Jesus lost his temper was with the hypocrites. Gay people who are visible in society are not hiding anything. The Church has made a decision to gamble the entire core of its existence, on their lust to sexually control a populace that is now, far more educated than many churchmen are themselves. In 2012, 57,000 US nuns were admonished by the Vatican for 'spending too much time on poverty and social justice...and not enough time opposing gay marriage and abortion'. Jesus would be proud!

I had seen such created hypocrisy first hand myself with Opus Dei, and in my contact and work inside the Church. I had also seen the other side, that of wonderful vocation and great work, but that always remained on the lowest step of this embittered, politicised, hierarchical and patriarchal institution. Hypocrisy is created by insisting on sin that doesn't actually exist. Once sin or crime is unjust (or natural) then the necessity to conceal is essential – hence the birth of the hypocrite. A Church which preaches shame instead of love, distorts vocation.

I was beside the late Frank Mc Cann in the Front Lounge when he was murdered one Tuesday night in Dublin. As I assisted clearing the shocked venue, I noticed a young priest who I knew, as he had attended some of my shows. I asked him to attend and to give the last rites to the dying Frank Mc Cann, as he lay on the floor, the blood oozing from his neck where he had been stabbed. As I ushered more people to leave, the young priest sped past me towards the front door and Frank, born a catholic, was left spiritually unattended. It shocked me to the core, maybe even more than the murder, that a young gay priest's vocation could be compromised, by administering the sacrament to a dying man. I see no faith in that, but I had also other experiences of religious hypocrisy.

Two young male friends of mine had a home together in Dublin for some years.

They were a lovely young gay couple with 'B' as a most charming young man – one I would describe as 'every Mother's son-in-law'. His partner 'C' alerted me to a fear he had about 'B's 'relationship' with a local priest. What evolved was worse, as 'B' declared he was leaving the home they had created, to become a priest! I reminded myself that ironically I had met them, both of my friends, first coming out of a pub, which had to close early on 'Holy Thursday' and 'B' was looking for a place to continue the party!

This revelation coincided with a John Paul ll's pastoral preaching against homosexuality in an uncharacteristic, condescending and offensive way (most likely penned by his controlling homophobic successor). This theme was later zealously continued by his elevated assistant, the disastrous Benedict XVI. The internalised homophobia of the Church was rampant in every phrase as the ailing Pope's infallibility was exposed to the interpretation of those who surrounded him. I had encountered and personally met John Paul and found his presence to be incredibly spiritual and sincere. In his later and ailing years, I could never reconcile that experience with the utterances published in his name. The Catholic church as an institution is a loveless place, as it is essential that political power is not challenged by the primacy of Christian love.

I challenged 'B' on whether he would preach that hateful sermon on the Pastoral letter. He said he would, as that was the commitment of his vocation. He made this statement in the kitchen of the home, he and his partner had made together and wonderfully so. I asked him further would he preach it, if I was present in the congregation. He said he would. I asked what would he do, if I then stood up and 'outed' him. He replied "I know you Brian, and you would not do that". I replied "You should not base your vocation on what I would or would not do". I wished him well and asked him to at least be truthful about his sexual identity at his acceptance interview, in order for me to respect him and for him to respect himself. He later told me, he did tell them he was gay at the interview and they moved swiftly on. They indeed had a 'catch'. He is a very charming guy!

Years later, I was approached in a pub (as the wiser owl) by two young men. One had come out to his parents in a local Dublin suburb. They were insisting that he go and seek the counsel of the local priest. I was asked what should he do? I enquired about his background and his location, and to the young man's astonishment, I advised him to go to see the priest. "But I don't want to. What will I say". I replied, just start the conversation with "Brian Merriman says hello" and you will be fine! That's how Ireland works. Fr 'B' as I would expect, was no further obstacle to him living his life. Another friend who was made go to see a priest was encouraged to live his life. When he said but that's against your beliefs, the Priest advised that that was something he would have to reconcile and not allow that to impinge on my friend's chance for happiness.

'Corpus Christi' was an important play for us and for gay people in Ireland. It was well produced and acted, though I did not appreciate the company taking the audience with them, for a follow-on discussion in another venue, thus depriving the play following them each night, of a potential audience! 'Jesus' definitely sinned in that action!

Interestingly, it was the female players that showed the greater strength of character onstage that year. Men find emotion the opposite of strength at times. Here in an emotionally charged scenario, it was the women who took hold and steadied the barometer, to allow the play to shine through. I had seen that happen in the scarred communities of Crossmaglen and surrounds, when I was doing musical theatre there, in a Catholic youth club in Sheelagh, at the height of the 'Troubles' and rampant local discrimination. Religion has been at the heart of our Irish culture and we have a right to claim it, if it remains part of our identity. No one needs permission to believe in a just God. No one needs permission to speak in theatre, but there are consequences if you choose to assert your right to do so!

'Corpus Christi' is a remarkable play, especially for those who grew up in a Church controlled State. This control and its effects on women later came out again in Eilish O' Carroll's 'Live, Love, Laugh' (Festival 2012) which dealt with women growing up in Catholic Ireland from the 1950s. It is part of who we are and only by revealing all its evolutions, will we move forward in the knowledge of the truth of the institutional flaws, which must be separated from the core message of any faith, based on respect and inclusion and the good works of those committed to its message.

The Sunday Tribune of May 11th headlined about 'Corpus Christi' "His legacy is bomb threats and bad press, but gay Jesus is now in Dublin" featuring the condemnatory comments of Sean Mullan, the Director of the Evangelical Alliance Ireland , whom I have never heard of before or since. Mullan did admit though that he had 'not seen the play as he had not had the opportunity…but he had studied the 'comments' of the author. I am unaware if Mr Mullan chose to enlighten himself by attending, or to more comfortably hold onto his beliefs. Why should he – he got his headlines, without ever having any direct knowledge of the subject – another disastrous outcome of lazy, confrontational advocacy which imitates 'balance' in journalism. I am always amused when asked to debate equal rights to find myself painted as an 'extremist' when I say I might like to marry some day!

The decent and socially conscious Bishop of Killaloe, Dr Willie Walsh, was quoted as saying " I have no intention of seeing it, as I would consider it offensive and I would not encourage other people to either" in 'The Irish News of the World'. None of them ever paused to consider that Mc Nally was spreading the good news, using well tried and traditional missionary techniques. Mc Nally's technique by making Jesus gay, to a gay audience, was similar to the approach of presenting Asian 'holy Families' in Asia. We all know that Mary was not the white faced, blushed cheeked, flowing robed, person embedded in our statuary. Effective missionaries, including St Patrick, have long used local and cultural references to explain the Christian message – in this Mc Nally out classed some followers of Christ, in his capacity to truthfully transmit an inclusive message, that claims we are all made in the imagery of Christ and 'Corpus Christi' proved it handsomely!

It was equally heart-warming to see so many of our audience engage emotionally with the play. Many were my peers and you could feel the scars of rejection by their religion of their deeply felt spirituality, coming out in the audience response to each performance. No Church can afford to lose such commitment. A man made Church doesn't see that.

The role of the Churches in preventing access to safe sex has resulted in possibly the greatest genocide since the Nazi holocaust. Not a word in any 'good book' can be rightly used to justify such devastating acts of cruelty and certain death, as the denial of contraceptive protection in HIV prone, poor and uneducated societies. In poor societies, the role and responsibilities of the educated are far more onerous in passing on the knowledge that saves lives. The ignorance of sexuality resulting from celibacy is the Church's most costly vanity. They denigrate gay life and culture as a lifestyle choice, when in fact that term can only appropriately be applied to compulsory celibacy.

Jesus Christ never required celibacy. Priests are not celibate – why should their followers be? The more visible advocates of celibacy in the Irish clergy in my youth, Bishop Eamonn Casey and Fr. Michael Cleary both preached celibacy and abstinence as they fathered their own sons. Their sin of course was not fatherhood in the truest sense of that word – it was the only Irish sin – they were caught. It is such a moral crises where Churches will put their lust to control people's sex lives ahead of their pastoral vocation, at the cost of many of the core teachings of the major religions, which map out a way to live a good life of peaceful co-existence. Millions of people have died from the ignorance of 'celibate' clergy in Africa today. Clergy were often educated. By their intellect they asserted control. Their families made huge financial sacrifices to facilitate the vocation.

My Great-Grandmother was known, like many of her generation, for her herbal cures. One young man had a veruka withered index finger when he applied to enlist at St Peter's College in Wexford, a hundred years ago. His vocation was refused on grounds of his disability. They would not want that withered finger near a host. He heard of my great Grand Mother (a devout catholic of original Quaker stock) and her cure. She administered it to him and the veruka and its tentacles were drawn out of his finger. He went back to the seminary cured and was admitted.

However a clerical troika delegation called to the family home and enquired of her method. It was herbal. 'Do you recite any words when collecting and preparing these herbs' enquired the controlling cleric? 'I do father' she replied. 'What would those words be' further ventured the Inquisitor? 'In the name of the Father, Son and Holy Ghost' was the reply! They left satisfied, but she never made the ointment again, nor would she reveal or pass on the curative recipe to the generations that followed her.

In 1961, her grand-daughter (My Mother) enquired late in her pregnancy (me!) at the beginning of the Lenten fast, could she eat a slice of toast to ease late night heartburn? No, was the answer, but radically, on requiring a second opinion from a Franciscan, she received another lecture, that Lent was not for her or her baby – her only duty was to ensure her own health and that of the child – it did however result in my having an ongoing legacy of reflux!

Finally, many years later, I was honoured to be asked to speak at the LGBT community's Christmas carol service organised by that most Christian of men – Brian Glennon and his team. There is a mixture of sadness and joy in this. The LGBT Christians (they can not be Catholics) are welcomed by that most inclusive church, the Unitarians on St Stephens Green, Dublin, whose joy is based solely on the commonality of belief. For me, it was like 'coming out' again to publically speak on religion to a dispossessed group. I had, as a young man working for the Catholic Youth council, been invited by my then girlfriend's father, a Unitarian, to do a 'lunchtime dialogue' in that Church with the Reverend Kenneth Wright. We spoke about the hopes and ambitions of young people in Ireland in the 1981.

At the LGBT Carol Service, I was a very changed man in one way, returning to that pulpit at the same venue, years later with a complete identity. It was truly an emotional challenge, almost like 'coming out again', but this time it was about my personal beliefs and in public. The feeling of loss and faith at the annual gathering is palpable and my words of righteous anger had to be put aside, to reassure those gathered, that we do not believe, by the permission of others. We can believe because we know our God. That was my Christmas gift to them that year. You do not need anyone else's permission to be who you rightly are, and if that is a gay person or a Christian, then the right is yours. The same is equally true for your right to be yourself in theatre.

In the new Republic, the control of the people by the Church, merely replaced the oppression by the British with that of the Vatican in the new Republic. The treatment of women and children was scandalous. Pregnant women could die. Mothers had to be 'churched' again to reinstate their purity after giving birth. Married people could not divorce. Pregnancy could not be avoided. Children were recruited for vocations in primary school. The imprisonment of women in the Magdalen laundries and the forced adoption of babies is one of the darkest episodes of a loveless religion and a compliant, obedient, ignorant, State. The exclusion of gay people and the creation of needless sin as a demeaning of status was a permitted mantra. The ill treatment and abuse of the children who could not be adopted, or who were simply poor, is well documented. These are issues theatrically explored by brave and insightful writers, which the Festival programming has attended to, admittedly with little appetite from our weary Irish audience, whose past is all too near.

So much horror was inflicted and concealed in that Ireland, that when I decided to engage in a mainstream dialogue of gay life and culture, there was a standard of truth required in the theatre. Theatre had been used effectively to construct the Irish identity the previous century. In a much tinier niche, could it still be of service in asserting our own identity as part of a modernising Ireland?

'Corpus Christi' was the right play at the right time to be presented in a rapidly changing and religiously suffering Ireland. 108's charismatic production was a timely reminder that, though some men may torture the message, others can still prove the words have a wider, more truthful, inclusive meaning. The right to a personal belief remains the right of the human soul. Terrence Mc Nally greatly honoured us with his work and with his esteemed presence at our Festival of which we are proud to call him a patron.

chapter 9

The Changing Cultural Context

We can not be them, because we are not them, so let us show them how

Cory Thorell on Harry Hay
(personal inscription on inside cover of 'Radically Gay' by Hay)

In arguing that LGB is not a distinct race, which it isn't, I have promoted this notion of us being a common culture. LBG refers to sexual orientation, whereas the traditionally associated 'T' for transgender is not – that is about gender identity. The 'glue' in that common experience worldwide is the similar construction of discrimination of LGBT people in all heterosexist societies. Hence, though our Festival theatre programme is selected from submissions worldwide, it never needs 'translation' for LGBT people who instantly recognise the positive and the negative construction in which they have been placed.

Gay people do not 'come out' into anything they create themselves. By 'coming out', we admit that we accept the narrowed heterosexist construction of what gay life is, in order to begin to live our own lives. No one has ever asked us to construct this for ourselves and that's where the theatre dialogue makes a contribution. In fact, we do not 'come out' at all, we 'go in' to a new construction created for us, from the residue of the negative stereotype and resulting shared stigma worldwide.

Things have changed radically and swiftly in Ireland for Lesbian and Gay citizens. There is some evidence today of overdue change for Transgendered people. There is protection from, discrimination in the workplace, from incitement to hatred, unfair dismissal, and in accessing goods, facilities and services. Frequently the police are called to pubs that refuse service to same sex couples or to same sex domestic situations. The role of the community police is crucial in presenting new societal values as expressed in law, rather than reinforcing residual, faith specific or current negative, cultural values. We rely on our State's Police in a safe democracy. Same sex couples or singles aged 18 and over, are entitled to enjoy a drink in any public house in Ireland. We can book a weekend away in a hotel, walk the streets together with increasing expectation of being left in peace. More people recognise that that is not only good for us, but good for a respectful and inclusive society. I am always pleased that the Festival flags and banners seem to encourage more visibility of gay couples on Dublin's streets each May. However in being visible, we are still the object of the curious voyeur.

The KAL case, where Katherine Zappone (now a Senator) and Anne Louise Gilligan, two legally married women in Canada, which only has one marriage law, are still battling in Court for equity in treatment, is ongoing here. It is extraordinary that Senator Zappone, the first married, gay politician in Ireland, still has to appeal to her parliamentary colleagues, for equal recognition of her partner. No other parliamentary colleague must appeal to her, for any similar acknowledgement. Opposite sex couples, married under that Canadian law have full rights in Ireland, same sex couples married under the identical law, do not. More stigma.

Invasiveness and voyeurism is now a prerequisite of heterosexist society that previously demanded concealment of sexuality by law. In the campaign for changing such laws, heterosexist society freely admits to having a limited knowledge of what it is, they so readily criminalised or prohibited, by their ongoing insistence on a voyeuristic examination of the lifestyles of brave advocates of legal change, when rights are pursued through the Courts.

There is still an exemption in employment equality legislation, sought and won by Fianna Fail as a special exemption from the EU, in the late 1990s, that allows employers with a religious ethos, to potentially discriminate in employment to protect that ethos, even if they are State funded. The Catholic Church though dwindling in numbers, still exerts great power over State funded education and health services, in facilities built by the 'pennies of the poor' of long ago. This exemption builds vulnerability and fear in our LGBT teachers and health workers, as many of these institutions are still nominally controlled by the Church. Legal amendment has been signalled politically by Justice Minister Alan Shatter and Education Minister Ruairi Quinn in 2013, which will have a choice of making the ethos test more difficult, which maintains the chilling impact, or of deletion of this 'Irish solution to an Irish problem, in equality legislation.

Our LGBT young people should be secure at school, in their homes, neighbourhoods and workplaces. That's the law. Schools are historically Church run in Ireland, but secular schooling is growing. Through dwindling vocations, there are five priests left in Leitrim under 50 years of age, the control still remains. Religious are no longer employed in great numbers by the State to teach subjects (creating unemployment in young qualified 'lay' teachers) as in my youth. In a time of recession, the State continues to fund a large portion of the work of teachers in State schools, engaged in communion and confirmation classes, exonerating the churches of the obligation of their clergy to prepare children for religious services, in safe, supervised environments. Irish vocations don't stretch to 'Sunday Schools' – it requires a State subsidy. The passing on of the faith is supposed to be one premise for vocation, but it only happens in Ireland, if it is State funded, at a time when harsh measures are being imposed on the public sector to increase productivity! Let the State educate and the Church indoctrinate.

Today though, the single cleric is often still in the powerful managerial role, surrounded by appointed citizens of the same religion. Sile de Valera, Minister of State at the Department of Education some years ago, supported the 'S/he's Gay and We are Cool with That' publication of positive gay student posters for secondary schools organised by Belong To LGBT youth service and the Equality Authority. It soon became evident that only 10% of schools actually put the free posters on display, even in an environment where homophobic bullying was finally being acknowledged as a serious cause of isolation, under academic achievement, substance abuse, bullying and even suicide, amongst students. Later the Equality Authority published a report on good practice for LGBT students in Irish schools but none were named. Law enforcers, public servants and those in privileged positions can not choose between law, criminal or civil, or between policy agreed by democratic forces – enforcement of equality law and agreed policy is compulsory too.

Many of our youth drama groups gave a voice to these serious school based incidents through drama, in innovative original productions encouraged and presented in the Festival, especially by Crooked House from Kildare and the Independent Youth Theatre, Dublin productions. Our first youngest playwrights were Shaun Dunne in 'Killed by Curriculum', Aaron Rogers 'Fragile' and Daniel Talbot's 'Slipping' whose fine works are discussed later. The presence of new young voices telling their own stories in theatre, has always been a priority for the IDGTF and it is great when they identify us as being their opportunity to be heard. The challenge in getting young, media driven audience in to theatres to see the plays, remains, with a distinct absence of gay youth group activity in supporting these relevant and well performed works by their peers, even when they have funding to do so.

Recently, a group of gay Irish police has formed a network called G Force. They made an impressive presentation to 18 young gay men from all around the country in 2011, who had undertaken public HIV charity events and given media interviews in their local and often rural communities. As facilitator, I suggested a scenario to the young men, where they might have met someone over the internet, or in a pub, and the following morning, might discover that their Iphone, Ipad or wallet was missing after a chance liaison. Having met and been hugely impressed by G Force, only two of the 18 said they would consider reporting the crime. The cultural legacy that exists in the entire LGBT community, is rooted in a minority's anticipation and expectation of discrimination or bad treatment. This is another key theme to be unpacked in much of the writing, especially by young writers.

Today, we have visible LGBT communities, Prides all over the country, GAZE an LGBT film Festival, the IDGTF - the biggest International Gay Theatre Festival in the world, gay sports teams, Limerick bidding for the 2018 gay games, the rugby Bingham cup staged in Dublin, advocacy and youth groups, thriving. Gay people are visible in the media, though many still succumb to the camp stereotype, which narrows the focus of the diversity within LGBTQI lives. It was quite an astonishing achievement to see a 'gay' musical on in the Abbey Theatre in 2012. Hugely hyped, 'Alice in Funderland' was well received by straight audiences and gay fans alike. Exploiting the parody of successful pantomime, with impressive resources, the characters rarely moved from the caricature. The women were either weak or one dimensional or if powerful, were played by men. The men, besides the colourless straight Warren, the evasive lead, all dug deep into the traditional camp caricature to sustain, over three hours of slow moving plot. Writing in gay theatre is changing but I worry when I see such limited progress emerge from the National Theatre's writing programme. We were back once again being entertaining to the masses, as the 'gay' roles minced their way from stereotype to stereotype. Clearly, much more work needs to be done which we continue, to amuse the masses, but also to progress.

The Gay Theatre Festival has many 'firsts' to its credit, but a few stand out as particularly dear. In 2006, we fundraised and persuaded easily Dublin City Council to fly Festival flags with the word 'gay' on them, on the Dublin Quays. In announcing this, as well as street banners and advertisements in Dublin airport (who gave us a great discount via Marie Therese Bourke) all with the word 'gay' on it, I laughingly assured our audience at the launch party in 'The Front Lounge', that we had 'greased the poles' as a precaution against interference! We had not of course, and indeed middle Ireland once again proved to be way ahead of perceived public opinion. The symbolism of the Festival's banners and flags in the city centre brings about a noticeable increase in same sex couples holding hands in public each May! No one stares at happiness anymore on Dublin's streets. The flags, banners and posters, not in any code, but celebrating our own identity, made a huge impact on gay people and the wider public, even if they don't end up at our plays!

The effect of such visibility in the community was substantial and liberating. People with little or no interest in theatre contacted us, saying how wonderful it was to see 'themselves', in our artwork, in public. Visiting companies were so impressed with the ads on arrival at the airport that they didn't seem to notice we had no funds to advertise in any more spaces on the nine mile journey from airport to city centre! They were so enthused seeing the ads on arrival, that they only recovered to see the flags on the Quays and hence had a sense we were 'everywhere'! Dublin City Council led the way in facilitating this shared citizenship and visibility that now sees other bodies like Pride and GAZE (film festival) use this facility and indeed other City Councils following suit at Pride time, regionally.

RTE, the national broadcaster supported us with a radio advertisement under the 'RTE Supporting the Arts' initiative and in 2012 hosted the first ever TV ad with the word 'gay' featured for our Festival, made by our young committee members, under the creative direction of volunteer, Siobhan Killen. No controversy – just more shared citizenship. I am not convinced it necessarily boosts tickets sales, as well disposed people still self-exclude themselves from a gay theatre programme, but it does include us centrally, in the completion of the cultural map and we are hugely grateful for that. There has been rapid progress and some admirable political leadership in Ireland. I am very proud of the Festival's small role in facilitating this intercultural dialogue and of the institutions that enabled it to happen, with ease.

Ireland is now multicultural and over 183 nationalities live in an Ireland, which was the isolated 'last rock' in Europe for centuries. Of course, people bring their cultures with them to their new countries. That has an impact in Ireland today, the new alliance between fundamental Catholicism and Islam is interesting, as they promote their zeal to control people's personal lives, especially that of women, through politics and law. We previously fought our electoral battles on Church/State separation, on access to contraception, divorce and abortion in Ireland especially in the nasty 1980s. We have finally dealt with the same issues, rarely ahead of and mostly following, the experiences in other Western countries.

We were all so 'the same' in Ireland, that we invented difference through parish and county boundaries, whether you lived in council or 'private' housing, which schools you attended, Travellers and of course religion distinguished us. Now and suddenly, by the 1990s, we were diverse, had access to new influences from media to travel, via education and affluence. We travelled and with our Irish humour, expected a warmer welcome as emigrants, than we had frequently offered our own immigrants. Some Irish abroad found it unusual to be seen as different. Some Irish at home have always been seen as different. It was an opportune time to explore why fear is a component of difference and why difference is unwelcome in Irish culture, at home and abroad. Building an international Festival and basing it in Dublin has been enlightening for all participants.

Today, New York celebrates its diversity and there is even an inclusive St Patrick's Day parade in the city, which welcomes gay people and acknowledges their diverse citizenship. Our IDGTF Ambassador, Kathleen Warnock, has held our Festival banner high in the 2012 parade on our behalf, to our great joy. In Ireland, it is a cause of great celebration, to see uniformed public servants from other countries, parade with us in celebrating our diaspora. We do it in their countries. It is a tradition here. It is reassuring and trust building.

The 6th European Gay Police Association held its LGBT Gala award winning, conference in Dublin Castle in June 2012 to coincide with celebrating Dublin Pride. It was to be a very powerful message, seeing European gay police proudly wear their uniforms, as they have done in previous Pride parades in other countries, in Dublin. Despite being hosted by President Michael D Higgins in his home, and a strong endorsement from Justice Minister, Alan Shatter TD, the Garda Commissioner Martin Callanan, personally intervened to attempt to prohibit the Irish and foreign police parading in uniform. Joining with our LGBT, Irish and police community in celebrating shared citizenship with pride, is a very positive action. The Deputy Prime Minister, Eamonn Gilmore, (Minister for Foreign Affairs) had to intervene on behalf of the foreign police for them to be allowed to march in uniform as in other cities. The Irish police were still prohibited from marching in uniform by a Commissioner, who had spoken at the conference, warmly, but through obvious gritted teeth. I look forward someday to seeing Garda uniforms marching with Pride as they do to celebrate the rest of their Irish identity each March 17th.

New proposals from Government indicate there will be a positive equality and human rights duty soon on the public sector. Policies and practices will have to reflect that ethnicity, sexual orientation, faith, civil or family status, gender identity, ability, membership of the Traveller Community, age, are not the things that separate us – they are the common characteristics of us all. The cultural differences of some ethnic or faith communities are frequently at odds with those in the LGBT community. The attempt by the Gardai in 2012, to confuse the skill of an ethnic liaison officer with those of an LGBT officer, through amalgamation, failed that test. The restoration of the distinct LGBT service was important. It is not a difficult task to identify conflicting needs and to respond accordingly, especially when backed up by important and strong equality legislation and crucially, managerial leadership. Leadership is the fuel on which effective community inclusion, can continue to progress. It takes just a little time and effort. Minorities will often welcome contact, based on respect.

The Festival is also leading that contact as we, the identifiable minority, present our theatre to all in the mainstream, in a reverse action to inform positive change and respect for difference. Of course, the celebration of such difference and the release of the stories, yields a rich harvest for writers, students of characters and storytellers in theatre today. It begins the exploration of masculinity and feminism that goes beyond the construction of heterosexuality – that is also liberating for many beyond the reach of theatre.

chapter 10

LGBT rights - the next Frontier

It does not seem fair or even reasonable, that one's personal intellectual ambition should be enforced as the legal limit of another person's activity

Eva Gore Booth

Traditional marriage of heterosexuals has broken down somewhat, in that people are divorcing, and many are refusing to get married. It is a pity, limiting and a lost opportunity, that gay equality is defined or confined, to having access to every right 'straight people' have, in a time when straight people are rejecting their own traditional, imposed structures. The 'gay marriage debate' should be an opportunity for society to develop new, appropriate structures to equally value and protect all of these new relationships, which is the failure of the mid-way concept of civil partnership. It is time to debate adult marriage, but we are not doing that. Instead, we are debating 'gay marriage', which rests the responsibility for change on a minority and absolves the majority of their role in achieving equality. This debate brings us right back to the notion that marriage should be based on the consent of others and not the parties involved. It is an odd convention.

The argument that traditional marriage has always only been 'between a man and a woman' is farcical, in that any other form of marriage was 'traditionally' prohibited. Therefore the traditional exclusion is the basis of the validation of a tradition, which was itself an invention for that purpose. Previously, traditional marriage excluded people of different races or religion. Should that remain so, or should marriage evolve as an accepted social structure, to include all consenting adults, who wish to commit their lives to love and care for each other? Modern society is inclusive – tradition proved not to be so, in many instances.

There are negative signals still in law, of an inequality in status for gay people. Civil partnership as a concept, first introduced in the Irish Senate by Senator Sheila Terry of Fine Gael (and defeated), is now eventually valid in law, after many other noble attempts by advocates and politicians. Unsurprisingly, it enjoys inclusive, wide celebration, though the law could not resist the stigmatisation of children of same sex couples, by putting in law for the first time, the legal barrier that creates a 'doubt' of gay parenting being 'acceptable'. It was a high cost for partnership rights. This new piece of rights legislation, formalised a lesser status for gay people, for the first time since criminalisation – a mean and unacceptable price, on the road towards equality.

In the civil partnership debate, some Fine Gael TDs initially saw some merit in a 'conscience clause' where a State employee could refuse to officiate at a same sex civil partnership. One younger parliamentary advocate never once considered had that same benchmark been in place in the 1970s, the marriage of his parents, one Irish, one from another continent, could equally have faced a 'conscience clause' and may never been registered. Later he toyed with promoting the primacy of the right of exertion of the personal choices and beliefs of public servants, despite its potential to have been applied to his own family circumstances previously. In one way, this 'blindness' is encouraging, as he does not see himself as being perceived 'different', in another way it is a marvel how quickly complacency sets in. Equality is personal.

As the 'traditional' family structures break down, this creates a huge 'caring cost' in society, as so much care is provided voluntarily, by families. The prevention of new family units in a society, where existing ones are falling apart, is at the least, economic nonsense. Prejudice is costly as official 'singlehood' or a partnership of lesser status, is enforced for 'non-compliant' consensual, adult relationships. The future financial cost could be crippling, as it means only the State will be obliged to care for people whose 'families' are not recognised. Such emotional costs have always been borne by gay people – they were a fact of their future.

The stigma of associating risk or disadvantage to the children of gay parents is sinister. It was created by those who were in fact often the source of proven risk. It creates another scenario to smokescreen the fact that so much abuse has been done to kids in their own 'heterosexual' homes or in approved religious institutions. Such stigma is false, morally redundant and deliberately damaging. It is an outcome of the approach that if you can't defeat an argument with facts

- create a fear. Equally, the perverse morality of confining abandoned kids to run down orphanages abroad, because potential gay adoptive parents are deemed, in some way, to be more morally offensive to society than abject poverty, is condemning these kids to a life of neglect and destitution to appease the comfort of the complacent. This is in itself an additional immorality and cruel to all concerned.

This debate is also misnamed as 'gay' adoption – that could possibly only exist of the child was gay, but who would call it that? There should only be one standard – good parenting, not straight or gay parenting – in these labels many dangers can be concealed, just as those who previously put their trust in the emblem of the clerical collar, realised all too late.

Heterosexuals as most of them know do not have a monopoly on love. We live in a society where we know children are suffering, ill and neglected, at home and in third world orphanages – this is their dreadful destiny required by a smug morality that objects to and prevents 'gay' parenting. The rights of children born through legal surrogacy remain absent in Irish law, even for the heterosexual, married donors of the gametes. The Courts once again must decide what the law means, as the lawmakers stick their heads in the sand. Cancer is also a creator of the need for surrogacy in young couples, so is same sex committed partnership.

Once again, we provide that the greatest victims of such immorality are the weakest – our children. We appear to be very slowly learning from the tortuous revelations of our concealed and murky past, that tarnished the many successes of the twentieth century, of the new nation, in complicit shame. We still pursue a policy that appears only to prioritise children up to the moment of their birth. 'Pro-life' clearly means up to the moment of birth, after which the baby is deafened by the rumble of running footsteps of those, who protected their right to be born, but abandon them, the moment their life begins.

Loving, consenting, same sex adult partnerships can still not marry as equals and are stigmatised as the only form of legal partnership not allowed to adopt children – even their partner's children in Ireland. What message does that send? The commitment of the Minister for Justice and Equality, Alan Shatter TD to amend this situation for children, given in June 2012 is welcome, commendable and reflects opinion polls which show 3 out of 4 people now support equal marriage. Submissions to the Irish Constitutional Convention to examine Constitutional change to marriage appear to be running three to one in favour of inclusive change. I am pleased that the Festival made a submission, which advocated gender neutral definition of marriage, thus ensuring the burden of legal change would be shared by more people under its remit, rather than demanding more of the ill resourced minority to change Irish society for the better.

I have a query that the current lack of rights for children of civil partnerships, may not satisfy the Constitutional provision on Children's rights, approved by referendum, if left unaddressed? The lack of children's rights in the civil partnership provision was a deliberate and shameful legal construction, which was the final damaging conservative tantrum of a process being dragged towards more equality.

The moral argument to defeat such narrow prejudice is clear, but so is the emerging economic one. Every time consenting adults agree to a formal family care structure for each other and their children – the State gains financially and society is more stable, as families tend to address well their own problems, in the first instance. New loving families can be built and sustained in an open, caring, inclusive, modern society. These topics, new families, also featured in our theatre programme, especially in a wonderful trilogy story called 'I Thee Wed' by Canada's Karen Lee Pickett, exploring the relationships of three female couples, one in 1903, one in 1953 and one in 2003, when same sex marriage was made legal and equal in Canada. It remains one of the Festival's most satisfying plays. However no one should underestimate the lingering grip, the perpetuated negative stereotype can have on decent people

In the late 1990s, I was directing the big Christmas show in the Olympia Theatre, Dublin, a rock pantomime 'Rockin' Hood'. We discovered two amazing juvenile leads to play 'Robin Hood' and 'Maid Marian' - Peter Smith and the 15 year old Samantha Mumba. The production nearly ground to a halt, because some of the 'adults' could not get their heads around, two Black Irish actors playing the leading roles. At one stage I stood alone in insisting on this proper, merit based casting. I pointed out the job specification of 'Robin Hood' was a capacity to 'rob from the rich and give to the poor' and I was sure that was not a skill confined to Caucasians! At brinkmanship level, and five sets of auditions later, with the complicit support of Producer, Gerry Sinnott, the casting was approved and not a single child of the 70,000 who attended, noticed anything, but Peter and Samantha's considerable skills!

Sadly, the Irish Times did refer to them as the 'Black actors' in a review, which also attacked a 5 year old child, because her mother starred in the show. I rarely ever respond to reviews or read them while the production is in progress, but this time I did ask the 'Newspaper of Record', what their opinion of the 'White actors' was, but unfortunately the letters page did not appear to have room for its publication! You can't always challenge the stereotype – you need permission for that too!

The fact that the Festival became a welcoming vehicle for the telling of international LGBT cultural experiences was a huge development. It was exciting to base such theatrical activity in Dublin, Ireland. It was radical and challenging and one which was well met by this modern city's audiences. One plus side of the 'fake' Celtic Tiger boom, is that many gay people came to Ireland and live freely, unlike in their countries of origin. Many of our EU colleagues also discover Ireland as a good place to live for LGBT people. The hospitality sector, language based services, the health sector and other tourist services would be the poorer without this linguistic diversity which contributes to our economic development.

Another of the Festival's great dividends is that many foreign people become vital volunteers, whose extraordinary commitment and skill, ensures our survival. They not only volunteer but double up as Guides, translators and friends for our visiting artists and guests. Such positive cultural interaction also reminds us of the 'differences' that exist within the LGBT community here.

There are Brazillians, Filipinos, Polish and so many more gay people in our community now. The Festival programme reaches out to these groups. There are LGBT people of all ethnicities in the world, and they too have specific cultural needs. Closer to home, the Irish Traveller culture is in itself, quite harsh, for gay people. They use the term 'dirty' for gay people and have been known to beat family members who 'come out', as wonderfully illustrated in Rosaleen Mac Donagh's play 'John and Josey' which had a staged reading in our Winter Festival in 2009. It was a memorably moving theatrical experience, that we have yet to succeed in finding a company to fully stage, in our programme. The capacity of the Festival to give a voice to these circumstances through drama is a core motivator of the voluntary work we do in the professional arts. It is particularly effective and honours our basic challenge – the stories must be told through quality artistic output. There is no point in hosting a gay theatre festival if the theatre is not good.

There are residual cultural issues arising from such constructed disdain that are also internalised by gay people and reflected by advocates in society to this day. The debate on 'gay marriage' on RTE's 'Late Late Show' in spring 2013 featured a young gay man, who opposed the legal extension, not only of his own rights, but of others like him. This did not indicate 'balance' in a debate, but was a sorry public illustration of residual shame. It is not the fact, it is the invented stigma – the constructed lesser status - the imposed negative stereotype that does the real harm. RTE 2FM, with declining listenership, finally embraced Pride and became a sponsor in 2013. They produced a series of rainbow striped images to demonstrate how in tune they were to the diversity of their audience. Advertising companies really do need to look beyond their own mirror to see all the colour of Irish society. The Transgender community have already successfully challenged negative advertising stereotypes. LGBTI groups, starved of resources, must not allow sponsors to dictate the stereotype, as we had to prove ourselves in 2009, to a harsh cost.

Here is the great challenge to any State. Which culture do you reflect – the individual and exclusive, faith culture (which has a right to exist) or the State laws that ensure and protect equality of participation and citizenship for all in a democracy? How is this reflected in practice, in our own workplaces, in the arts and in the community? Is diversity recognised or understood, or is it a 'concession' that we are allowed hold our Festival at its minimalist level? How much does the silent sneering reinforce the negative, in order to keep the successful event small and in a 'ghetto'? Is the existence of this unique theatrical event pro-active positive action by a modernised and inclusive society, or does the lack of resources confine it to a new form of 'ghetto'? Ten years of trying to mainstream this good theatre work, prompts this reflection, with no clear emerging answer.

There are other identity challenges for a society emerging from the shadows of concealment. A transgendered Irish doctor, Lydia Foy's incredibly brave, invasive and long court battle resulted in the possibility of change like, new passports and birth certificates and full legal acknowledgement of the true gender of a person. People must be allowed tell us who they really are. Over five years later, Foy still hasn't seen the Court's judgement enacted, repeating the legislative tardiness of the Norris case, 25 years later.

Transgender activists and actions will result in a new law in the anticipated

Transgender Recognition Act. The Equality Authority successfully supported Louise Hannon as she vindicated her rights to gender transition while in the workplace, in a ground breaking case in 2011, before the Equality Tribunal. There is great and rapid change, but it has had to be fought for, step by step. There is no ripple effect in achieving progress – at times it appears the process of change starts from scratch, each time change is required. Ireland hosted the 4th European Transgender conference in Dublin in 2012, which debated change, but also saw some of the delegates attacked in the city centre. There has been progress, but it is done in the light of on-going stigma.

The legal notion that a married transgendered person who needs to transition into their real identity, may be forced by law to divorce, in the absence of same sex marriage, is an astonishing test for a country that struggled to introduce divorce, if couples lived apart for four out of the previous five years, in 1996! This test must surely breach human rights and is easily solvable by the introduction of one marriage law for all consenting adults, not based on gender, but on commitment. Bad law makes for more bad law. The Catholic Church which already supported an abortion amendment to our Constitution, which in fact created the legal circumstances which permitted abortion, may now be pursuing policies on equal marriage that will introduce in law, the principle of forced divorce – the folly of fundamentalism!

'Rachel's Café' by Lucy Danser, told a true life transgendered story in Festival 2012, and the trans community drama group gave a free show some years earlier in 'The Front Lounge'. In Australia's 'Girly Side of Butch', transsexual Vonnie Watkins also gave a moving account of her own transition as did Amanda Munroe from 'Drags Aloud' some years later. An actor who once performed with us as a woman, returns in his true male identity to perform in 2013.

There is also a debate to be had on the association between gender identity and the distinct nature of sexual orientation – two more separate groups brought together, by the common culture of experienced and constructed discrimination. There has been a price paid for this support. It associates gay men and women's sexuality with some confusion over their gender identity, when it is clearly not the case. Such is the price exacted for solidarity in the face of constructed discrimination. It is a price that can add to the confusion of an emerging gay or 'trans' young person, trying to see themselves reflected in their surrounding society.

The response of society has been proactive in embracing many of the facets of the changing Ireland. But is it embedded yet? The real test of change remains for Government, parliament, media and in our case, senior management in our artistic and public services. Is the good work done to date, still vulnerable to, or reliant upon, personality change at senior levels, or is it truly embedded and proactive in a public service ethic, wanting to serve all who make up the community in Ireland today? Is the arts truly leading the way in teaching us about the completeness of the Irish and human identity, as it has in instances in the past? Can a small festival like ours make a valid contribution to that change? That is the task of each annual programme - good theatre and good subjects unwrapping a concealed history, as it unveils the space for new voices and for new audiences.

This human rights through artistic dialogue event, just like the songs, plays and poetry of the fight for women's rights, which gave momentum to the fight for black and ethnic minority rights, which gave momentum to the fight for Gay rights, which gave momentum to the fight for transgendered rights, all have one common result. People live better and fairer lives. People are also recognised as part of their own society through the initial medium of a presence and value in the arts.

The arts civilise a society, as they inform it of the parts that make up its complete identity. Inclusion benefits society by challenging the potential for criminal exploitation of the economically and socially excluded. Those advocates and artists for change, create the space for society to shake off the imposed value system that insists on different statuses being placed on people. Their success creates a more open and equal society, one that develops and values distinct and respectful cultures. This is the community our artistic work strives to facilitate today. We are here and in an artistic conversation.

We know you can not fully participate in society unless you know, embed and embrace the opportunity, knowledge and culture of equality. Good theatre enables such change to be relayed and understood. The privileged, deliberately charge each minority with finding its own space to be heard. In that, they exert further control, as space is limited. We provide our own space to release our stories into the mainstream, so that they can be heard through theatre as an artform, valid in a modern society. We are supported in this endeavour.

When voices are heard and the commonality of releasing information and preventing discrimination is shared, then more people are empowered to take up the cudgels on behalf of minorities. Privilege is replaced by participation. Prejudice prevents that change. Prejudice prevents good policy. Equality is the opportunity to do better. Equality in the arts is maximising the truth of good theatre, to inform change and bring a broader artistic citizenship out of the shadows to be celebrated.

We are all challenged by our cultural past. We see the opportunity for equality in a modern context, not offered to many previous generations, to get to know our diverse community, as it exists today, in every locality. Nothing can be revealed, as long as people have to hide their identity and truth. Nothing will be entrusted by people who don't trust you. Nothing can be achieved for equality and diversity, if you do not experience it, first hand. Theatre provides a space to speak, a space to be heard and an invitation to listen.

Prejudice, hate, discrimination and crime thrive in the security of unchallenged and enforced prejudice. It is up to all of us to work to achieve that goal, within our communities, revealing and respecting distinct identities. Gay people have for generations expressed themselves, their talents and worth, safely in the arts, to the benefit of many. This contribution was not always fairly recognised as it was dangerous for the artist to reveal his or her complete identity. This current stage in that development, facilitated by gay theatre, ensures the validation of that immense contribution, in the complete identity of the artist, in theatre. People are listening. People are writing. People are performing. People are attending.

Traditional intimate communities have been broken down during the 'Celtic Tiger' as many Irish neighbourhoods asserted their economic advantage and built gates to separate themselves from each other. In 2012, in county Wexford, two cases of men who lived alone, remained dead in their homes for months, in small rural, intimate towns. This is a shocking change for a traditionally intimate society, like Ireland.

There is a high rate, particularly of young male suicide, in rural Ireland. Often, only in such tragic cases, do families sit down and for the first time, consider their son or daughter might have been gay. An appeal, all too late, is made to the gay community for information. Then notices of missing teenagers and adults go up in gay bars. This is a tragic cultural residue, often made too late by a family, who believed the shame. These young people have internalised the traditional shame inflicted on so many, with one nasty far reaching, result. By being visible, being inclusive and being truthful, our form of theatre asserts our position in the mainstream artistic discourse, that enlightens and liberates many more beyond the LGBT community. It liberates families too.

As artists, we must have the courage and the capacity to speak. We must not speak solely to ourselves – we must provide the opportunity for others to know and learn. If that strategy fails, then other approaches will evolve, but we must try to speak first. Theatre is the natural home for voices to be heard. It has a natural accessible structure for stories to be recounted. If theatre fails to reflect the society which it examines and questions, then it hastens its journey towards redundancy.

It is important that having contributed to, and learned our trade in theatre, that gay artists now use these skills and talents to contribute to theatre's next evolutionary phase - inclusivity. It is important to evolve a space where difference is not an oddity, but a new opportunity for a more complete and truthful exploration of identity. It can inspire a new commentary on the emotional diversity that defines men and women of all sexual identities in the twenty first century. What a broad and brave ambition for a small sector, in a small country, with a small audience, and a small budget, in Dublin today?

To fail to contribute to this opportunity in Dublin, would be to revert to the intent of all the legal and religious controls, we are finally shaking towards freedom. To inspire the new generations to begin from this moment of opportunity, allows us to accelerate our own cultural recovery and confine the sore lessons to the past, that restricted older generations and often choked the truth of their creativity. In this theatre event, there is a new potential. In the mainstream, there is a much more viable channel for its ambitious realisation, which we can only hope to influence and access. The complacent fear potential. We are not complacent about the task. The ambition is to have it shared by those who can ensure it future success.

As gay artists, we have overcome much greater controlling mechanisms. We use new media well and our Festival works to include more people in the arts, than ever before. We have done so like many other identities, without the permission of the privileged, who feel we are all enhanced by the limitations of their own stories. We, by starting this unique event in Dublin, assert that artistically we have more to say, more to see and more to learn. This time we will write our own scripts and produce our own stories, for our own audiences of liberated citizens, who no longer benignly exclude themselves, but will be open to including gay theatre in their spectrum of interest. With all that 'Wilde' ambition at heart, we proceeded to unfold the scenes that would bring over 2,000 performances of gay theatre to the good people of Dublin and our international visitors to enable the conversation to begin, through theatre in Dublin in May 2004.

scene 1

'In the Beginning' 2004

I did not want to offend other people's prejudices

Noel Coward (on failing to 'come out').

In late 2003, I was persuaded to accept (having turned down many) an offer from an ambitious young group to stage 'Sweeney Todd' in the Theatre Royal in Waterford. Working with young people can be refreshing. I liked a challenge and it's great to do wonderful work with enthusiastic people, who want to learn. Following intensive auditions in the above manner, this approach was clearly not fulfilling all local ambition and the production was 'postponed'. At last I had a gap in my schedule. The embryonic idea of a Festival celebrating gay identity through theatre as an artform, finally had a space to emerge in a previously crammed schedule.

The learning from my Masters in Equality Studies, on the visibility of LGBT people in modern Ireland, the Pride exhibition, playing and writing Oscar Wilde, the memory of discovery and confiding from 'La Cage Aux Folles', all culminated at the end of January 2004 with the idea of the first 'Dublin Gay Theatre Festival'. I drew a line on the calendar between what was a weekend Lesbian Arts Festival (ALAF) and Dublin Pride and found the May Bank holiday weekend was free. I set that as the date with a little regret, as it was a challenging time for students whose voices and talents I wanted to include, though this respect for the scheduling of existing events has not always been reciprocated. In having the freedom to do what you wish, you must not encroach on space or time, already inhabited by others. The first full fortnight in May was chosen, beginning Bank Holiday Monday. Now a Festival had to be planned and delivered. The context of the first five years is published later (Interval Act) so I will add the following memories of a hectic first year in 2004 as we announced ourselves to an unsuspecting theatre and LGBT public.

Eddie Devoy, (aka drag star, 'Dolly Grip') had been one of my talented, fellow travellers on the amateur musical circuit, through the years. He was full of theatre. A most reliable company member, but he was not a strong singer, like many drawn to the genre who make up the bedrock of the musical ensemble, as a dancer and intelligent actor. Eddie gets his theatrical moments now as 'Dolly Grip' and is the 'last bastion' of the drag interpretation of the Broadway musical in Ireland, tap dancing included!

Eddie was the only other 'theatre person', I had in the first event – all the rest were gifted enthusiasts and generous well wishers. He was, de facto, our first technical manager, as he not only knew what sound and lighting equipment looked like, but also knew where to borrow it at last minute notice, for free! I always remember his kindness in his running around, when he would call to my house and offer me a lift in to a venue, unprompted, despite his own workload.

I too was in a different situation employment wise. I had spent my early decades living out of suitcase in the company of strangers, in various theatres throughout the Islands. I had a desire to settle. I knew how hard it was to sustain a living from theatre, hence my traipsing throughout the UK and rural Ireland with my suitcase from week to week, directing and making ends meet. I now had returned to Dublin and had another decade of professional theatre behind me in the Olympia. I did not want to teach – though I have offered to teach a module on the 'business of theatre'- the glaring gap of any academic course that prepares artists for employment in an industry many just do not understand, financially and legally. I never ceased to be amazed by the number of 'teachers' that had 'schools' in Ireland, many had done very little theatre work, but they survived and I admire that. What they taught though wasn't always accurate or preparatory.

I had evolved DAYMS into the Musical Company in the early 1990s, which was my professional entity, committed to staging works with 'all Irish' casts. I had previously faulted the 'Olympia' policy of bringing in artists from abroad, when Irish artists were available. I soon came to understand that policy. Some Irish artists who have stayed in this small pond, are led by ego and not practicality. I concur that many should have enjoyed more success in their careers as they had the talent. But, it is not the fault or task of that rare species, an Irish producer to address these issues, just to create interesting and fairly remunerated work.

Many young actors leave after a decade of frustration eeking out a living in theatre. Some do not understand the finances of theatre or what it is really important to ask for in a contract. In three seasons of my own productions at the Olympia, I had generated £1.3million at the box office in Irish productions, but unfortunately paid out £1.4 million, meaning little of no income for my year's work, endless grief at the disappointment, and a loss for myself and my principal backer my friend, Richard Dunne. The convenient perception of those who can't do the finances is of course that I was 'on the take' – even when the theatre seats were empty!

It was amazing how Irish Actors Equity would query my basic compliant contracts and charge the young people 'dues', when I was paying four times the salary of other main theatres who were recruiting skilled and qualified young performers, on derisory 'student contracts'. On top of that, some 'agents' who had done nothing to get the gig for the young actor or negotiating the contract, would take, at times, up to 20% of their wages in 'commission' – there really is a need for a business module in all acting courses!

The teaching of artists how a production is budgeted, what expenses are involved and what the end result is between a budget, when you multiply the anticipated attendance rates, and the eventual box office outturn might be, is non-existent. If it was explained, then the actor could establish what portion their contribution might earn and be entitled to and negotiate for that. The Irish aren't good at that.

The more a sector is starved of opportunity, the more fragile the ego becomes, through the harshness of unemployment. I had one Irish actor's UK agent address me, as the producer, as 'Young Man'. I told her I would sign her actor's cheque 'Young man' and let her find a bank to cash it! To be fair, she made an instant appointment to meet with me, flew in from London, had done her research, and proved to be amongst the best to deal with! She established that I had produced Olivier award winner David Heneker's last musical 'Peg O'My Heart' which David attended. As a kid she had played at his feet as he composed. John Kander (Chicago / Cabaret) had later been David's rehearsal pianist for 'Irma la Douce' which, together with his 'Half A Sixpence', made him a UK Broadway success, long before Lloyd Webber! It was a joy to work with and be trusted by him in his later years.

I had also decided in the 1980s that I would not move to London despite the support of producer David Turner, Nic Walsh Manager of the Theatre Royal in York who acted as my agent and Virginia Kerr who lent me her flat, to see if I could live in the city. I didn't like that city as a home, its expense and its very low levels of remuneration for directors. Ireland was much more lucrative and I needed to live!

I was once offered the graduation class production at Mountview Drama School at £200 per week, but I had to pay all my transport and accommodation expenses etc and stay 6 weeks! I would usually put up a good production in 3-4 weeks, as I was a meticulous planner and kept a very detailed book on each of my 300+ productions. On that fee, I would have starved!

As a result, by 2004, I was in the fortunate position of having done what I set out to do as a director. Increasingly, I found I was more in a position of 'teaching' rather than directing, especially as the good artists had left and the new ones were pursuing fame, rather than learning a lifetime craft, and I didn't want to be part of that.

The Festival idea was definitely a response to my need for a next stage in my theatrical development. I feared burn out and was close when I decided to go to UCD to tax my academic brain with a challenging masters' degree. I needed a new direction to apply a considerable catalogue of skill. It didn't matter if theatre did not sustain me financially, it didn't need to, as I had other resources through my work for equality and human rights. I wondered had I run out of avenues to make any further contribution to theatre?

I get a great kick out of the success of others. I like to see people I know or even may have assisted, do well. I can't understand a contrary view, as it reflects well on the entire sector and augurs well for good theatre. I also was not one of those people who talked down their perceived opposition. I could never understand a director who rubbished the work of another, in an unfair way. One pressed me for seats to my 'King & I' in the Olympia and I gave him a box in which he decided to sleep his way through the production!

I always learned from good theatre. Sometimes I learned more from bad theatre! No one has a monopoly on talent or theatre – it's a worldwide industry that needs so many contributions to evolve, create and compete, especially in the multimedia age.

I also understood the premise, that if there were 5 plays on in Dublin and four were good, the five tended to be lifted and do well, as the audience reaction was positive to the overall standard of theatre available. If there were five plays on in Dublin and one was good – it too struggled more than it should, because of the paucity of good productions on offer in other venues. So for me, if I went into a company that had been directed well, then half of my preliminary work on stage craft was done, as I anticipated they at least know the basics. I always teach or check stage craft before I begin to direct especially young people. It is time well spent.

I didn't resent success in others, especially success fairly acquired. The first patron of the Festival, Senator David Norris is a fine example of generosity. I wonder has he learned from his Presidential campaign, that some of the recipients of his immense generosity, were not always worthy or loyal in return!

I was very conscious also that having earned a fulltime living from theatre for almost two decades, that once in fulltime employment, it was not fair to continue to compete with colleagues who depend on it, for their livelihood. I recall in my final year of professional theatre, this being my main source of income - the Millennium pantomime 'Cinderella' at the Olympia, with a budget of 1 million euros, I directed that in just under 4 weeks, including technical and preview. Simultaneously, I also produced, devised and directed the Waterford Millennium celebrations, attended by over 50,000 people, with 15 hours of free events featuring Waterford artists and celebrities, like Tony Award winner Anna Manahan and chart topper Val Doonican, funded generously by the City and local business. We bucked the national trend of greed on that day and inspired over 1000 performers to work with us, in outdoor events (on a mild New Year's Eve) the last light sunset event, A Gala Concert in the Theatre Royal broadcast on local radio, which I presented, and the huge outdoor rock and community concert and fireworks on The Quay. The numerous community and cultural events involving most local artists in an action packed programme, administered by Patsy Meade and promoted by Annette Birthwhistle, was a year-long labour of love for a city that had been good to me. I had done my bit, earned a good living and believed I had delivered good artistic results. I was moving on.

I decided that whatever I did for the Festival, it would be on a voluntary basis, with no expectation of payment or even expenses. I aimed to inspire others to do the same, therefore I was happy to set the example. It had been the hallmark of my professional career. I had two 'rates of pay' – what I was worth and what I was willing to give. Don't do it cheaply – giving is more satisfying, if you can afford to. When they can not afford to remunerate you properly, but the project is still of interest to you – give with a smile. The Festival (like DAYMS) was to be a creative endeavour where we would release new voices, by using our skills to provide space, channels and a standard where new voices, authors, actors, volunteers and audience could begin an exploratory journey in Ireland, to complete our portion of the cultural map.

The clash with the 'profit' ethic and the volunteer ethic, was later to haunt us a bit. It immediately created the space for those to consider it not to be a professional endeavour, which it was, from the outset. Had I relied on salaries being available, it never would have gone on stage, and other professionals clearly and selflessly related to that ambition. I relied on the concept of service to the sector and many people responded and contributed to that generously.

All companies would be financially rewarded for their endeavour and we would also fundraise to provide further supports to them, to eliminate or reduce the main financial risks associated with presenting theatre. The ambition was defined, created and the word spread. The response continues to amaze and is appreciated.

The bureaucracy was kept to an essential minimum, but I did invite a businessman who had been a commercial promoter some years previously, to join the company, at the outset. He had an interest in administration and kindly became the AD (Administrative Director and Company Secretary). It was noticeable though, even by 2004 that people were loath to sign up for 'gay' things, so my home address became the company office and usually my name appended everything.

I had successfully run my own theatre business for many years but it is always good to have another set of eyes and expertise available in a company that had at its core – transparency. I was used to working with groups and was very conscious of my job as a civil servant, as good governance is an essential part of public service. If we were to be handling public funds, or holding box office funds for companies, then it was crucial that a few people would have access, the processes were transparent and accountable at all stages. We appointed auditors and a solicitor.

I indicated that most such companies I knew, had about seven members, but asked the AD to explore the appropriate structure for this new venture. What

I was referring to indistinctly, was the structure of a 'not for profit, limited by guarantee' company, but I was assured that a limited company would suffice. I was also asked by him, would I agree to accepting a 50% shareholding in the new venture and that the other 50% would be held 'in trust', to be given out, as I saw fit to new directors, as they came on stream. Naively, as I was focussed so clearly on the theatrical output, I agreed and soon found, when I nominated Eddie Devoy as a director, no shares were transferred to him – a matter of principle that almost brought the event to a halt, two years later. This selective exclusion ultimately led to the demise of Eddie's involvement, which I greatly regret. His was exactly the kind of spirit the event needed and still does. I missed his humour, understanding, talents and support.

I set about booking venues. I also learned about stereotype. I wanted to book the Teachers Club, a small well equipped studio in Parnell Square for the first Festival. I was told to meet a non-drinking, Irish speaking Tadgh Mac Phaidin. I arrived with a copy of the Equal status Acts in my pocket expecting perhaps, a negative reaction. How wrong I was and indeed how shameful my expectant stereotype - but it wasn't an unreasonable expectation, when trying to present gay events in mainstream Ireland in 2004! We were sincerely welcomed, not only on our merits, but with enthusiasm and it is our most lasting relationship to date.

I also had the good fortune of meeting Jack Gilligan (introduced by Derek Byrne), the Dublin City Arts Officer. He lent his support to the first event. Dublin City Council, from officials to elected representatives has been a source of endorsement for the Festival since its inception. The Council has contributed so much to many an important historical milestone in our evolution.

In year one, with no funds (due to our sudden start) we made a deal with companies that the first contra against the box office would be the venue rental and then a 70/30 split in favour of the production company. Everyone was making their contribution to get us off the ground. In the event of the rental not being met, no loss would be incurred by the production company for this – our incentive to work hard to avoid a Festival loss. We have continued to build-in this incentive in later years, by accepting full liability for rental costs with no box office contra. Too many Festivals become swamped and leave companies to their own devices. I was determined that we would not act as a 'promoter' but as a partner or co-producer, to ensure their individual success was also in our best interests. That was our incentive to acquire the seeds to sow for the following year.

Also as an egalitarian, I knew of the theatrical practice of exaggerating the terms of one's deal, to emphasise one's own importance! I published the deal on offer online, for all to see and adhered to it in all cases. This has proven to be of immense stability to the Festival, as each promoter or producer or performer tries to edge a little bit more out of us and then of course is at pains to tell everyone they got it. In fact no one has – we give away everything we have in an open and fair way. At times, I have helped people personally with accommodation in my house, but even that practice had to stop, for my own sanity, as I needed a safe haven to return to, Festival free, every night! Also as the box office progressed, the efforts of the Festival went into promoting the weakest selling plays, often with great effort and little success. Lots had to be done and a lot has been achieved by our hard working volunteer corps.

I had the pleasure of casting and directing Senator David Norris in his first professional theatre role, that of the narrator in 'Side by Side by Sondheim' with Tony Kenny, Joyce Teevan, Marian Duane and Jim Doherty in 1993. Choreographed by co-producer Joan Kenny, it ran three weeks in Clontarf castle and was very favourably reviewed by a previous narrator, Gay Byrne. It transferred into the 'Olympia' with West End Star Glyn Kerslake succeeding Tony Kenny who was midway through his US tour. I invited David as an artist, a Joycean scholar and as the bravest of gay activists to be the Festival's first patron. He honoured us with his agreement and has been a generous supporter ever since. ALAF's demise certainly spurred us to broaden our definition of 'gay' in a more public way, very soon into our evolution. The first programme did not have any particular lesbian input and that became a key focus of my own work, shortly after.

The imagery for the event was created with our first young designer Geoff Mc Grath. Though not the greatest proof reader, Geoff's talents got us up and running and we stickered out any published errors! It was a huge undertaking for a young man and adaptations of his early creative concepts still survive today.

I wanted to link the Irish identity with Oscar Wilde. Part of my process of visibility research, yielded no pictures of young Irish gay people, even on the internet. There was a distinct absence of faces! Even in the art exhibition on the railings of public parks like Merrion Square and St Stephens Green, I noted the absence of male imagery. On one stroll around the Green exhibition one summer, I counted three male images amongst thousands of painting. I wanted to use a visible modern Irish image. The handsome blonde form of artist (to be) Steven Mannion was developed, holding a green carnation – which was to be an emblem of the Festival. The first programme produced notes that the 'Green Carnation' emerged in Paris of the 1880s and was later adopted (and claimed) by Wilde as a marketing technique, for his opening nights at the theatre. He used to dye white carnations overnight, but ours came in a box from China sourced by Geoff! Wilde was first publically exposed in Robert Hitchen's nasty novel called 'The Green Carnation' in 1894. We were building our historical links and placing them into a modern context.

This wonderful homoerotic image was a first class communicator with the gay community. It was thoughtful, sexy and artistic. What I discovered within a year or so was, that the young naked male torso appeared to discourage many straight people from looking at the Festival literature. I reached out to artist Will St Ledger to evolve the Wildean form of our logo for 2006. He did with a cheeky 'Mona Lisa' twist and it was excellent. Now people began to pose for photographs beside our posters in Temple Bar – Wilde is a great linguistic currency to have on side. Straight people feel comfortable with his image. Though, when speaking about him to Steven Baitson our youngest Mr Gay Ireland in 2012, he politely enquired of me had Oscar 'been your boyfriend?'! He later was the only person to get a question on Wilde correct in the quiz set by the Mr Gay World team. How quickly we can forget or realise that his history was rarely taught to the succeeding generations.

We launched the first programme on April Fools' day 2004! I referred to my experience having played Albin/Zaza in 'La Cage Aux Folles' a decade previously in the Olympia, months after decriminalisation and bringing the show home to the International Festival in Waterford. The adjudicator RTE's Head of Music, Cathal Mac Cabe, declared that the WIFLO 'would never be the same again'! I had the same ambition for Dublin and this renewed incarnation of gay theatre. My launch speeches became legendary in themselves, with many thinking them far too long and boring, or indeed a mini thesis on gay theatre and why we do, what we do! However, I noted at the first launch:

"Theatre itself has often given a safe haven to gay people in less accepting times. Very often gay artists were only tolerated in society because of their exceptional talents to amuse or entertain... I would be proud to see this Festival develop into an event that would continue to increase the visibility, and celebrate the contribution of gay people to theatre in Ireland and abroad".

"Theatre has always offered a voice to the voiceless. Comedy and Drama have often been used to powerfully challenge prevailing societal mores. It was the forum used by nationalist playwrights to challenge the appropriateness of the British administration in Ireland. One of its codes for Ireland in its political struggle, was the invention of "Kathleen Ni Houlihan". Gay people have also used codes to be heard in society and theatre. The First International Dublin Gay Theatre Festival is designed, not to present these works in any different way, but to offer the possibility to hear and see these works in a different context – perhaps allowing them to be decoded".

"The best advice young writers get when starting out, is to write with confidence about what you know best. Use your own life experience - it is your own truth. Too often, when gay authors wrote about love, life, hopes, disappointments, whether in comedy or tragedy, they had to shroud their presentation of their life experiences, or social commentary, to conform to the norm of, and to be accepted by, a heterosexually constructed society. In our very modest first Festival, we can present them in the context in which they were written....I believe the Festival opens the possibility of taking another small step on the road to theatrical truth". The stage was set. The capacity to achieve was ambitious, but lacking resources, other than gifted volunteers. We ventured forth.

The first thing we did in publishing and using the word 'gay', was to introduce each play each night in every venue. It was a way of promoting to a committed audience the rest of the programme, but it was also important to use the gay word in the theatre, before the actor did. I used to comment 'we get rid of all the gay stuff before the performance begins'.

I noticed one woman in the lobby of a play and obviously she had come to see someone she knew. When she saw the male images, she visibly baulked, but went ahead into the auditorium. I announced, of course without any reference to her, 'though some of you may not realise it, you are at the first ever Gay Theatre Festival'! Later in the bar she was sitting in the corner with her husband and on leaving the premises, she parted from her husband and approached to congratulate us on the Festival – a big change in a short time period and exactly what we had set out to achieve! Another older man approached after a play and asked to speak to me. He began "I'm gay". I replied "Many of us are". "No" he said, "You don't understand, I have never told anyone that before". I replied "well you've come to the right place" and talked him through the rest of the programme, many of the plays, he later attended.

The programme went up from May 4th to 16th 2004 in a format that remains trusted, but evolved, today. Two weeks of theatre, with an entire change of programme mid-run. The first Festival programme began in four venues with at times, three committee volunteers, but thanks to staggered opening times, we made it!

We inaugurated an idea I had enjoyed at the LGB Film Festival, a variation on the short movies programme. By instigating a 'theatre shorts' programme, I not only encouraged emerging playwrights, but maintained the interest of a curious, but unconvinced, audience. It remains a great vehicle today. The Teachers Club housed the first 'Theatre Shorts' Programme featuring 'Don't Take Your Coat off' by Dark Horse Productions Dublin, a story of a young man (Robert Power) coming out as he cared for his elderly grandmother (Eileen Fennell) who had raised him, in a heart-warming well-acted piece. It featured for the first time our valued association with a remarkable youth drama company 'Crooked House' Productions from Kildare. Under the direction of Peter Hussey, they presented 'Karamazoo' by Philip Ridley. This was two 'firsts' for us, one it was youth drama and I had a strong commitment to showcasing that and secondly it was not a gay play! It was a gay relevant play, in that it dealt with masculinity and the concept of the 'Alpha male', played strongly by a young Ger Brady. As it was presented in the gay theatre context, no one ever said to me that it wasn't 'gay'. This was an important development in including the concept of the masculinity and the place of gay men on its continuum, in our repertoire. As gay men are constructed as failing the 'masculinity test' in some way, it was a ground breaking inclusion on the programme. The 'shorts' ran for three nights, as unlike in later years, we did not open on the bank holiday Monday, in the first year, that was our 'get-in' day!

The 'shorts' also heralded another pattern for the Festival. Plays that sign up for the programme do not necessarily materialise on the day! This didn't bother me much for ourselves, but as the competition increased for spaces, I was disappointed that companies accepted a place in the programme they were ill prepared to realise, thus depriving another well-run company the opportunity to participate. That did annoy and upset me, as they always left it late to renage on their agreements. All this effort was put into creating a performance opportunity and some do not respect that, depriving others, who do need that vital scarce space to be seen and heard, in a supportive atmosphere. In this, the theatre community is not always considerate of their colleagues. Here, between brochure printing and first night, we replaced the scheduled short 'Monster' with 'Patient b' a George Bush, health policy short, supported by a stellar group including Jimmy Fay, Bedrock Fringe and TCD. The cast list of actors who went on to impress professionally, included Aengus Og Mac Nally, Will O Connell and Dylan Tighe. George W Bush was to prove instrumental in our international development later, as his view of the USA, meant gay theatre groups increasingly looked abroad for opportunities to express and perform their artform, to our benefit!

Jonathan Harvey, author of 'Beautiful Thing' also wrote 'Hushabye Mountain'. I had first auditioned director/actor Sharon Sexton for the title part in 'Annie' in my nationwide hunt for 'Annie' for my 1994 production in the Olympia, which eventually saw Susan Mc Fadden (West End credits) get her first leading role alongside 'Twink' (Miss Hannigan) Austin Gaffney (Daddy Warbucks) and Honor Heffernan (Grace Farrell). Years later, I remembered this little girl from Naas who got to the very final stage of the 'Annie'. Another successful applicant was Carly Hennessy, later to emerge as a finalist in 'American Idol' as Carly Smithson. I can spot talent! I was also instrumental in recommending Susan's brother Bryan into the process that saw him emerge later, in 'Westlife'. It was a talented time.

I noted later in a launch speech "I recall an excellent production of Jonathan Harvey's 'Hushabye Mountain' last year, which in this Festival was as hilarious as it was moving. I then went to see it in another venue in mainstream theatre, and the response was noticeably different. One felt that people could hardly breathe because the plot had gay characters with AIDS, let alone laugh at their observations. There was almost an atmosphere in the Andrew's Lane Theatre audience that if you laughed at the comedy, you were either gay or politically incorrect".

Sharon had re-emerged, graduating in the DIT drama course, directed by my brother Dr Victor Merriman, former Arts Council member and member of the IDGTF board. Her boyfriend (now husband) Irish actor Cillian O Donnachdha (TG4) and colleagues set up 'Biscuits for Breakfast', I think inspired by the opportunity created by the Festival. Cillian had played my 'son' 'Jean Michel' in the revival of 'La Cage Aux Folles' in the SFX City Theatre in 2003. 'Hushabye

Mountain' is a hard hitting play about three friends, Connor, Lana and Lee who are trying to deal with the recent loss from AIDS of their friend Danny. It ran two nights to full houses with memorable performances, especially Clare Barrett as the Mother.

My musical company DAYMS had attracted many directors as performers, so we can not claim credit for that, but I did reach out to the DAYMS diaspora. Two distinguished young directors did emerge from the DAYMS crew, Alan Kinsella and Mark Pollard. Both were now to present two significant plays in the programme. Mark had forged a career in musicals on the West End in 'Joseph', 'Starlight Express' 'Half a Sixpence' etc and had set up his own professional company in London. He answered my call with a tight production of the romantic comedy 'Personals' from the Actors Circle, London – making us truly 'international' from day one. The cast stayed in my home for the duration and packed the Teachers Club. Alan Kinsella collaborated with THEame Paris adding to our international outlook in 'Water Drops on Burning Rocks' in the Players Theatre, in Trinity College (Wilde's Alma Mater). It was a fine piece of drama, well directed, introducing Gary Murphy and adding substance to the first programme. The TCD student players also did 'Salome' that year in association with the Festival cementing our Wildean association.

I took to the stage in Bewleys café, to bring music into the Festival with my long time collaborator David Wray. David and I created a 'one man show' (with five singers!) celebrating the music of gay composers called 'Singing Out'. It was to evolve into a series over many of the Festivals, until my own workload made it impossible for me to be in any fit performance mode, in future hectic years. I was joined by the talented sisters Roisin and Aisling Sullivan, Patrick Kelliher and Ryan Sheridan, many had appeared in La Cage with me previously. The music of Cole Porter, Noel Coward, Lorenz Hart, Stephen Sondheim, Leonard Bernstein etc all featured in the programme for two nights. I loved Coward's explanation for not coming out publically. "I did not want to offend other people's prejudices". It is a phrase and an explanation that resonated with me and spurred us into action, to ensure that benchmark would not dominate our efforts to be seen and heard. Visibility is a powerful counterbalance to prejudice.

We had brought the Festival's identity into the theatre, by David Norris launching it in Andrews Lane Theatre on April 1st 2004, and we brought theatre into the LGBT community, by holding two free play readings in The George bar – Dublin's biggest and oldest gay bar. The venue opened early on a Sunday afternoon. 'Please be Quiet' signs were put on the doors and even the ring in the cash till was turned off – for the next two hours, in the noisiest of venues, only the actors voices were audible. Peter Mc Loughlin, the manager, told me later that this featured very highly amongst the staff favourite events of the year there. Aiden Harney's play the 'Monarch of Hollywood', later successfully produced in 2011, was read there for the first time. Writer Warren Meyler's comedy 'Some Woman For One Woman' showcased the comedic talent of 'Heather Boa' aka Sheila Hamilton to popular acclaim.

We were honoured by the celebrated playwright Mark Ravenhill's association with 'Crooked House', who allowed his draft of 'Citizenship' to be read by these young (straight) actors in a gay venue, with audience response noted for transmission to the author. The free play readings too became an integral part of the programme.

Finally we had our first 'independent' production, where a company stages its own production of a play and associates it with the Festival, on more limited financial terms. AboutFACE Theatre Company staged the 'Laramie Project' directed by Paul Brennan, in the Space at the Helix. It was a strong and true production with many fine performances. They invited me to facilitate a 'post performance' talk which I found very difficult. A few weeks prior to this, I had to give a character reference to a member of my own staff, who had been convicted of killing her husband. It was in the Criminal Court, in front of the media, who were salivating at a woman killing her husband. Her two sons and her husband's family were present in the packed courtroom when I spoke up for her. I told the truth and that same night I went out to the Front Lounge for a drink, to recover from the ordeal. I was standing beside Frank Mc Cann, known as 'Rosie' who was murdered within an hour. Those incidents were very raw in me when I was asked to facilitate that discussion about Matthew Shepherd and his 'crucifictional' death in Laramie – it remains my strongest memory of year one.

We took to the stage of Liberty Hall Theatre to celebrate our first venture in our Gala final night concert. I also commissioned that theatre, with the premiere production of Brian Gallagher and Sean Purcell's 'Larkin, the Musical', on the life of trade unionist, Jim Larkin. Strangely it was reviewed by Industrial correspondents in the national newspapers! Our first Gala celebrated with guests and artists in 5 minute clips of the shows, our diverse and extraordinary achievement, in assembling gay theatre and presenting it over a fortnight in

Dublin, as we began our second decade, post decriminalisation. There were new artists, companies and voices on an Irish theatre stage. New audience members cheered.

The recorded credits for year one are sparse and included the three original directors, our designer and Karl Hayden, John Kavanagh and Alan Kinsella. We had six good citizens make a donation to us and thanked a small but vital group who assisted us, including The George and the gay media. 'Scene City' magazine in particular, gave us great space to preview the plays and afterwards to review the plays.

The financial outcome was like the Festival itself, modest but successful. Programme adverts raised 1,000.00 euros, Programme sales 476.00, sponsorship including grants 3,600.00. We recorded ticket sales of 5,607.00 with adjustments of 49.00 with our total income of 10,372. Of this, we spent 140.00 on a website, 25.00 on paint, 1,230.00 on printing, and paid 2,795.00 for theatre hire. The 'big sellers' that year, according to our excellent records kept by our Administrative Director (AD) were ' Personals' grossing 1,655.00, 'Hushabye Mountain' 1,188.00 (in only 2 nights!) and 'Water Drops On Burning Rocks' 908.00. We ended up with some seed capital for next year – and according to our announcement in our first programme, we set the dates for year two - we were on our way!

The work never stopped from then on. The potential of the event was clear and the learning rapidly advancing. I was accredited as a producer with the Edinburgh Fringe Festival, which I had visited previously. Having paid the bills, the AD and I headed off to Edinburgh where I was anxious to establish a presence for ourselves and to illuminate our administrative side, to the real skills of a viable and valid theatre festival. I read through over 1,700 fringe play synopses and together we constructed a gruelling schedule. We would start as early as 10am and finish past 1am each day – taking in 8 plays and some grossly over priced, mass produced food snacks were grabbed on the way to the next venue. We presented good companies with our brochure and the 2005 criteria. As we didn't know Edinburgh that well, we, often found that our next venue was miles away. On the Edinburgh map, a road that should be next door, but was in fact two or three flights upwards, carved into the many cliffs of the city! We were exhausted, but promoting and learning. The Festival could not fully fund this visit, where very basic accommodation costs multiplied by 5 for the month of August, so once again, we subsidised ourselves.

The Edinburgh Festival and the British Council assisted us in every way and invited us to many events, including the valued 'promoters breakfast'. There the two of us worked as a team, with people queuing up to speak with us and me being organised in strict ten minute slots, to get through the maximum number of companies. All our ticket requests were kindly approved which helped our finances, except from some of the Irish companies! We were not invited to any of the Irish promotional events that year in Edinburgh. However we were establishing ourselves well in the international community.

It was interesting to note that very few programme synopses used the term 'gay' or 'lgbt' or any easy code in the Edinburgh programme. I found out about some plays by recognising audience members and asking them had they seen any other relevant plays, invariably finding a good lead or two. Edinburgh was rewarding, exhausting and fruitful in that we identified some good prospective productions and as a programmer. I had now the rare luxury of having seen them on stage. It is a challenge to maintain an August production until the following May, but Edinburgh opened doors for us and continues to do so generously!

chapter 10

The Sequel 2005

Pretty Boys, Witty boys too, too, too… and We all wore a Green Carnation

lyrics by Noel Coward 1929

By the end of 2004, I was using every opportunity to promote the identity of the Festival and realised it would run down my own professional theatre involvement, if it was to succeed. I proceeded as planned. I did take up one professional engagement back in the Olympia. The Adele King Theatre School was staging its performances in the Olympia in the week after Christmas 2004. I had a huge love and regard for Adele, whom I had directed many times, for her passion, talent and energy. She had started three schools called AKTS and they were a roaring success. Her plan was to do the same show each night with an entirely different cast of hundreds of kids. It was a monumental task and reminded me of how much I did not miss working in theatre at Christmas, when gridlocked Dublin made it impossible to do get-ins etc. But the kids were great! After taking a director's cleaver to the clumsy pieces, borrowing sets and bringing in my own crew, we were up and running.

Each year, having successfully got the huge budget Olympia pantomime up and running, I would head to the beaches of Asia to recover. The appalling tragedy of the Tsunami occurred on St Stephen's day in an area known to me and where I had been on that day, previously. It is not right to compare tragedies – they are equally appalling to the victims and their mourners. As time goes on, the 3,000 victims of the 9/11 atrocity are remembered and rightly so, but the 250,000 poor people, represented by less powerful governments are not. It was the biggest single disaster of our time, with footage recorded too dreadful to broadcast. The scenes broadcast still haunt me on my return visits to Asia.

I knocked on the stage door in the Olympia and Tommy the doorman said "Brian we thought you were there". I wasn't but I had to act. Millions of euros were pouring into buckets in an unaccountable way in Dublin, as decent people wanted to help. The images of the poor people reaching into the torrents to rescue drowning tourists and the heroic stories of Irish survivors were astoundingly moving. Brian Whitehead, the manager of the Olympia approached me to ask was I alright and I said "Brian I need the venue to do something for the tsunami". Brian agreed immediately, with further details to follow.

One of Adele's most loyal and supportive friends was to attend the show that night. I have always found Linda Martin, Ireland's Eurovision winner, to be one of the most sincere and admirable artists around. When Linda works for charity, she does it for the right reasons. Her interests were animals, mine was AIDS fundraising and we always supported each other's causes, now I approached her for Asia. Previously I had put together a celebration of Irish success in the Eurovision Song Contest for World Aids Day. I suggested we might expand this and with Brian's agreement, Sunday January 23rd was selected – three weeks hence. Linda worked tirelessly with me to build and promote the fundraiser. I went on the Joe Duffy show 'Liveline', the following day to announce it and we had sold tickets before I had finished on air. We had not even finalised the events details, but it was happening. That year was my first direct experience of corporate Ireland opening its doors. Many of my friends were now in senior positions and they responded generously to my call. Fleishmann Hillard took on the public relations gratis. 'Riverdance' agreed to perform, along with all the artists, for free. The security team in 'The George' led by John Kelliher, offered their services and thanks to Brian Whitehead the venue came on board for free. Three hectic weeks followed. I insisted that every cent raised would go directly on the ground, to these afflicted communities. If you bought a boat in Dublin for Sri Lanka, it cost 3,000.00 euros, if you bought it there, it cost 300.00 euros.

I rekindled my friendship with Siva, a UCD fellow Equality Studies graduate from Sri Lanka, whose own home in Batacloa province was flooded. Music is central to the local community there – it heralds births, deaths and marriages. He explained the Island is similar in size to Ireland and the tsunami had travelled from 'Belfast' to 'Kerry' in 20 minutes. He said 'you will understand this, I need money to replace musical instruments, some over 400 years old and in the same family, that have been washed away'. I happily agreed and over the next months developed an arts project and refuge with him and his team, for his local community. In all this, I appealed to my Festival and DAYMS colleagues for help. We put both logos on the flyer, brilliantly created by Festival designer Danny

Lane.

I gave out the Gay Theatre Festival tagged flyers in AKTS and parents and children took them and promoted the event. One parent gave me a donation of 5,000 euros for the cause. I researched the 36 best winning songs of the Eurovision for the programme. Eurovision is a trademark and we were raising Euros we called the event 'Euro Vision for Asia'. Linda got fellow winners Niamh Kavanagh, Paul Harrington, Charlie Mc Gettigan and Eimear Quinn to learn a selection of other winning songs. Linda's 'Non Ho L'eta' and Niamh's 'Ne Partex Pas San Moi' (Outdoing Celine Dion) were among my favourite renditions of the night. Twink, Shirley Temple Bar, Mickey Harte, Chris Doran and Brendan O Carroll joined us in a night, hosted by Carrie Crowley and Mary Kennedy. Edmund Lynch and Karl Hayden created archive clips and without rehearsal, we went 'live' to a packed theatre at 8.00pm. I remember calling the show live and asking the tech crew to decipher my instructions amongst the expletives!

The atmosphere was electric and after 10pm, I noted other artists from other theatres come into the back of the stalls, to witness this first public gathering for such an enormous tragedy. I was very proud of one thing as I knew the Festival would lead to the eventual demise of my beloved DAYMS, to see a DAYMS chorus back Niamh Kavanagh's tsunami anthem rendition of 'Love Shine A Light'.

One hitch came when a technical operator refused to work for nothing on the night and demanded 400 euros of a fee at the last moment. This meant my commitment that 100% of the fundraising would go directly to the cause would not be honoured. That was too high a price, so I got DAYMS and the Festival to each pay him 200.00 euros from our own funds. Our commitment remained intact and the show could proceed as promised. It was later televised by RTE. To see gay theatre being credited in a mainstream event was a joyful but unintended consequence that also rewarded our efforts. We had raised 107,000 euros in one night.

Placing the money on the ground was a real challenge. I had met the representatives of the Indonesian Government in Ireland. Many people were unhappy with the policies of the recovery there, especially as Aceh, the main area of devastation had been a separatist province. On my next holiday to Asia, I contacted some of the Indonesian charities, most of whom were headquartered in Bangkok to learn more. It was going to take time to ensure this money was spent properly. My mother then came up with a suggestion. Having a commitment to development, I wanted where possible, for the money to be used to hire local people to build and provide their own facilities – to give them a reason to face the day and to invest in their own recovery. The Irish Carmelites had parishes in Aceh for over a century. My father's first cousin Rev. John Keating was a senior Carmelite. I contacted him and he put me in touch with their worldwide fund in Rome. Having established that our approach to recovery was similar to theirs, we made a direct donation of 35,000 euros to their on the ground fund, rebuilding the homes and facilities in their parishes in Aceh.

Matthias James Des Lauriers O. Carm wrote to me from Rome: "I did receive the 35,000.00 for the tsunami relief you sent in August. All I know at this point is the Carmelites have been helping specific villages to rebuild and obtain the means of income (building boats for fishing etc). One of our Carmelites living here in Rome, Antonio de Silva Costa visited Aceh in July and August and verified the work being done…"

In Sri Lanka, Siva and his colleagues identified a specific developmental need which fitted in very well with the ethos of the Festival. As a holiday maker, I am fully aware of the economic value of a beach and the sea in this part of the world. Surviving children were now terrified of the sea. The arts group FAST developed a programme of arts and dance to bring children safely back into the ocean. We then assisted them, as they were in the Tamil region, and not necessarily a Government priority, to acquire a 7 acre cashew nut farm and to develop on it a preschool, an arts space and womens' refuge and at my suggestion, an outdoor amphitheatre for performance. With high interest rates there, we eventually donated 70,000 euros to this project and it was wonderful to be consulted by Sri Lankan people in Dublin who were drawing up the plans etc. for the accommodation in the refuge and the school. We transferred over the money to benefit from the high Sri Lankan interest rates and that dividend funded the salaries of the pre-school teachers. In all this is was striking to see how much work Siva and his friends did here in Ireland, before and after he left, and sad to witness the huge emotional strain it was on him. They all did great humanitarian work.

DAYMS stalwart, Michelle Kavanagh, our secretary of 17 years was the chief guardian of the funds. An exemplorary civil servant, her astute administration of the account meant that, when we were closing it down a year later, we had a surplus raised by interest on our deposit account. The Pakistani earthquake hit a very poor region that year and many facilities, like clinics, were levelled. We sent a Marist priest working in a remote area, our final 7,000 euros, which helped him keep his clinic open for the next six months. In was a year's additional work, but Linda, Michelle and I did honour the work of all our contributors in placing the money in good hands, directly on the ground, where it could buy up to ten times the amount being sent by suppliers from abroad. It also created local employment and incentive and allowed local people the right to decide the infrastructure they needed to recover.

Some day I hope to visit the areas to see the work for myself. 'Euro Vision for Asia' is another very proud contribution by our Festival colleagues and demonstrates again the generosity and capacity to mobilise the arts for a tremendous cause.

2005

Starving artists in attics may make for entertaining operatic librettos but it is a destructive myth. Really you do not need poverty for brilliance in art

President Michael D Higgins at UNESCO France February 19th 2013.

Year two had begun before year one was over and fitting in the tsunami work and its great responsibility was an added challenge. Work began on evolving our structure and raising our ambition. Many who had thought or hoped for a 'one hit wonder' were now beginning to take notice in a positive and negative way. Dublin City Council were on board but there was a resentment by a few gay artists of our insistence of the artist's full identity being acknowledged. "It is not acceptable to laud the art and loath the artist" I was quoted as saying in the media. If gay people's negative stereotype was to be used as a benchmark for discrimination, and I don't offer an excuse for bad behaviour, it is only fair that it is balanced with the extraordinary contribution made by gay people to a decent society. It is all the more laudable when they found ways of making that good contribution in a hostile environment. ALAF the lesbian arts festival was struggling and we felt we now had more space to broaden our inclusivity, without treading on toes. In fact ALAF welcomed our involvement generously.

UCD's Katherine O Donnell gave a paper to our academic seminar on lesbian theatre and she noted that gay women had remained 'in the shadows' of gay life and culture and mainstream society. I am a feminist. I wanted to ensure that our use of the word 'gay' was inclusive. I set about looking for women's theatre. My first port of call was the award winning Irish playwright and novelist Emma Donoghue. Emma is typical of what it means to be Irish. Irish people, especially those who attain success abroad, do lend their support to home initiatives. She kindly and readily agreed to be our second patron but extraordinarily, when I outlined to her the difficulty in getting women's theatre, she 'donated' the use of her catalogue for companies who wished to produce her work in the theatre festival.

A most generous similar act followed some years later by US playwrights Carolyn Gage and Kerric Harvey. It is typical of those who write for the right reason, to offer such incredible support to gay theatre. However like many artists they also have to eat!

Finding women's theatre groups or groups interested in women's theatre was less easy and eventually I had to act as the covert executive producer of the 'womens' plays in the early years to ensure their presence on the programme. I took an extraordinary action, having been the sole director of DAYMS productions for over 20 years, I invited Philippa Alford to direct under the DAYMS mantle and she presented Donoghue's 'Don't Die Wondering' in the second Festival. Emma's considerable standing meant that when she attended the production so too did one of Ireland's leading social commentators Fintan O Toole, who subsequently reviewed the play in the Irish Times – another breakthrough! It took some years for the situation of women's theatre to remedy itself, but it did and handsomely in later years.

By 2005, I had pushed my way into another iconic gay theatre venue and hired the Gate Theatre for our launch on April 11th in the presence of the Deputy Lord Mayor. The gay couple who co-founded the Gate Theatre Hilton Edwards and Micheal Mac Liammoir were about to have their legacy partially hijacked in public!

"it is also very important to us that we launch this year's festival in the theatrical home of two of the greatest gay theatrical practitioners of the first half of the twentieth century – Hilton Edwards and Micheal Mac Liammoir…In some way we are 'hijacking' the great contribution of these artists known as 'The Boys' in acting as an heir to their legacy. I hope they would approve". Michael Colgan director of the Gate, who was the last visitor to the ill Edwards, later mused that they probably would not! Like many of that generation, acknowledgement was impossible. But I did recall an important acknowledgement that did happen led by Mac Liammoir.

"Mac Liammoir first presented in Dublin, London and New York 'The Importance of being Oscar' – a rather timid telling nowadays of the story of Oscar Wilde. In order to perform such a piece he too was wise enough to construct it to fit in with the heterosexually structured and homophobic society. Mac Liammoir declared in his play that Wilde was in love with Lillie Langtry and his wife Constance. He does not quote the infamous calling card left by Queensbury which prompted the trials accusing Wilde of 'posing as a somdomite'. The actual trials occur in the interval with Act Two opening with the sentence given for a crime which isn't mentioned. The rest of the Act dwells on Wilde's religious fervour in 'de Profundis' and the 'Ballad of Reading Gaol'.

"The intention was however noble – he declared that to so many thousands of people today the name of Oscar Wilde merely conjures up an immediate image of shame and scandal. It is time not to forget the scandal or the shame, but to place them in their correct relationship with the subsequent development as an artist and a human soul".

This was an extraordinarily brave undertaking by Mac Liammoir. Had he not been an actor of such excellence, he might have been 'outed' and his future as an artist suffer the same fate as the unfortunate Wilde, in the hostile 1960s. Dr Eibhear Walshe further enlightened the Festival in later years by his papers on Mac Liammoir during our academic seminar, which he also acted as a valued Guide and mentor.

Mac Liammoir, as Wilde, had given us a language in which being gay could be acknowledged. He constantly and in public referred to Hilton Edwards as his partner. People took it to mean in business. I noted "At Mac Liammoir's funeral the President of Ireland was amongst the first to sympathise with Hilton Edwards at the loss of his partner. Over thirty years later Senator David Norris still battles to have such partnerships recognised"

I added further as the topic of partnership rights was so prominent in Ireland. The Festival had to be contemporary and relevant. Very often we were among the few entities that could gather an audience of politicians and decision makers, so our responsibility to air important issues was important not to let the opportunity to clarify go by. " "Why shouldn't all consenting adults who care and commit to each other be treated equally, by validating both socially and in terms of partnership rights, their relationship? Why does this still prove so difficult for some political and other minds to embrace? Yet the on-going discrimination of not validating such relationships on an equal footing with heterosexual ones, seem to prove no difficulty at all? Is it still the case that in Ireland at least, the

'Marquis of Queensbury' rules still prevail? We live in hope and wish you well David!"

David Norris had just had his partnership rights bill defeated in the Senate. I didn't agree with his inclusion of rights for opposite sex co-habitants as that broadened the church of opposition. Heterosexual couples had marriage and divorce, we had nothing. Though probably inevitably destined for defeat, I would have preferred the clear focus on same sex rights in the ill-fated but ground breaking Bill, which he did his best to progress, typical of the man's generosity in believing the decency of others!

I placed year two in the following context in my launch speech in the Gate Theatre. "Theatre was and is important as a place where society was exhibited and recognised itself. Wilde's plays were obsessed with the boundaries of society. If you were in society you could leave cards, visit people of good standing, attend receptions. Fear of exclusion from society led Wilde to sue the Marquis of Queensbury for libel. Wilde's brother Willie later told WB Yeats that Wilde considered that his crime was not vice itself but that he should have brought misery upon his wife and children. He was bound to accept any chance however slight to re-establish his position. Later the Wilde trials established homosexuality not just generally but at the heart of theatre. It had an effect.

In the 1920s, Jocelyn Burke writes of a nurse, a devout Baptist, who insisted that theatre had 'an aura of wickedness and that playhouses were sinks of iniquity".

Following the almost extinction of a generation of young men in particular in World War One, I noted the "emergence of other social locations which supported alternative even oppositional attitudes. Bohemia, which afforded principled justification for disrespectful behaviour. George Chauncey remarked that Bohemians generally were believed to be queer, in some contexts calling men 'artistic' became a code for calling them homosexual"

A.T. Fitzroy's earlier novel had linked all this and Dublin nicely. His novel 'Despised and Rejected in 1918 was " set in a pacifist, socialist, artistic, bohemian tea shop which included flappers, actors, poets, Jews, people living in sin and Sinn Feiners with mournful lilting Irish accents!". Theatre being outside society and being gay are historically and intrinsically interlinked, I argued that launch day.

Launches gave me a captive audience and one annual opportunity to try to posit what it was that drove the Festival. The standing audience and the cheapest of wines did not greatly incentivise the listnership. "If you don't believe our lack of resources wait until you experience the quality of the wine!

Year two was a chance to set out what we had learned and to broaden the definition of our own ambition. "I believe if it is appropriate to have a national theatre to celebrate the unique contribution of Irish artists to theatre, and it is, then it is equally appropriate to have a Festival celebrating the contribution of gay people to theatre. It is entirely appropriate that this international Festival has its home in the birthplace of Oscar Wilde – Dublin".

"But let me place the context in a more real and modern plain. One of our Festival plays showcased in a country town last month. It is entitled 'Citizenship' a premiere by Mark Ravenhill is an important play also for us in that it brings young people into this Festival and it spreads the impact of the Festival beyond 'The Pale'. It is also important because in a democracy many people take the right of citizenship for granted. Many others go out of their way to construct a lesser 'degree of citizenship' for anyone who is perceived or constructed as different. This is what mainstreaming gay theatre can help to address. In its pre festival run, these gifted and talented young people learned the lesson that even in a modern democracy there are different levels of citizenship.

Mid performance some other young people broke into the venue and ran onto the stage shouting 'faggots' at the cast. This is hardly akin to the Abbey Theatre riots, but it reinforces my belief that much work needs to be done to truly embrace the diversity that is Ireland, and to counteract the enemies of human rights. They thrive when information is concealed. It is our responsibility to present the reality of lives and not to hide them behind the exclusively heterosexual or homophobically constructed 'norms' that exist, to insist upon our difference being a deviance".

It was thrilling to see the response of parents, some gave chase to retrieve the stolen costumes, many packed the Festival audience in support of their sons and daughters as they explored true citizenship!

I knew we were building audience for gay theatre. It was a struggle and not a lucrative one. I wanted once we had gotten them into the theatre, to expose them as much as possible to gay culture. I began to assemble themed programmes. This meant you got two plays for the price of one – a huge but shared sacrifice by our participating companies. It allowed us to reach out more with the programme but seriously limited the financial rewards for productions.

There was somewhat of a male/female divide in the early years which I appealed for assistance with from our lesbian supporters. If I did a coming out programme, featuring a male and female story, the women would stay for the female story and then invariably leave. The men would stay for both and if the women's play was better would mark it higher in their audience response forms. I noted early that we were getting mixed audiences. Irish people tend to like to know someone in a play – this attracted in a straight audience as many of our actors had straight friends or were straight themselves. Our limited publicity was also targeted at the mainstream to diversify audiences. This was a critical success factor and we were achieving it. In 2004 I would estimate 70% of our audience was a loyal following of gay men. By 2005 this demographic changed and we began to realise a 50/50 diversity rate. Much to our delight, the intercultural dialogue had begun.

Secondly our first Festival had not sufficiently recognised the considerable achievement of this theatre work. Awards create an opportunity to turn some decent human beings into hypocritical monsters. I had known this to my cost every time I won a truckload at AIMS or WIFLO! However we were dealing with mainly young professionals. I also curated the programme and without any resources to truly verify, I had to take a risk as to whether a good script would be badly produced or whether a reasonable play would be brilliantly presented.

I did not want to descend into a competition which would take the focus off the new work, valuable networking and camaraderie of the participants. This was hugely important to our success and sustenance of our voluntary work. I decided after much soul searching to create some 'rewards' – accolades that would be of use to our talented participants. It was also an opportunity for me as curator to give a final assessment of what I deemed to have been worthwhile in the selection process. The Festival was about new writing – post 2000, but gay history is also important, so I chose to construct the rewards around those pioneers of history. I kept the focus very narrow to reduce the competitiveness of the nature of the actor and the ego. I was not always successful in this. I launched four awards 'Oscar Wilde' for writing, 'Hilton Edwards' for an aspect of production and two 'Micheal Mac Liammoir' for performance by a male and female. The deliberately narrow focus with only three nominees was almost choking, considering the diversity of the event. I had to refine that outward in future years. It took many years though for even some actors to fully credit the awards in their CV. I often read that someone had won a particular award in 'Dublin' or at a 'theatre festival in Dublin', but it is still a rarity to see the Gay Theatre Festival credited in CVs, no matter how much the award was deserved and appreciated – fear of type casting, I assume.

In 2005, we presented eight Irish premieres including four world premieres. Eddie Kenny, patriarch of the Cobalt Café, our main music venue, would always loudly comment on my 'Singing Out' series "What have you done this time – changed one song and called it another world premiere? Well, at least someone was reading the programme! 'Singing Out Too' with Eddie Devoy, Alan O Sullivan and Brendan Spratt joining me onstage, was an entirely new show concentrating on the music of new gay composers and artists.

We had theatre companies from Dublin, Kildare and Cork and three international companies. We managed to feature plays by three women writers, sadly our first play 'About Face' did not go on due to the tragic suicide of author Jinny Mc Allister of Almeida Theatre London, the week before the Festival launch. This dreadful tragedy for her cast and family was a serious and noted loss to the Festival. We attempted to facilitate the performers but they hadn't the heart to go on in such circumstances.

Willie White is a canny man. He is welcoming and shrewd and did open the Project Arts Centre to the Festival – admonishing us for not having approached him the first year – we had not the funds to do so. With Willie's elevation to greater things as the Director of the Dublin Theatre Festival, and the appointment of a new openly gay director in the Project, we have been unable to renew our booking for this venue in 2012 and 2013. Willie did support the Festival fairly and through challenges of multiple get-ins and political difficulties. We were delighted to be informed by his box office that our opening night play in 2010 was the first 'full house' of that year.

In the 1970s, Dublin Corporation's Arts Committee Chairman, Councillor Ned Brennan, famously tried not only to stop a show, but to close the building, following a performance by Gay Sweatshop London at the Project. Times had changed! We also added the Focus Theatre (though sadly very run down) and Andrews Lane Theatre to our list of performance spaces that year, bringing us into the heart of theatre.

Wonderland's production of the 'Love Doctor' proved to be equally memorable for its unhappy cast. At times I had to intervene to get them to go on! Gay domestic violence was the theme of 'Say Sorry' an uncomfortable but well played drama from 'Slice of Life' productions in London, written and directed by Alex Baker. This was an important and often hidden story of same sex partnerships that fitted our 'tell it warts and all' ethos well. 'Biscuits for Breakfast' returned with 'Naked Will' by Blair Fell, exploring the much queried sexuality of William Shakespeare and his love interest Mr W.H - a topic of interest to Oscar Wilde.

Alan Kinsella once again proved his skill when he directed a powerful production of Steven Berkoff's 'Decadence' in The Focus, which was paired with 'Harlequins Lesson in Love' directed by Caroline Staunton. David Wray returned with' Simply Sondheim', a devised musical feast with Ellen Mc Elroy, Danna Davis, Andrew Holden and John Matthews also directed by Alan Kinsella.

I had an approach from Jack Gilligan to include a late entry into the programme. That was strange as the author was Neil Watkin, had played a wonderful 'Bosie' opposite my Oscar in the premiere of 'A Chelsea Affair' and I knew him well. I met with Neil and producer Philip Mac Mahon and by seriously squeezing extra performance times, they fitted out the Centre Stage Café in Parliament Street and presented Watkins 'A Cure For Homosexuality' whose style was to inspire so much of Watkins future performances and writing. Neil was on a roll and in the meantime won the 'Alternative Miss Ireland' (AMI) where I had provided some of his costumes.

I remember a launch party at 'Glitz' at Break for the Border – kindly hosted by our supporter Declan Mac Gregor and Scene City Magazine. I had done a full day's work, then attended and was the sole responder to a debate on inequality in the Royal College of Surgeons – a bastion of privilege. I then rushed to the launch party and without notes announced the entire programme and named accurately the entire voluntary group. Our Administrator handed me a well earned pint and told me Neil, despite the late accommodation of his work, still hadn't signed the standard contract. I approached him and asked him to sign it immediately – if for nothing else – for his insurance protection. His reply was 'I'll talk to you when you are sober'! I hadn't even had a tablespoon of beer! I realised we might be in for a bit of a journey!

Despite such AMI distractions, Mac Mahon was concerned about the final product, pre-performance, when he alerted me to its many merits but wondered was it in fact finished? I think the author had availed of a week in the Tyrone Guthrie Centre to concentrate on the play. His early analysis proved correct in my view, though the acclamation it inspired was truly admirable. There are certain performers and authors who truly inspire zealous devotees and that is indeed admirable and deserved. Watkins and later Mac Mahon, take a bow.

The play went on and was glowingly received in many quarters. To me it was still somewhat incomplete. Act four was really a hurried tidying up of a hugely entertaining fantasy. It was greatly helped by Watkin's diverse performance of stamina, designed to shock at all costs - a trademark he would later evolve and stamp on all his work. It was good theatre, great to see it emerge in Ireland, and his many friends, including Mark O Halloran, continued to refer to it during the Festival years later, at every opportunity, as if it was in some way unrecognised. Here's where my first awards structure became somewhat unstuck.

'Crooked House' (and Kildare Youth Theatre) continued our tradition of bringing a previous play reading from page to stage when they got permission to stage Mark Ravenhill's 'Citizenship' with its 14 strong wonderful young cast this year. The support coming from those who had only seen his play, was so loyal that any objective discussion was unwelcome. Such insistence is hugely unfair to the works presented by the many other distinguished companies in the Festival. Neil in fact came in a hugely creditable fourth in the writing category, and also fourth in the performance category – the latter won by professional TV actor Tom O'Leary for a heroic performance in 'Decadence'.

It is difficult to appear not to succeed when so many well-wishers are affirming you and deservedly so. It was my 'unfortunate task' to adjudicate and be fair to all the productions, and to stand over my view in public. I was most pleased to see the Festival assist a play of this merit and a gay Irish performer of impact like Neil Watkin. It was not a slight when others are judged to have been excellent in their field, as if the Festival was to be used in any way to denigrate any performer, it would be a nasty and worthless endeavour. I remain unconvinced that the perceived lack of honour in four narrow categories was every forgiven. I amended the nominations to five in each category the following year, though I doubt that would have satisfied in that year!

Aiden Harney once again allowed a play reading of his work 'Being Miss Ross' in The George to success! The support of this core of Irish artists was essential to the early success of the Festival and set a high standard for those who followed. The 'Actors Circle' returned with 'the New Boy' (adapted by Russell Labey) with an award winning performance from stunning, pint sized comic, Clare Kissane (as the Teacher). Emma Donoghue conveyed its participation in our event to the author William Sutcliffe, with whom she had toured, spreading our network further.

A Dublin and Catholic guilt setting surrounded the 'Dark Horse' presentation of 'Torch Song Trilogy' programmed. A rather bizarre scenario evolved here with personnel going missing and out of contact and the play involving a community based arts programme never made it to the stage. I had wondered about the rights to adapt such a piece and ensured that performance rights and permissions were a core guarantee of each contract. We were to be plagued by some unreliability in each Festival.

The shorts that year fused two 'coming out' stories. Initially the only plot I was not interested in was 'coming out' – I was more interested in what was done when you emerged as a gay citizen. However a broad programmer must remember to be the first to break the rule! 'Three Wise Women' presented Verity Alicia Mavenawitz's (director, Nuala Kelly) well written and 'Then There was Me' performed by the pioneering Irish lesbian actress, Suzanne Lakes. I coupled this with a terrific piece from 'Be Your Own Banana' Production of 'The Self Obsessed Tragedy of Ed Malone". This show had toured in its own right and the company noted the difference in response from a gay theatre audience. Their director Brian Desmond commented "they get it – they even see things in this we did not – a great way to end our tour". Here both plays were worthy participants, but once again all the women did not stay to take in the deliberate combination of the two interwoven tales.

The Festival had made the breakthrough with women writers, directors and performers who laid a great foundation on which we could build our inclusivity, promote visibility and produce good theatre relevant to women's lives and experience.

Emma Donoghue's legacy was well presented in 'Don't Die Wondering' which Fintan O'Toole reported "The existence and obvious success of the Festival is a mark of cultural change" a view not always adhered to by his fellow journalistic colleagues in the 'Irish Times' in later years. O Toole noted "And the shift is more evident in the capacity of youth companies, who don't have a specific gay or lesbian focus, to engage in confidence with work which does. The old fear that the young would be corrupted by contact with such shocking material has been replaced by cheering evidence that the young have in fact had their morals deepened". O'Toole's eloquence and openness got what the Festival was about.

That year's Festival committee expanded to about nine people. Joining the original three directors were Chris Fildes and Danny Lane who ran the Queerid website, Stephen Wallace, Declan Coogan, Connell Kennedy and a deeply committed new recruit, Gareth Hurley who would emerge as a key and loyal player in future years, while he led our online evolution. We had sixteen productions on over a fortnight and the quality continued to grow in a resource starved innovative event. To cap it all RTE TV showed 'Euro Vision For Asia' during the Festival in May that year.

We paid our bills, had enough seed capital for next year and began looking for new opportunities to develop. My business ethic, because theatre and our ill resourced Festival was so financially fragile, was that all our bills had to be covered by opening night. Depending how hard we worked at box office, we would end the Festival with a foundation for the following year, so Edinburgh and the Audit could be paid for and venues secured by December - the closing date for submissions. Coinciding with this we were now receiving enquiries worldwide. George Bush's America was not kind to gay theatre and in one year alone we had 60 applications from the USA. We could have run the US gay theatre festival from Dublin!

I acted as a dramaturg for all these submissions. This took an enormous amount of time and effort and many a winter's night by the fire reading. The hard copy plays would invariably not fit into my letterbox so at times, daily, I had to make my way to James's Street Post office to collect a package. Recently the collection office has been moved much closer to home on the South Circular Road which helps!

I appreciate writing. I trained and qualified as a professional journalist in the only such course run at the College of Commerce, Rathmines in 1980. I like writers, they are brave and without them there could be no theatre. I respect that. Not everyone is a writer and not all my opinions are correct! The work that went into turning a submission down was far more intense at this stage, than those that thrilled and were accepted. Very often my only tool of communication was email and that can very much rely on the mood of the reader, rather than the correspondent. Some amusing general trends did emerge from reading in excess of 100 plays annually.

'Coming out' plays are generally not of interest and very personal. People can write about deeply felt emotion or incidence, but not communicate that in any dramatic way. People don't like being told their personal stories don't make good theatre. There was an abundance of these similar, one person stories from the US in particular - all very similar in plot and outcome. Some people write a play and tell me they don't know how to end it. This requires a very careful reading, if alerted to the problem. My first read of a script has me keenly listen to the story being told. I inevitably end up identifying the ending the writer has lost sight of, in his or her immersion into the detail of the plot. It is vital that the dramaturg does not become the writer. One must release the voice of the writer to be of value to the process.

In essence and a little flippantly, I would summarise that American writers are obsessed with the 'Walnut Creek'/ 'Walton's Mountain' approach. No matter how dreadful the experience related, it must have a moral outcome and preferably a 'goodnight Johnboy' ending. Americans love it when things turn out ok, because generally they are a generous and good hearted people. To get the American author to maintain his/her edge was often quite a struggle. Most Americans do appreciate the time and effort put into analysing their script. They are mannerly, even in their disappointment. I tried always to offer suggestions of editing or indeed a new journey for a character, or plot, to assist the evolution of the embryonic play.

Some writers have two or three plays in one and these also need to be separated into distinct works. Others write a part for their actor friend whose influence can be seen on the script and not always for the ultimate merit of the piece. There a few writers who respond to a critique that every item you analyse as being weak, happened to be the very thing that each of their best friends loved, when they read it!

The British are different too. They tend to collaborate more and often the presenter feels obliged to 'defend' the work of his/her collaborators with a sense that anything else would be to let them down. They also tend not to react quickly like the Americans to an analysis. However as they do consider the matter, it frequently emerges some week later that they have taken on board what had been said and move on graciously. I am always delighted to receive a further draft of a work and some have then been accepted for performance. It is also important to note that it is the individual play that was not successful, not the writer and they must distinguish that in the perceived rejection. Keep writing and apply again and again!

The Irish are different too. I understand that they do not like 'submitting' work to someone they may know. In the mountain of scripts, I have often finished it before I realise who the author is or whether I may or may not know them. I am of the firm conviction that you do not do your 'friends' any favour by putting up any work, as a writer or actor, in which they are not guaranteed every possible opportunity to shine. That ethos is not always acknowledged or appreciated and some never speak to you again, if you query in anyway the Shakesperian quality of their very first work! The Irish do not take well to perceived criticism and even when they do, they invariably have 'friends' who will re-interpret my advice in a negative way. That is why I try to meet with Irish writers if I can, to assist them in that process of script development and some have graciously accepted my guidance. I too learn so much from their work and am privileged to invest in its production.

There are other trends emerging. I had a strong commitment to telling the stories of the Holocaust. We are their descendent by culture and just as I witnessed ageing Hiroshima survivors speak to schoolchildren in the Peace Park in Japan, we too have an obligation to ensure the Nazi holocaust on gay people is never forgotten. I also am interested in issues such as mental health. Stigma, abuse and exclusion does so much psychological damage. It is clear that our audiences do not want to attend such personal stories. We have had some wonderful pieces of theatre like 'Funny in the Head' from Canada whose final night full house rose in standing ovation, almost before the final word was spoken. Yet two performances earlier in the week were cancelled due to non-attendance. Colin Clay Chace's 2012 piece 'Rock n Wrestle' equally struggled despite the edge and alternativeness of this strong piece of theatre. Our efforts to get mental health organisations to support these productions have also failed. Child abuse and its connections to gay people are also hard to sell. "The Tricky Part" from South Africa paid horrendously high royalties to stage this play in Dublin in 2011. It was well acted Peter Hayes and wonderfully contextualised by Irish abuse survivor Andrew Madden in a rare post show talk. We could not sell it to an exhausted Irish public frustrated at the total failure of any Institution to take full responsibility for their abuse of children.

Light comedy, music and naked performances sell. The lure of the naked body still appeals and the challenge for straight actors to perform naked to gay audiences, has resulted in many an interesting examination of masculinity in after show chats at the Festival Club. I spoke on Newstalks 'Culture Shock' show with Fionn Davenport about 'Brokeback Mountain'. I said 'Brokeback Mountain did as much for gay people as Al Jolson did for Black people by 'blacking up as a minstrel'. I had been particularly incensed by Gyllenhaal and Ledger's appearance on Oprah where they hardly looked at each other, sat apart, and emphasised their heterosexuality in an interview allegedly to promote the movie. Their 'love' scenes were a borderline on aggression passing as passion. In the Festival, straight actors often discuss with me how much confidence they get about their own bodies when they come to terms with doing nude scenes in a gay Festival. Invariably some also tend to overkill by trying to find a straight woman in our volunteer corps, and there are many!

We have used some plays performed in their own language. I appreciate greatly the trouble companies go to provide me with English translations. Unfortunately as we struggle so much to sell a gay play to our audience, it is almost impossible to further sub divide that audience into a category who may want to see gay theatre in a foreign language. It is not yet sustainable. We did present one performance in Ukranian, another in Russian though it was 95% dance, about 'Tschaikovsky's Wife' which did sell and one in Spanish about the life of Joe Orton complete with electric subtitles, 'Noel Road,25'. However the dialogue in Spanish was delivered with such passion and speed, it made the reading challenge very difficult for our audience, though we also marketed it to the strong gay deaf community.

At the DGTF, it is the case that the author is king. We need our stories to be told and we are relying on their creativity in the first instance. The Festival itself has inspired some plays. The 'Artscape' new writing programme made an early connection with us and presented some fine plays in our programme, directed by Roy Sargeant. The visits to Dublin became sought after in South Africa and one day Roy received an anxious phone call from a legendary older actress decrying the well established fact, that older women have fewer options in leading roles in theatre (or film). She enquired about the Dublin event and in exasperation said 'I'm even willing to play lesbian!". In Roy's company that day was the eminent TV presenter and journalist Fiona Coyne. Intrigued by the statement, Coyne was inspired to write the play 'Careful' and set it in the context of a tour to our

Festival. It is a hilarious two hander between an older actress who contacts a lesbian reviewer who once described her as 'a national treasure' to use her as a reference point for 'playing lesbian'. It is a wonderful entertaining comedy that doesn't fail in any way to make its more serious points. Diane Wilson won the best female performance that year, with Coyne being nominated for best writing. Tragically Coyne took her own life sometime later, to the shock of many and denying our world further output from this talented writer.

Renowned US lesbian feminist playwright Carolyn Gage performed her own works 'Joan of Arc' and a short 'Calamity Jane Writes a Letter to her Daughter' in Festival 2006. We did a radio interview and while we were chatting, I explained to her about the 90th anniversary celebrations of the 1916 Rising visible in the city. I told her about the role of women in the struggle and how Nurse Elizabeth Farrell who surrendered with Pearse, had been airbrushed out of the surrender picture (except for her shoes) and as a result history. Some months later Carolyn produced the play 'The Countess and The Lesbians' about Constance Markiewicz, her sister Eva Gore Booth and her partner Esther Roper, which was a highlight of Festival 2007. I secured Gina Costigan to produce and this three-hander went on appropriately in Liberty Hall, where Markievicz had such a strong connection. The real hero was Eve Gore Booth and subsequently thanks to Dr Sonja Tiernan and Katherine O Donnell's illumination, we learned of our first lesbian historical artist.

Mr Mac Liammoir was stripped of his best female performance award and Eva Gore Booth was proudly instated as an award title. Sonja Tiernan subsequently published the first biography of Gore Booth and Roper which is an excellent and enlightening read – another piece of gay history uncovered and honoured. This later inspired Alan Flanagan to write 'I Run, I Sing, I Swim, I Dive' the life story of Eva, based on Tiernan's book, for its world premiere in Festival 2013.

The Festival also instituted the Dr Aiden Rogers memorial lecture to honour an eccentric (because he was gay in the 1970s?) but renowned teacher at St Patricks Teacher Training College in Drumcondra. Aiden was a brilliant Shakesperian interpreter and found time to educate that rarest of individual, the male primary school teacher into the realms of dramatic interpretation. Male teachers in particular have an additional burden of being the ambassadors of Gaelic sports in our schools. It was Aiden's gifts that shaped these student minds and put many on an artistic road. He also directed me in 'The Arcadians' where his outrageous behaviour was a source of constant shock to the suburban singing housewives of northside Catholic Dublin. He was a principled man and died alone in unfortunate circumstances, having finally being unable to survive in that most Catholic of worlds. Like so many gay people of his generation he lost his battle with alcohol. I hope he would be honoured with our occasional lecture series, often introduced by a former student or colleague.

We also honour the late Patrick Murray from Cork. Pat was a most generous and talented set designer, dance advocate and Arts Council member. He was always kind to me as a young director, especially when I visited his native and beloved Cork. The 'Patrick Murray Award' for outstanding contribution to Irish gay theatre was initially generously sponsored by the Labour Party, of which he was a member, and where he designed their rose logo and conference platforms. His unexpected death at Christmastime meant so much of his Jacob's award winning art catalogue is now feared lost. He is well remembered by us. The Festival set out to encourage an intercultural dialogue and Dublin City Council sponsored the award initially.

By the end of 2005 and another exhausting visit to Edinburgh, I had over 130 submissions to read through when the deadline passed on December 1st. The administration side showed some impatience that I couldn't make up a programme immediately, clearly not allowing for any form of in depth analysis or dramaturg service, which I know from responses, has assisted playwrights yet to have their work appear in the programme.

The end of the year also brought other administrative issues to a head that decided me not to proceed with the event unless these matters were addressed. Matters intervened to resolve the issues of the shares 'held in trust' not being passed onto nominated directors in the limited company. There was a refusal to do so and ownership of what I had established as a shared event, was clearly becoming an issue. I had simultaneously established that in order to be grant-aided, we should have been (as I thought) a 'not for profit, limited by guarantee' company. We proceeded to evolve towards that and formally registered the name the 'International Dublin Gay Theatre Festival Ltd'.

I managed in this new structure to reflect the ownership as per the original intent. I had learned the lesson and wanted to find people who would protect the corporate entity for its core purpose – theatre and the gay and arts community. Without challenge, I invited Barbara Cashen, who had Chaired the Equality Authority's first ever LGB 'Implementing Equality' Group which published a far reaching rights based report, Eddie Devoy, Dr Victor Merriman and Gearoid O Byrne from TP Robinson Solicitors as my nominees. I also appointed our Administrator as a co-director and offered him one place on the Board. To my complete surprise he did not appoint his partner of many years, who was an asset on our Executive Committee, but his daughter who never consequently took any role in the company. The ownership of the company was now in safe hands. The membership seceded the day to day running of the event to the Voluntary Executive Committee who continued to be the key players in delivering the event. The membership of the Board was purely supervisory, to ensure good governance, to protect the corporate entity from theft or damage and to ensure proper auditing etc. Little did they realise that they would play a key role in stabilising the entity when it was subject to attack. The Administrative Director was appointed Company Secretary with statutory responsibilities for corporate compliance and I as Executive Chairman became the Managing Director as well as the Artistic Director. We were finally properly established, and the crises of the shareholding averted, with all funds from one company being made available to the new corporate entity. We continued to recruit the skills needed for the Executive to deliver an event that was to take a further dramatic turn in 2006.

2006

Strangely moving to hear an Irish TD refer to his male partner on radio in passing and no one bats an eye-lid

Abie Philbin Bowman @AbiePB 2013

I was acutely conscious that Irish people support theatre more, when they know someone in the cast. The quality of the submissions merited a radical change in our programming. Also the initial surge of quality productions was beginning to wane a little and I wanted to create an opportunity, a centre where Irish writers, directors and actors could experience first-hand what was happening in gay theatre worldwide. With all these plusses overcoming the minuses, I decided to jump off the theatrical cliff and programme a fully international Festival. It was a huge risk and I still had a bias towards Irish theatre that I have maintained, however it would now have to be of the standard of the entire programme and vice versa.

The main demand for participation came from the US. I had an enormous amount of one person shows, many autobiographical, and I could only facilitate a few, if any. We set up a new financial structure whereby the Festival now assumed full responsibility for the theatre rentals, regardless of the box office and the Festival grant aided the companies on a 70/30 basis, reflecting the box office take with no contras. I was also hugely stressed by also offering actors accommodation in my home and our Administrative side did a great deal with Travelodge, where for every room we hired we got one free. Each room could house up to three people. It was now an attractive deal to come to this Festival and the Travelodge deal was a huge achievement. All the companies had to do was to fly here and to feed themselves, as our voluntary technical people went to every length to assist in sets, costumes, props, stage management and operating gratis.

The high submission rate meant about one in six was selected. I did it on the basis of the script, the subject matter, and any research that I could find out about the personnel. It was a risk, but we had no resources to fund a proper programming development scheme. We also launched a new logo. Talented artist Will St Ledger embraced the Oscar ideal and produced a wonderful Mona Lisa-esque image of Oscar smiling with a green carnation in his mouth. The general public loved it and so did I. At last people looked at us and indeed took it as a souvenir or had themselves photographed beside it! We were reaching out and being seen.

The Executive Committee had now grown to 13 and our volunteer corps to 30. Interestingly that included a large portion of foreign people who felt included in the diversity of the event to our delight and benefit. If the audience wasn't going to know many in the casts, they weren't going to know the plays either and we had 19 of the 20 productions as Irish premieres. It is difficult to market a new show, but to market 19 simultaneously was a real challenge.

We approached 2006 with a new vigour and the work of all involved was exceptional. My local representative and later TD, Catherine Byrne of Fine Gael had been elected Lord Mayor of Dublin. She is a woman with deep community roots. We wrote and met her in the locality and she agreed to let us launch the Festival in her home in The Mansion House. This was a huge honour. It was a most opportune year. 2006 was the 90th anniversary of the 1916 Rising which was to create a nation of equals. We also had made great efforts to get some State support. This mainly fell on deaf ears. We invited and got acceptances from over 80 important people in the arts, administration and the gay community for our launch. We were told the Lord Mayor would attend 'for two minutes'.

When her anxious handlers arrived, I took to the podium. I set the launch in the context of 1916 and an egalitarian Republic. I reminded them that many speculated that the leader Padraig Pearse may have been gay. We were in the Oak Room panelled with portraits and coats of arms of previous Lord Mayors. We were in the room next door to where the first Irish Dail (parliament) met in 1922. I began:

"When citizens are perceived as being different, then society can utilise this difference to discriminate. When such a difference is deliberately structured what chances have the discriminated? Well there is a chance…for the brave. One must take on those who insist on the stereotype and exploit the fear. Theatre enriches a civilised society. It is a forum where life can be portrayed and understood from its many diverse perspectives. It is a forum that allows you to make up your own mind".

"Society too can give validation by offering the supports granted to the mainstream, to those who operate to the same standards, outside what is perceived to be the mainstream. The role of national arts and cultural funding bodies is crucial if citizenship, diversity, freedom to express, communicate and human rights are to be embedded into the core of a society – especially when one seeks to follow the values and human rights so eloquently set out in the Proclamation, to cherish and treat all its citizens equally. The only principle should be the merit principle – the bedrock of equal opportunity. We have looked to national arts and cultural funding bodies to assist us in partnership in fulfilling our citizenship and our cultural expression to no avail. In this the anniversary month of 1916, I am very pleased however to acknowledge the only support we got from an arts and cultural institution operating in the Republic is the partnership between the Festival and…the British Council".

There was an audible gasp. I let the impact sink in and then noted. "Sure why wouldn't they, wasn't it their funds that maintained and developed the work of Edwards and Mac Liammoir as they toured internationally, when work at home was limited and not lucrative enough to maintain the viability of their theatrical company?".

The Lord Mayor had now been with us for over 20 minutes having waved away her handlers. She had no prepared speech but she spoke from the heart, endorsing our concept of the right to citizenship. She pointed out "I am the first citizen and this is my home and you are welcome in my home and always will be as citizens of Dublin". The point was made and understood. We did eventually get the smallest of grants, but of course a price would be paid for the public exposure of the weaknesses of the State process.

Change was happening in the programme too. 'Gay and Confused' by Patrick Walshe was to be a six part live soap opera staged in 'The George' at weekends. Directors Sharon Sexton and Vinny Moran were put to the pin of their collar to make the material valid and entertaining in such a short time. Our first Israeli play dealt with the autobiographical play 'Somewhere in Between' of the gender transition of Ronny Almog, a female Israeli soldier into her male identity. They were a strange group and did not get the concept of sharing a venue. They wanted to erect a permanent set, but insisted the South African company that followed them, could not act in front of it! Added to that they had no capacity to rig, so they spent almost 24 hours staring at the lighting rig in a tight shared get-in. Our technical director Naoise O Reilly eventually had to leave her demanding station, getting two plays into The Project and rigged 80 lamps in about 90 minutes. When they continued to create obstacles, I opened my lungs and told them I would close the show and they could go home. I was embarrassed to discover my threat had an audience – the South Africans who immediately burst into applause!

We were learning about multi-cultural theatre instantly. We always said to our volunteers that they were not to involve themselves in dispute – that was the Artistic Director's job and my decision was contractually final. In my absence, the Administrative Director would intervene in what is a difficult task in an event relying on goodwill.

The South African play 'Happy Endings Are Extra' by Ashraf Johaardien was a story of a bisexual man, his fiancée and his escort lover. It was a very strong piece of theatre and began a trend of South African female actors winning successive performance awards at the Festival, with Deirdre Wolhuters claiming the honours. It included a scene where rent boy Chris (Pieter Jacobs) nakedly eating a bowl of strawberries,that lives in Festival legend to this day!

The expanded programme also allowed us to take a shot at Eurovision, the iconic event that enraptured a generation of gays. 'A Night of a thousand Jay Astons' marked writer/actor, Jonny Woo's, first (of many) appearances in Dublin. The cheesy 'Sing-a-long –a-Eurovision' appropriately included some instantly forgettable UK entries, introduced us to Andrew Norris, another artist of note from Manchester and 'Emmerdale' actor Steve Swift.

'Minor Irritations' was a gay play I had discovered, thanks to an audience member in Edinburgh. Writer Sam Peter Jackson had not used the word gay in his synopsis and we almost missed it. It was a tight comedy that ultimately won nominations for three of its four cast. The fourth, Nick White, the diversity officer of the Yvonne Arnaud Theatre in the UK, became a great Festival friend and a member of our Festival reviews team, who also penned many a poetic tribute for the Gala night. He is now the manager of the new St James Theatre in London. Once again, I covertly acted as executive producer of Emma Donoghue's 'I Know My Own Heart' co-produced by DAYMS and played in Liberty hall. This period piece attracted a mixed audience of men and women. I had always been very uncomfortable at film festivals where audiences were segregated by the gender of the film. We set out to ensure that men and women would attend all plays and in much of this we succeeded, especially with Emma Donoghue plays. Linda Gough's last minute stand in, playing of 'Isabella Norcliffe' ,was one highlight of this fine production.

One of my all time favourite plays is 'The Drowning Room' marking the return of Irish writer 'Verity Alicia Mavenawitz'. This play is set on a hillside where a group of family and friends gather with the ashes of 'Sean Roche' who was murdered for wearing 'fancy fuckin' boots'. The perpetrators get a very light sentence and the grieving group have their remembrance night interrupted by the arrival of the father of the accomplice, with a shattering admission. It's a great play. Mavenawitz's strength here was definitely in the writing and not in the direction, but the play gripped the audience. It transferred later to mainstream and once again the layers of the experience recounted were not as readily recognised, as the fact that the victim was gay, appeared to dominate the mainly straight audiences. This is one of the plays I received without an ending and it was an honour to assist in suggesting that dramatic finale.

Patricia Hartshorne had thrilled Edinburgh audiences with her 'Me and Marlene'. On our first meeting in Dublin, she rather markedly commented that she hadn't seen many of her posters about. I replied there is no need – you are sold out! 2006 was also the year we held our first academic seminar in Trinity College in the presence of Professor Alan Sinfield, renowned author and academic. He was joined by Dr Victor Merriman (WIT) Professor Colm O'Cleirigh, Dr Eibhear Walshe (UCC), Professor Brian Singleton (TCD), Dr Katherine O Donnell (UCD), Dr Vincent Quinn (University of Sussex). We included an audience and panel discussion after a series of inspiring gay theatre related papers from our distinguished guests. This was followed by the free play reading of Harlan Didrickson's 'Four of a Kind' about two same sex couples who wish to have a child. The critical advancement of our audience led to a much better in-depth analysis of the piece, which demonstrated to me that our audience was maturing, even at the expense of the author's work!

Possibly the longest internet discourse took place this year between myself and the award winning playwright Nick Patricca. His play 'O Holy Alan Ginsberg…' was a revealing piece about healthcare for HIV priests in the US Catholic Church and property development. I loved it, but felt strongly he was pulling his punches with the happy ending. We wrote challenging tomes to each other and as Nick stated at the seminar "I knew I finally had to make my own decision when Brian signed off, and this is my final word on the matter". He did as all writers must do, make his own decisions. The play won the Best writing award that year, followed by a commendation in the Onassis awards later that year.

We did another transgender piece this year by hosting (our 2006 production award winner) Brad Louryk's reproduction of an old LP recording of Christine Jorgensen's gender reassignment. This former GI made international headlines and the discovery and performance of 'Christine Jorgensen Reveals' was masterful. Joining it in The Project was Gene David Kirk's internet grooming drama 'All Alone'. I loved this. On stage are two actors (award winners Ben Carpenter and Andrew Barron) playing their own alter egos, one is beautiful physically and the other a lout. Man A and B lure young underage girls for sex by grooming them on the internet with an interchangeable and surprising ending each night. This caused our first audience reaction. I was accused of confusing paedophilia with homosexuality, but I had not. This play was about a straight man seducing a young girl, but had a huge resonance to a community that used the internet, often dangerously, for portraying their own identity falsely online, in a fantasy where they too can not be certain of the outcome. Finally, my well-wishing audience were engaging with the issues presented and were challenging back – creating a new programming dynamic to infuse my own work.

I did select some one man shows, including a show where we made up two of the three audience at Edinburgh - the tale of a mentally ill, gay homeless man in Alex Kitay's 'Charles Manson Where Are You'? Kitay's performance was excellent – he uses space so well. His audiences were better than Edinburgh in Dublin, but deserved more. Another solo show 'Lay Down and Love me Again' was bizarre and bad. To my horror at the next Edinburgh Festival, it cited its appearance at our Festival to promote its production. You win some, you lose some!

'Crooked House' most prolific year was 2006 when they presented two dramas about young people 'The Spiderman' by Irish writer, Ursula Rani Sarma accounted for teenage fears and anxieties in an adult world. This was coupled with 'Mouth to Mouth' by Kevin Elyot and featuring fine performances about an older man's relationship with a 15 year old, sexually charged boy. I had coupled plays that year again in a 'two for one' programme and sometimes they were viewed purely in the context I had placed them. This fusion was one of our strongest ever contributions by youth drama, directed by Peter Hussey. I finished the Festival up with my late night 'Singing Out Three' ably supported by Thomas Creighton, Niall O Dwyer, Fiona Cullen and Clare Barret.

This Festival was a breakthrough and defining event. The income had jumped to about 45,000 euros and we were still solvent at the end of it, having improved the range of theatres available and our marketing. The talent was obvious from writing, to professional theatre to academic achievement, but the 'knives were out' to talk us down, as some sort of amateur gay ghetto celebrating itself. That view only pertained in a small segment of the Irish theatre and gay community. We could no longer be fairly ignored and now the objections to our presence became political. The challenge to further evolve was considerable.

One final note from 2006, I was present at our academic seminar when the distinguished panel discussed the significance of our title and mused how visible the word gay was in it. I found this exercise intriguing. Instead of being asked why the word 'gay' was at the centre of the new title, a long discussion was held ignoring the primary source. It concluded that it was not as visible as would be desired. I eventually got a word in to clarify. We had been the 'Dublin Gay Theatre Festival LTD' and because we needed to change the name to a new entity, I stuck in the word 'International' in front of the title, which already had some name recognition and registered the new entity. Simple as that, nothing academic about it!

At the same event, a young doctorate student registered his disagreement with the concept of a gay theatre festival. He is gay. I responded giving a brief summary of the points being made in this book, to a huge applause. I was never to be forgiven. It is important that people study theatre but when we vest accreditation in those who do not create anything and possibly do not know how, we take a serious risk. The response was to come and to be maintained in the pages of the 'Irish Theatre Magazine' amidst fairly good reviews of productions, especially those by artists whose eminence preceded them, the writer chillingly noted:

"The International Dublin Gay Theatre Festival raises a lot of difficult but important questions. If we grant it an experimental licence and space to grow, and accept that it can not be all things to all people, where do we locate its value now"? A chilling and breath-taking assertion, but firmly recording that permission had not been granted (and by whom) and it would need to be, in order to be granted the 'space to grow'. Threat received loud and clear (and often repeated!).

The writer added "I suggest that it is more interesting as a cultural event alongside the 'Alternative Miss Ireland'". AMI is affectionately known as 'Gay Christmas'. It packed out the Olympia for one night each St Patricks Week up to 2012 and launched the most entertaining and motley crew of alternative drag acts for an immensely important cause HIV. It is hilarious, edgy and is a stunning success as a fundraiser. The audience are fully aware they will be treated to acts from the sublime to abysmal! I love it! It is a wonderful celebration and produced by the writer's flatmate.

This is the true risk of writing in an intimate society, but the writer was consistent in promoting AMI on a par with our theatre Festival at every opportunity. He even faulted us about the position of the toilets in one of the venues we hired, which rendered a review of the play being shown impossible! Interestingly and to be fair to the Irish Theatre Magazine, if a play to be featured in our Festival was reviewed, before it reached our stage, it usually faired a lot better in its appreciation. Some local 'knives were out' and were never to be replaced in their scabbards. But we were getting coverage. We must have been doing something impactful to warrant such attention.

However the constant attack did dis-incentivise emerging Irish production companies, who would now have to consider such a potential reaction in any collaboration with us. The small negative must not counteract the hugely positive coverage and reception for our efforts at home and abroad. Happily in many other quarters, our reputation grew as we continued to work hard, inspire and push out our own boundaries. The international interest and support grew at a fast pace. Soon a programme selection for the Dublin Festival was taken as an international standard in gay theatre. Coincidentally, the Abbey theatre was flourishing with its own programme of 'gay theatre' but unacknowledged of course. Alan Stanford returned by popular demand with a new interpretation of 'The Importance of Being Earnest' from July 8th - September 9th. The all male cast produced a triumphant and edgy interpretation of the 'wetter' roles of Cecily and Gwendolyn to huge effect. Director Gerry Stembridge, himself a distinguished writer of 'The Gay Detective' one of the earliest gay plays I attended in the mainstream, was directing John Patrick Shanleys 'Doubt' in the

Abbey that October/November.

In June, in my role as Managing Director and Chairman and conscious as the financial base was now expanding, I proposed a further re-organisation of what was still an entirely voluntary endeavour. We had grown rapidly and it was essential to ensure transparent and good governance. I tried to set out a broader structure. Instead of the two directors and though there was some agreement, I wanted to ensure others had access to and monitoring of, our finances. I suggested one committee member might also take on the role of Treasurer to work with the two Directors. It met with the following response "the suggested appointment of a Treasurer is completely unnecessary and is an absolute insult to me! If we ever reach the stage where I am either unable or unwilling to continue producing proper accounts – then you may bring up the subject of treasurer again."

My call to bring in a position whereby our sections would produce purchase orders for approval by the Directors was equally opposed by our Administrative director: "this is unnecessary red tape and paper work which would be found impractical in such a small organisation". I responded. "It is precisely because this didn't happen this year that I am making proposals to change current practices and to revert to our previous agreed shared principles. I am very unhappy with this situation – we had no idea of a budget, of a cash flow plan and what commitments were entered into, up to the last minute. Some were committed without my knowledge or approval, therefore we, as directors, never had the opportunity to allot resources into priority areas. This can not continue. Secondly, I don't know what cheques I signed for this year – and this is reckless on my behalf as we both have legal responsibilities to the members and the Companies Office. We also clearly need access to a third signature in emergency – this could possibly be a company member"?

I warned my colleague "We have a deal and I have stuck to it and in this area I have very little control. This must change and will. If not, it will be a future area of deep conflict between us and my proposals are designed to avoid that at all costs. No one should want to put themselves into a situation where only one person handles monies collected publically – We need an open, planned and accountable system of financial management which we do not have at all at the moment. I will welcome a proposal from you as to how this can be attained".

I also had to address some other issues. Our deal was published on the website and adhered to fairly for all companies. I uncovered some matters of concern. Our Administrative Director had in fact, without my knowledge, agreed to cover additional expenses for one company and in doing so implied to the US producer that my role was peripheral to the business of the Festival. I also discovered that as one play was getting additional resources, another was told they could not have a bed, essential to the plot and were coping with a mattress on beer crates on The Project stage. I intervened and corrected this. Artistic concerns were emerging too.

In getting Jonny Woo to Ireland first, I failed to get Taylor Mac whom I dearly wanted. Mac is an alternative, gender inconclusive, anarchic artist and a master of language. His Producer later informed me that he had been told by my colleague that 'if he wanted to come to Dublin, he would have to make many changes to his act as it wasn't good enough'! I had no knowledge of this conversation and we lost out on a serious artist, who later played Dublin to packed houses and great acclaim. As the Festival grew not only was I struggling to find good theatre, but I was fighting for access, apparently needing 'permission' to exist, but from whom? Now I was insisting on transparency and finding that an alternative artistic policy was being pressed behind my back. I would later visit New York to be asked who I was, that they had already met the Festival's director!

As success gathered, these issues would stress the voluntary structure which I believed strongly must be collaborative and collective, if it was to succeed. As the counter-attack formed, the word was whispered that my attempts at good governance were in fact some lust for micro management. Truthfully it was anything but, I was losing access to key areas like finance, payments, budgets and accountability. No one else, other than the two directors, had such access. I never believed funds were being misused in anyway but I had seen a Taoiseach being damaged for a 'signing blank cheques culture', I did not want to perish the same way – regretfully for us all, I did not succeed in that ambition. These issues would simmer in the background as we progressed. The following year I no longer signed the 'welcome address' in the programme, but jointly did so.

However, following an innovative and quality Festival outwardly, as we headed again to Edinburgh, all was well in Irish gay theatre, where we networked, offered contracts and exhausted ourselves in promoting a cause still very much at the heart of our work! Edinburgh was forming a significant proportion of our annual programme, which meant that at least I could now appraise some of the production companies as well as the scripts being performed. That was an evolutionary luxury for a resource poor curator of the biggest programme of gay theatre staged worldwide.

scene 4

2007

From being a 'cold house' for lesbians
and gay men in 1993, Ireland is now
one of the most accepting and inclusive
countries in the world

Kieron Rose GLEN

The fourth Festival began with an influx of submissions from around the world.
The trip to Edinburgh had yielded fewer plays than we had hoped but a stuffed
mailbox spoiled us for choice. 101 plays from the USA, UK, Spain, Italy, Jersey,
Ukraine, Australia, Canada, Ghana, South Africa, Iran and Ivory Coast. We were
also delighted to be approached by Philip Mac Mahon and Ireland's multi-talented
and skilled drag artiste Panti, who wanted to include Panti's first one person
show in our Programme. 'In These Shoes' was a jewel in the programme that
year and marked what I hoped would be a more inclusive element of connection
within the Irish gay artistic community. I recommended that it play in 'Smock
Alley' which would accommodate over 90 seats, but Mac Mahon preferred the
'New Theatre'. This was the venue adjoining the Connolly book shop – it had
embraced capitalism well, as it proved to be our most expensive rental that year
for its 66 seats! I was correct in my optimism and we had to turn away audience
from this sell-out show. We now had the confidence in our audience numbers,
no longer to link plays in a loose theme and sell them as a package. We risked all
standing alone as we programmed 171 performances of gay theatre in Ireland
over a fortnight.

In my 2007 Festival launch speech, I confidently sent a clear message. "Most
importantly, we are here and are here to stay. We will drive forward this event
because we have something of value to give to the arts, to our living, diverse
democracy, to our own community, to the society in which we contribute an

enormous amount to, and to you. We do so out of a passion, a commitment and a drive that would infuse and reenergise many an arts event. We have reached out way beyond our country and our community and we have inspired an international response to which we have spared no physical effort to accommodate. That is art, this is a living culture and this is a culture that we will bring people together to define and to present gay theatre in the years to come"

"On stage you will meet old people, young people, parents, children, prostitutes, rent boys, naked men, naked women, gaydar diarists, divas, beauty queens, singers, dancers, kidnappers, musicians, telephone sex line hosts, men with small appendages, suicide victims, servants, aunts, cousins, 'bunburyists', sons, daughters, lovers, liars, feminists, wives, husbands, partners, historical people, ordinary people, cheater, clients, students, black people, people with disabilities, foreigners, married people, single people, available people, volunteers, naked singers, clothed singers, professionals, amateur enthusiasts, academics, politicians, actors, abductees, transgendered, university students, playwrights, wannabes, experts, and ordinary people and of course, your friends, neighbours and family".

"We have straight men playing gay roles, gay men playing straight roles, gay playwrights writing about straight life, straight playwrights writing about gay life, international writers writing about Ireland, Irish writers writing about other societies, young people performing, older people performing, international people performing and volunteering, artistic directors of other theatre Festivals, venues and events attending from home and abroad, people in dialogue, making new contacts and friends, creating new production companies, casting new plays, encouraging to stage their work again in other venues, friendships made, stories told, a community given a voice and an audience hugely entertained".

Sir Ian Mc Kellern kindly wrote: "I am in full support of your Festival. It would have been wonderful to join you in May but my main responsibility is playing King Lear in Stratford, so it won't be possible for me to get over. I send all my best wishes for a hugely successful event".

Renowned Irish actor/director, Adrian Dunbar was connected to us by a young actor Robert O Connor. Adrian honoured us greatly by launching the Festival that year commenting "So here is an open, inclusive theatrical event bringing together as it does, artists and their ideas from all over the world to Dublin - the only event of its kind – and contributing to the city's calendar of events in a very special way. The Festival runs on goodwill and generosity by people who give their time and energy for the love of the arts and as such is worthy of all our support. I wish Brian and John and the other committee organisers lots of late nights and fun, and hopes this year's Festival is a huge success and gets the audience it deserves".

We set up a walk through billboard exhibition of gay theatre Festival posters in the 'Front Lounge' sponsored by Absolut, who were later to play a most destructive role in our event. RTE's soap drama 'Fair City's actors presented a free play reading of Ken Gray Scolari's 'Something's Missing' directed by our good friend Alan Kinsella. I had seen this in Edinburgh was not impressed by the direction, but liked the play about a child abductor and his victim who is rescued as a teenager. On his release from jail, the perpetrator meets up with the kidnapped boy, now an adult and a gripping drama of role changing takes place.

We had a clash of personalities in 'The Project' that year. I had seen a wonderfully tight one hour long, two hander play 'Jack the Lad' written and devised by Matt Harris in Edinburgh, a spin on the tale of 'Jack and the Beanstalk'. What arrived in Dublin was now 90 minutes long. It had an additional female character. The onstage action was replaced with long speeches about what was happening off stage and the director Phil Setren certainly left his mark on this formerly fine piece of drama. His cooperation with the other company sharing the space 'Dream Man' was also misrepresented to me and I reacted wrongly and badly to Micheal Kearns and Jimmy Shaw's very significant play. I tried to remedy that as the week went on and as Setren's destructive role became more clear. 'The Project's' technical staff were also seriously under pressure as we discovered that this new 50% longer version had never been set or fully played before. However a version went up, helped by Alaister Barton's performance in the title role of Jack. 'Dream Man' became a dream team for cooperation and I included a 'no changes' clause in all future contracts!

Dublin's maverick collection of burlesque and drag talent 'The Dopplegang' did their cabaret 'Mein Camp!' for four nights, introducing us to Emma Weafer who later joined our Board. I had been persuaded to direct 'Pageant – The Musical' written by Bill Russell and Frank Kelly, on the condition that my role would be more consultant, as a team would put it together. They all didn't turn up on time, so this was an extra burden on me and choreographer Thomas Creighton. The musical where men dressed as women (as opposed to drag) compete for the title of 'Miss Glamouresse' was one of the Festival's biggest sellers ever, proudly under the DAYMS banner. It was budgeted at 18 euros a seat, but I later discovered it had been mainly sold in a package of 5 plays for 65 euros. This put a huge strain on the finances as it packed out, but struggled to break even. It was super fun and the audience got to choose the winner each night to cut throat on stage competition!

Andrew Norris quickly transformed from Eurovision groupie last year to his own one man show 'On The Sidelines' about a one child family where the mother was the 'glue'. She dies and leaves an incommunicative father and a 'coming out' son try to forge a relationship. Menno Kuijper is a modern Danny Kaye. He brought his play 'The Gaydar Diaries' to the Festival to sell-out audiences. The six actors hilariously acted out the scenarios and fantasies played out in Gaydar chat rooms – including the lightly populated 'Gaydar Antartica'!

'Kildare Youth Theatre' returned again with a sell-out production of 'The Importance of Being Earnest' in Andrews Lane Theatre. Women's theatre advanced again this year with some exciting and innovative theatre from Ireland and abroad. Possibly the strongest pairing in 2007 was 'The Dress' by Irish writer Teresa Hudson about three women of different ages and stature, who all own the same dress. A wonderful study of a beauty queen and her obsessed mother, a butch lesbian and a middle aged party animal portrayed by a company of six women actors. 'I Thee Wed' was scheduled to open on Tuesday to allow one of the actors to leave the stage in Vancouver, Canada and to get to us and onstage within 24 hours. This was a beautiful study of three relationships each 50 years apart in history between two women. Karen Lee Pickett and Lisa Hitch's wonderful play (by Pickett) was appropriate in an Ireland openly debating partnership rights. It remains one of my favourites in its simplicity and its impact. The Monday night was well utilised by Suzirya Theatre from Kiev, who travelled all the way to play 'Last Year's Snow' on one man's personal journey using the 'Ballad of Reading Gaol' as its base, with simultaneous translation into English – quite an international accomplishment.

Another controversial piece emerged from the unlikely source of 'Lorena Hickok and Eleanor Roosevelt'. The play itself traced the relationship between these two extraordinary women well. However performer Marj Conn proved a handful. Highly tempremental, she had a penchant for addressing the audience and complaining about us as the next play queued to get in. One night I discovered her in the lobby of the 'Cobalt Café' while the next play was on and I enquired as to what was wrong? She stated she had left a cassette tape inside and now 'would have to wait an hour' to retrieve it. I offered to do so and to leave it for her in the box office tomorrow. She indignantly enquired 'And how will it get to my hotel (which we were paying for!). To which I replied 'in your pocket'. She duly went to the box office and caused a major scene threatening to commit suicide, if we did not allow her to use (our sole telephone line for ticket bookings) for her to call the USA. It transpired she wished to speak to her dog! Later she railed about us on US gay websites only to inspire an avalanche of supportive commentary from other artists for our event across the USA! Marj called her production company 'Connartists' – a point on which I can not disagree! Memorable!

The long suffering partner to this play sharing the Cobalt was Chicagoan David Kodeski. David had found a series of scrap books and diaries belonging to an industrial worker Dolores, who frequently signed off each diary page with the note 'another lousy day' – which became the play's title. His story telling skill was empathetic, respectful and highly entertaining. His patience with the 'goings on' in the venue, combined with that of the owners Eddie and Dorothy Kenny, were exemplorary and appreciated!

Thomas Creighton, Paul Monaghan and Mark Power all who had worked on 'Pageant' joined me for 'Singing Out 4' where we used the songs of gay composers to tease out 'love and marriage' in this the year of partnership rights. John Matthews who had sung with 'Riverdance' delivered his own musical late night cabaret in the Cobalt café that week.

Dr Eibhear walshe (UCC), Peter Mc Dermott (DIT) and Dr Katherine O Donnell (UCD) once again directed the debate in the academic seminar on Irish gay theatre, past and present. We continued our free programme by giving a stage for the first time to the community transgender drama group who devised "Who the hell does She Think She is" - a cabaret. It was wonderful to hear transgendered voices speaking through theatre and a highlight was a young transitioning male whose life story was recounted in a self composed song 'As the Hammer Falls'. It was ground-breaking and a very moving call for action.

We got a surprise offer from the 'University of Pennsylvania Glee Club' (long before the TV series) who were coming to Ireland and heard of our event. I found a space in the 'Front Lounge' and about 40 well groomed and tailored, Ivy League young men marched in and gave us a 30 minute choral treat on Thursday, May 17th at 6.30pm. Nothing like this in presentation and performance had ever been seen by us before. The bar's manager Tony was so impressed he offered them a case of beer as payment. They burst into choral thanks singing 'Hail Tony our gracious host' which saw our bald host, blush bright red. They also honoured their former director who was of Irish descent, by having him conduct them in 'Danny Boy'. The pub erupted in appreciation.

Another crises hit when a play I saw in Edinburgh called the 'Irish Curse' began engaging in a bizarre correspondence from director Stephen Henry. Henry tried to pull out and used the unavailability of the rights, at the last moment, as the excuse. I followed this up and immediately established it was more likely a desire to continue drinking tequila in a Mexican beach resort that was the real issue at hand. It was my good fortune to encounter the writer Marty Casella and his agents. On hearing of the plight, he immediately waived the rights, and facilitated us in becoming a joint producer and the cast who were depending on this for their income, were able to perform. To top it all, Casella flew to Dublin and attended and enthused about the Festival – a real theatrical gentleman!

'The Irish Curse' is a discussion group of men in the US whose Irish heritage has resulted in small appendages! ! I was later happy to facilitate its Tasmanian premiere. It was a hectic year of people welshing on contracts in some form or other and just as we sorted one week out, those companies leave and an entire new group of 'strangers' descend upon the event to perform. It is to the great credit of all involved that these 'strangers' soon become friends and supporters, no matter how unpredictably some of the offstage drama plays out! But the stories are regularly recalled with laughter and exaggeration afterwards.

Our friends in South Africa returned with Juliet Jenkin's magnificent 'The Boy Who Fell from the Roof', dealing with teenage inter racial love and psyche. They used the term 'coloured' in their synopsis and an interesting intercultural debate ensued between us, easily resolved. RTE's 'The View' came in to review the play for the prestigious TV arts programme and it was favourably received. Once again, the women actors were to the fore in this beautifully presented piece from the Artscape new writing programme in Cape Town.

Panti as expected sold out, but what was unexpected was her revelation of her HIV status, which added an edge to this night of clever comedy and autobiographical drama. She was visibly nervous, which is so rare for such a consummate performer. 'In These Shoes' was to lead onto many more distinguished stage appearances including in the short lived 'Queer Notions

Festival' in later years.

Daniel Austin is a committed theatre practitioner and skilled writer based in Jersey. We met in Edinburgh where his naked play 'apollo/dionysus' packed out with the curious, the female and the titillated. It was much more than that. It was a colourful and powerful portrayal of the relationship of two brothers, sons of the Gods passionately and physically presented by real brothers Johnny Liron and Joshua Liron, joined by Jack Speckleton as the child and Francesca Carlton as the woman. It was a visual and powerful piece of theatre and the masculine image of Johnny made him the front cover of 'The Event Guide' in Dublin. Our friendship with Austin was to progress over the years as he completed the trilogy work.

Rick Skye is a 'Slice O'Minelli'. This hilarious and not so kind impersonation of Liza Minnelli had the audience rolling in the aisles for this live drag performance, which eventually won the best performance award. It rivalled the naked cabaret from David Zak's prestigious 'Bailiewick Repertory Theatre' of Chicago's presentation 'Bare Naked Lads Singing' where I as the adjudicator, had to sit on a step in the packed auditorium. I was later to comment at the awards ceremony, that I would have loved to give a nomination to a costume department this year, but nobody really made an effort!

Intense women's stories filled the Teachers Club with Gail Miller Correa's 'Elysium'. This was a tormented tale of heaven in the midst of hell and was an example of when you are too desperate and angst driven in your synopsis, you may in fact turn away a potential audience. It was well presented, designed and physical in its interpretation. It joined the accomplished 'Joan of Arc' by the excellent Carolyn Gage of whom I have written earlier. This was Carolyn's first ever opportunity to do 8 consecutive performances and one woman returned with her daughters in tow, to see the play again!

2007 possibly had one of the best theatre shorts programme. I had encouraged our volunteers to engage with the Festival as writers and this was well reflected in some debuts of promise, in this 'seeds' programme. 8 short plays from Australia, Ireland and USA packed and entertained the audience. Sean Mc Intyre's 'The Pickup' revealed the voice of a guitar to its owner. Vickey Curtis's writing debut 'A Magina Vonologue' was strongly played by Iris Meehan aka 'Funtime Gustavo'. My own debut one man show, 'The Gentleman Caller' telling the story of a deceased bachelor church sacristan was delivered skilfully by Sean Mac Nally. 'The Goldie Boy' by Diane Searls was an Irish story of young suicide. Carolyn Gage fascinated with 'Calamity Jane Sends a Message to her Daughter', directly after playing the demanding 'Joan of Arc' each night. The talented Aiden Harney's comedy pulled no punches with the hilarious 'Unsuccessful Suicide of Trish O Malley' brilliantly played by David Gilna and Niamh Shaw. Shawn Sturnick a talented Irish resident from the USA contributed two plays. 'Solomon, A Life' and to the surprise of many including himself, the best writing award winning 'A Closet Flung Wide Ope' a poetic delivery, near perfection in its construction. So overwhelmed was he at the awards night that this prolific writer was stuck for words. As ever, Marty Cassella voiced his congratulations on the award. Edinburgh beckoned and each year the queue to come to Dublin grew and grew as producers and promoters invited us to attend their performances. British Equity and the Festival were hugely supportive and many good people began to recommend our event or good plays to me to attend. The Festival as a theatre event was firmly established and its identity was clear, relevant and artistically based.

2008

I'm not the first gay man to say I miss spirituality

Terrence Mc Nally to GCN

The next Festival relied on a significant data base of artists and audience to continue to evolve. We listened to and welcomed feedback. The impression was because I chose the play (often on the basis of a paper submission) meant I saw the presented product as meritorious, was not based on fact. Therefore it was important for me to reward excellence through the award system and also to heed reaction and encourage discussion through our audience response forms.

We had begun to engage in serious analysis in order to concentrate on developing opportunities for new voices to be heard. We did not play safe with our friends and ask them to perform again and again. Indeed some of our favourite players were not accepted, if their submission the following year was not suitable – but of course the door always remained open.

The Festival invites its audience to assist in the programming of the event by completing an audience response form at each production. A Total of 1,787 audience response forms were received (double the amount completed in 2005) showing an 86.2% excellence rating for the 2006 Festival productions. Marks are awarded for each production on a grid of 5 for excellent, 4 for very good, 3 for good, 2 for average and 1 for not of interest to me. This grew again in 2007 and consistently generated an excellence rating of over 85%, first recorded in 2004. There were however interesting notes written on some of the forms that indicated areas of improvement and indeed the positivity in which this event was being appreciated. I read them all.

There are a few things to note about this type of audience survey:

- Many Irish plays will know some of their audience so this might positively influence their rating.

- Some people who support the Festival may refrain from making a negative comment.

- A controversial play very well staged may be appraised on its content and the audience member's emotional reaction to the subject matter, rather than on an appraisal of the production values, writing and acting etc.

- The more forms that were returned, the more likely it is that the average mark would fall.

Percentage totals are calculated at the 5/5 rate, so all papers are counted and then multiplied by 5. The total number of marks is then given as a percentage of the maximum number of marks available, if everyone had marked it at 5/5. It is always interesting to count a pile of 5/5s and 4/5 and to get a single 1/5 – it can all depend on the mood you are in on the night!

There were some negative comments about the venues – particularly the ones without a stage, when full houses meant people at the back had poor visibility. Also heat inside the venues featured especially during the 'heat wave' that challenged our box office mid Festival. We had four sunny days and one play had 57 prepaid seats and only 17 turned up, as the lure of the rare sunny evening triumphed over theatre! The happy sun-kissed people did not look for any refund! The busy line in the box office irked a few people but delighted us, as the box office set-up was very costly to the Festival and not altogether efficient. We read and recorded all the comments and take them on board, where possible.

We asked our audience to let us know about their nationality. This helps with tourism funding. It is also an important indicator of what an event like this can mean to people who come to visit, or are living, in Ireland. Does this Festival give people a sense of inclusion and participation? We had many nationalities in our volunteer corps and for example our Italian volunteers were a brilliant asset in assisting our Italian speaking company – a great additional service from the Festival to our participants.

People of all ages, beliefs and sexual orientations attended the Festival. We had in total 64 different declared nationalities who attended the Festival. We did not include the ones who described themselves as members of the human race or the global community!

The Festival made a significant breakthrough this year. We allowed all plays to 'stand alone' there were no double bills. We also staged the most 'drama' led programme ever. It is very difficult to sell a new play. It is very difficult to sell an unknown cast (as in not local) to do that 35 times, was quite an achievement. In 2007 the box office rose by a staggering 150% on our successful year in 2006. This year we were drama led and we were also hit by two mini heat waves, but the 'Celtic Tiger' was roaring and disposable income was high.

The introduction of online booking buffered us very much against the impact of the good weather. On the hottest night, some prepaid tickets were not collected, and the number of 'walk-ups' to the doors fell significantly – the moment the weather changed these bounced back. We are still challenged by the audience tendency to 'wait and see' how the Festival is going, before booking and this means that people miss out on many great plays from week one. The programme is deliberately and carefully balanced to ensure there is not a difference in standard in either week.

Our box office growth demonstrated that approval in 'Celtic Tiger' Ireland. Our analysis, led by volunteer Gareth Hurley, indicated that audience members were booking on average 5 plays out of the programme. It still did not rid us of the problem that each year about three plays (often solo shows) did not sell well. There was an unevenness in the spread of the box office across the programme, meaning we worked extremely hard to support the weaker selling shows. To add to this analysis, there was no indication that the weaker selling shows were not good. In fact they frequently scored very highly with their small audience. Success one year did not guarantee another success. Ricardo Melendez's stunning 'Nijinsky' sold 'The Project' out to the roof to award winning acclaim. His follow up play a wonderful renaissance cross gender drama 'Queen Sofia' defied every known marketing strategy available to us and proved almost impossible, to sell despite its opulence and excellence.

The highlight of Festival 2008 was this message from President Mary Mc Aleese. "It gives me great pleasure to send warmest good wishes to the International Dublin Gay Theatre Festival 2008. The Festival, since its establishment in 2004, has served to build important bridges of cultural understanding across Irish society, and to offer a fuller picture of cultural life on our island. I congratulate all involved, and send my best wishes for a successful programme". The US participants in particular were hugely impressed by this great honour, noting it would not have been the action of George W Bush! It was a high note on which to start our fifth anniversary year.

We had also brought the lack of State funding to the attention of the Department of Arts and Culture. They too endorsed our efforts by giving us a once off grant to promote the anniversary year. The Minister for Communications Eamon Ryan TD enthusiastically launched the programme. He arrived early at the event and engaged with my thesis of our distinct cultural identity. The Green Party, of which he was a member, was promoting civil partnership in Government and his endorsement of our distinct cultural identity at the launch, was most progressive.

Our jewel in the crown that year was the inclusion of 5 times Tony Award winner Terrence Mc Nally's 'Corpus Christi'. At the last minute Mc Nally himself could not come over but agreed to become our third Patron. His husband Tom Kirdahy did attend and was a most positive presence on our event leading to a long personal friendship. Terrence wrote " I am deeply honoured that the International Dublin Gay Theatre Festival is welcoming my play CORPUS CHISTI to the festivities. I hope we stir some hearts (and minds) with it. I am proud that queer theatre has grown so incredibly over the past decades. We are telling our stories and the world is listening. I wish you a glorious Festival and am eagerly awaiting to attend next year's celebration" – which he did!

There was no doubt but that tensions behind the scenes were rising. It is difficult to run a volunteer led event, especially when it is growing at such a rapid rate and receiving positive attention. The zeal to control, in an exclusionary manner, became stronger in our Administrative area to the point that Committee members began to sit back when enquiries were shouted down. It proved impossible for the group to meet in the final few weeks, despite the very good output of the Administrative Director - his was now a detached fiefdom. I felt in order to keep some sort of solidarity that I should not push the matter, but the absence or withholding of important transparency information was of great concern. The politicisation of positioning was also divisive and a clash seemed inevitable. My own encouragement of individual members was yielding results, but my attempts to promote them to 'director' level completely dismissed. Not only was it difficult to motivate them, but my own motivation was waning in the face of constant acrimony. I began to devise a succession plan which would ensure, as I hoped, that the Festival would survive all existing directors, in the short term.

The 'headline' play of the fifth Festival is well covered in the chapter on religion. 'Corpus Christi' was by no means the only play in this extensive and ambitious programme of 2008. We were affluent in the 'Celtic Tiger' years and commercial venues knew that if we attracted a crowd, their bar tills filled, so there was good cooperation all round. We had free events including a free green vodka cocktail the 'drama queen' launch party. Our walk through billboard of gay theatre posters was held in The Front Lounge for three weeks. We had a free play reading 'Dancing With the Minotaur' by Max Hafler and later 'The Crown Jewels' by Shawn Sturnick and Christiaan Feehan. The Gaiety School of Acting reading Mark Ward's play 'A Stint in Your Spotlight' in The George.

Our seminar featured Dr Eibhear Walshe (UCC), Nick White (Diversity Officer Yvonne Arnaud Theatre) Dr Katherine O Donnell (UCD) and the beginning of a relationship and understanding of lesbian poet, activist and playwright Eva Gore Booth, thanks to her biographer Dr Sonja Tiernan. Jazz duo of renown 'Zrazy' linked their free Sunday jazz sessions in 'The George' with us, as I encouraged them to tell the story of their music and group, as part of the Festival.

Companies who went all the way through the application process, sent all their details, agreed the terms, asked us about flights and accommodations, continued to let us down. We had secured a great production of 'I Am My Own Wife' from our trip to Edinburgh. We were delighted in its standard and that it had packed out a short run in the Dublin Theatre Festival's programme some years previously, to great acclaim. I was always looking to outreach and mainstream and this was a good opportunity. We stuck our financial neck out and hired the main stage in The Project – 200+ seats. After months of cooperation with the UK producer, I was told at the last moment, there was in fact another 'producer' an American company whom we had never heard of previously. The British producer now disappeared!

Always beware of anyone who calls themselves the Executive Producer, a long time into the arrangements – it means trouble. I had the misfortune to call the most rude woman I have ever dealt with in Theatre and suddenly there was no show coming. Clearly she claimed she had never been consulted by the British partner and though he had signed the contract, she had not and that was that. We were caught in their dispute and were not as lucky to meet a Marty Cassella again! Yes, we could sue, but we hadn't the resources to go international. Many theatre companies are fully aware of that, when they mess us around!

It was to be the benefit of 'Lightning Strikes' by Matt Ian Kelly, directed by the celebrated Patrick Wilde. This play, set in the dreams of two gay men in different eras, was a most creditable 'replacement', with a good performance by young David Ames, but could not reel in the mainstream as we had hoped. The other beneficiary was Australia's 'The Girly Side of Butch' starring Vonnie Brit Watkins, Rochelle La More and Fifi La Douche. These girls knew how to build an audience for their somewhat traditional drag act. They worked the Festival clubs and filled each night, overnight. Vonnie's transgendered life story was particularly memorable amongst all the 'Priscilla-esque' glitz and glam.

Even though we went to 'The Project' believing we had a shared 'cutting edge' audience, there was no evidence that their audience did engage with us in any significant way. One evening I asked the box office how many tickets they had sold for our show in 'The Cube' and she replied 'two''. Just as well as we had sold the other 68 then! Ricardo Melendez's passionate portrayal of 'Nijinsky's Last Dance' sold out at 'The Project', where even I had to access the lighting box and call the cues in order to see it and his best Actor winning performance.

I had placed Jeff Key's one man autobiographical show "The Eyes of Babylon" in 'The Project' too. I met Jeff on night two of his week's run, and he said "75 seats tonight". I said "great." He replied "no there are 75 left"! I headed to the nearest hostelry and 'papered' the show. They loved it! Jeff was a US marine who served in Iraq. So driven was he about what he witnessed there, that he used the 'coming out' clause to be discharged and then to oppose the war. We were at the height of the rendition flights at Shannon airport and we still could not get this play across to 'The Project's or Irish audiences! We eventually got Jeff on the prime time Pat Kenny radio show and finally attracted the highest quality Irish theatre audience we ever got, and he get a huge response. The play was hugely relevant to Irish society, so why the hard sell? Is it that people exclude themselves, not negatively, when they see the 'Gay' theatre emblem on our work? 'That's obviously not for me then' – and that is the challenge to get more mainstream theatre not to self-exclude themselves from our inter-cultural dialogue. We need to bring people to the stage where they recognise, we don't just talk about sexuality, but our citizenship is as valid in any other areas of life aswell.

I loved attracting theatre by experienced actors of all ages. The commercial gay scene is very ageist and it is important to let modern gay young people realise their cultural history and to meet the people whose early emerging voices set the stage for so much to follow. Bob Kingdom's study of 'Truman Capote" much complicated by lack of permission from the writer's estate, was one of those classic pieces of theatre, originally directed for Bob, by Sir Anthony Hopkins!

It was time to challenge the reliably positive consistency of the audience response. 'Shackled' was a controversial new play. It was written and directed by Fergus Ford and starred Lee Hunter and James Ashton, who wake up shackled and naked in bed together. A gripping drama enfolded about their previously unknown inter-relationship with a brutal outcome. The exploitation of homophobia in a straight man, heightened the tensions in the plot. Which was worse, calling for help from his macho father or trying to explain why he was in bed naked with another young man? A classic example of how homophobia can boomerang back on its perpetrators. At last my audience was talking and analysing. It provoked perceptive debate with responses on the forms from 5 to 1 being recorded at the same performance! Here we saw how the content influenced the reaction. Here we began to create the space for more critical comment, to help us create more innovative future programming.

'Big Sister' was originally a youth project developed with adults in partnership with London's Queen Mary Theatre Company. It was a female version of 'Big Brother' with eight young women on stage. Co-writer/director/producer Charlotte Graper showed all the signs of making a significant contribution to theatre, but her mainly straight cast did not mix well at the Festival Club and tended to distance themselves from engaging in the network that builds an audience at our event. Women writers are rare. All female companies with decent roles are equally rare. This approach of disengagement was also the case with other and mainly London companies. They tended to be on overdrive with each other and not take advantage of us placing them in contact with the wider audience in our Festival club each night. London companies had an internal competitiveness that preoccupied their visit to Dublin and cost them audience. Those plays that did engage with our audience were rewarded with a busy box office. Those that had good imagery on their posters and in their artwork in the programmes, also showed a significant advantage in advance booking. This advice was always given, but not always heeded, and then companies were on the back foot from the start, in a highly competitive niche market!

I had assisted the Gay Community Centre 'Outhouse' in Capel Street, with the conversion of their derelict Georgian basement into a performance space, thanks to the vision of successive Chairpersons, George Rowbotham and Malcolm Hickson. It was a tight venue, well equipped thanks to Tony Murphy, but as with all community centres, there was often a 'one hour' weekly booking commitment which could not facilitate a week's run. It was also very expensive – surpassing 'The Project' on rental fees. However, it had the most marvellous welcome, it was important we were there and staff and volunteers like Martha White and Tiffany Brosnan Fitzgerald did do their utmost to support us. "Yesterday, when I was Young" was an electric one woman show on the life of Josie Pickering who went from back street housewife to lesbian dominatrix. Sexily played by bodice clad Erin Shanagher, this play stretched Outhouses 75 seat capacity each night, as it deservedly packed out.

I have a strong commitment to remembering the Holocaust. In 2012, I was honoured to read the testimonial on behalf of gay victims of this atrocity at the National Holocaust Memorial Ceremony in the Mansion House. I was delighted to get a submission from Italy called 'The Night Faeries" the story of some of the forgotten 250,000 gay victims of the Holocaust. The story centred about a young Belgian, Dirk and his life in Sachsenhausen Concentration Camp and the demand of his last will "Do Not Forget". The play was written by Claudio Massimo Paterno who was joined onstage by Marcello Manuali and Alan Peppoloni. Helen Regan, our beloved volunteer met me after a performance clutching her chest saying " I still can't breathe after that". The passion was added to by their more precise phonetic delivery of the English language, at the insistence of myself, by the talented and deeply committed cast. It was a huge task and an amazing theatrical achievement, that is one of my all time programming highlights.

Comedy actor Menno Kuijper (Gaydar Diaries) returned with "BUTCH – a Queen's Struggle to become a King" – a personal comedy of a skinny gay guy trying to muscle-up. His 'Danny Kaye' like quality on stage lifted an incomplete piece of comedy theatre in an engaging manner.

It was the year of civil partnership and 'Knotty Together' an opera by Njo Kong Kie and Anna Chatterton from Canada, fitted the bill nicely. It was a financial risk as gay opera is a niche within a niche, but our audience was well up for high art. Classical singers, Keith Klassen and Paul White gave us a musical 'Brokeback Mountain' relationship, but I had the most insightful discussions with them about masculinity after their performances. They openly engaged with playing to a gay audience, with a gay subject matter, when they were both straight. Their body confidence grew too, as towels once impaled into the waistline, began to fall as they broadened their own continuum of being faithful to the plot, being more open to the diversity of the audience and more confident in themselves. It was a challenge for straight men to go naked to a predominantly gay audience, but one which our in depth discussions on masculinity brought about a change in the performance, and restored it to the way in which the Opera had be staged in front of audience whose sexual orientation was not as clearly pre-determined. As a former student of the College of Music, I was delighted to have an opera of such standard in the programme and for it to book well.

Our final offering from Kildare Youth theatre – a stalwart of the Festival was to be 'Burying Your Brother in the Pavement' by Jack Thorne, directed again by Peter Hussey. A terrific youth drama with a strong cast, but unfairly deserted by its support base. I fear the repeated participation in the Festival later put a strain on the programming of this great company, which is regrettable. Their adult company 'Crooked House' also presented 'Down Dangerous Passes Road' a tale of three very different brothers on the eve of a marriage, who drive out to the fishing spot where their father drowned. It was a gripping drama written by Michel Marc Bouchard, directed by Michelle Panella, and acted by Keith Burke, Stephen Wilson and Nick Devlin, skilfully staged in Liberty Hall with huge impact.

Musical Director David Wray returned with West End star Paul Monaghan and Eoin Cannon for a delicious programme of gay musical theatre which ran two nights only, to standing ovation. 'Memoirs of a Gayshow' was a delight and heralded the first ever offer by me to run again the following year. The imagery of the poster must rank amongst the best ever in capturing the show and enthralling the audience with wonderful arrangements, magnificently sung. Many of these images are still visible in our archive on www.gaytheatre.ie.

New Irish writer Alison Martin did a site specific murder mystery "Bed Death" in the Georgian drawingroom of the 'Cobalt Café' which recorded full houses. I had been a pioneer of murder mysteries in the Park Hotel, Kenmare and renowned playwright Hugh Leonard attended one and promptly wrote two more for me to stage. He enjoyed them so much, he gave us a full page in his column in the Sunday Independent on a New Year's Eve, some years previously.

'Imaginary Forces' UK, did 'The Iron Eyelashes' in 'The Cobalt'. This was the story of Pieter who lives in East Berlin in 1961 but works as a young drag artist in the West. The wall goes up and he makes a life changing choice to stay in the West and not return home. Pieter was well portrayed by Simon Stephens with good direction by Sarah Niven of the delightful and 'hands on' Imogen Brodie's, sensitive script.

Every now and again there is a hidden gem in a programme. Daniel Talbot's "Slipping" defines this tag. It almost ran unnoticed in the very full programme and it was excellent theatre. Adam Webster was fortunate in his cast of Rose Buckner, Daniel Caffrey, Adrian Conzalez, and Nate Santana as the lead Eli. This group slipped into Dublin, but should have made much more noise. Eli's father dies and his abusive lover abandons him, so he sets out for a new life in Iowa. Talbot's writing is inspiring and I regret that this play may win the title of the 'one that got away' – it deserved to top the bill! Unsurprisingly this play has gone on to get significant attention in the USA, as has Talbot was a writer. He was to make it to Dublin, which might have helped the publicity, but his appendix burst! The fact that it followed 'Corpus Christi' may have also militated against it, as that play lured audiences away for unprogrammed after-show discussions, as Talbot's play was running, but the play, production and performance was true quality.

I have previously written about Carolyn Gage's 'The Countess and the Lesbians'. The interconnection between three women rehearsing a play about our heroes explores the story of the life of Eva Gore Booth and her partner Esther Roper and Eva's revolutionary sister Countess Markievicz and that of the three actors. The cast delivered substantial roles in style with Jill Mongey's award winning (Nan), Lynn Rafferty's (Kathleen, a towering Countess) and the empathetic Grace by Gina Costigan, who was the talented flame behind this world premiere production. It was so exciting to see this international collaboration of women's theatre, facilitated by the Festival and directed by Sheila O Reilly – another ambition delivered. However it too was not without controversy. The Sunday Independent's Emer O Kelly headlined it "Self indulgent turged rubbish beggars belief" while the Metro gave it five stars, with the Irish Times' Sara Keating assures "There is enough depth in the historical material and the performances of Gina Costigan as 'Eva' and Jill Mongey as 'Esther' to keep the audience engaged for 50 minutes. The erasure of their role – the erasure of feminist history entirely from the burgeoning nation's narrative – was surely one of 1916's greatest failures". Dublin City Council's Arts Committee later supported another performance of this production in the city. At last we were filling column inches and being talked about in theatre circles!

2008 was a Festival known for its quality drama. Many of the 35 productions (from 42 events) got four and five star reviews in the national media. 'Best Man' by Greg Owen and Nick Mc Garrigle was a wonderful story of male friendship. Set in Northern Ireland it evolved from childhood best friends to shared, then divergent sexuality, to an invitation to an engagement party where memories were relived, but the best man would win! It was a beautiful and powerful two-hander that emerged in the ruthless competition of works like 'Slipping' and 'The Countess and the Lesbians' to win the Best Writing award that year. The competition was so close that I had made all my final decisions by the Saturday evening. Volunteers had warned me that they had noticed an 'improvement' in performance when casts knew I was present with my adjudicator's hat on. To be sure of my decision, I crept in as the lights went down, to watch 'Best Man' again, in the 'New Theatre' at 8.00pm and slept soundly on my earlier writing decision that night!

American Mormon, father and male escort Steven Fales is a strong presence in real life and on stage. He recounts his autobiographical tale truthfully, skilfully and is a clever artist. 'Confessions of A Mormon Boy' made a worthy impact on this rich programme of theatre. Bringing this other perspective of religion into a 'Corpus Christi' dominated programme was very important. Fales' strong piece more than held its own in relevance and impact. It is also a fine insight as to the commonality of how bigotry constructs its negativity towards gay family members. The diversity office of Dublin City Council assisted us in our first story of growing up black and gay with Les Kurkendall's funny 'Christmas in Bakersfield! Pioneers of gay theatre in NYC, the respected partnership of David Pumo and Moe Bertram introduced us to Pumo's creations of six gay characters from the NYC scene, expertly acted by Bertram in six seperate 'Love Scenes' that blend into a valid theatrical storytelling unit.

We initiated an ambassadorship to recognise the international support we were getting, the good steers, insights on production companies and the promotion abroad from some committed theatre friends. None can hold a candle to New Yorker, Kathleen Warnock. Warnock is associated with companies like, 'Emerging Artists', 'The Other Side of Silence', Drunken Careering Writers, in NYC, but most importantly she is that rare thing – an enabler of theatre.

Kathleen prefers her own title of 'Ambassador of Love' – love of the theatre and what we aim to achieve. She certainly has delivered for us in abundance and is a treasured colleague. I was delighted to programme her own play – a light comedy 'Some Are People' that year, directed by another Festival favourite the distinguished Mark Finley.

Once again the popular 'Theatre Shorts' programme brought out more new writing talent and full houses. 'Blind Mating' by Vicky Curtis was a hilarious comedy about partnership. Matt Casarino's 'Emily Breathes' is a confessional confrontation between a young man and a priest, about the boy's dead mother Emily, brilliantly acted by Hunter Gilmore and Greg Homison. 'Tumbling Down' was my own 1980s homage to the camp men who survived in dark days in working class Dublin and Linda Martin records, starring James Barrie, Mark Yeates and Rian Corrigan. Irish Actress, Suzanne Lakes penned 'Mammy's Boy' which was to grow into a full length comedy later. Here Elijah Egan's (Tim) gets a job as a waiter to escape his Mother (Lakes) and her friend Alice (Ciara Mc Guinness), but they have other and hilarious ideas. Kevin Brofsky's 'Tom Cruise – Get Off the Couch' with James Mc Dougall, Kaolin Bass and the (human) dog 'Cruise', Jason O'Donnell, was EAT's comic offering with Shawn Sturnick's unpredictable turn on matters in 'Connubial Celts' a tale of King Brian Boru and a same sex marriage, finishing off the full and diverse programme where Irish emerging playwrights more than held their own against international competition.

The South African Artscape contribution was important to the Festival and this year's offering was another step forward with Peter Jacon's rich tapestry of characters in 'Dalliances'. This time a change of director to Matthew Wilde brought a young, fresh and sensual imagery to the stage, while maintaining their earned prowess in acting. Four interpersonal charged relationships emerged onstage through the talents of Claytono Boyd, Stephen Jubber, Keenan Arrison and the delicious Daleen van Der Walt s 'Janet'. The black and lemon imagery was the source of the only ever complaint we had from the 'Teachers Club' who were not happy with the stage drenched with lemon juice each night – apologies once again!

Mark Power, Thomas Creighton and David Wray joined me again in 'Singing Out Five' – a look at chorus boys, gay codes, divas and new writing for musical theatre in the Cobalt Café late at night. The Gala Awards night was a great vehicle for our handsome young host Darren Kennedy, who later carved out a career in TV to no one's surprise. He was joined on stage by emerging comedian Gearoid Farrelly who later became an Edinburgh hit, and award winning stage and screen actor and writer Mark O Halloran. Undoubtedly, 'Corpus Christi' won the Intercultural dialogue Award for 2008. The Festival began with one headline play and ended up delivering many more, in a rich programme of drama, which confirmed our status as first and foremost, a new theatre driven festival of significant standard.

Our committee and volunteer corps were stretched to their limits and it is hard to believe how such a strong and diverse programme of theatre was delivered that year. Naoise O Reilly led the technical delivery with a valiant, patient and creative crew, joined in all other areas with the support of Gareth Hurley, Eddie Devoy, Chris Nugent, Eoin Wilson, Declan Coogan, David Lee, Thomas Creighton, Connell Kennedy, Gary Tiernan and Mark Banchansky and almost 60 people to run our front of house and support services – all free to theatre.

A Gay Jesus, a Gay Mormon and a Gay Marine soaked up a lot of the publicity, but the engagement by mainstream media was curious, respectful and disseminating. Sue Conley interviewed me for the Evening Herald:

"When asked if he thought the Big Smoke needed yet another festival, Brian Merriman did not hesitate for a millisecond: "I think theatre needed it. I think theatre at the moment is not hugely dynamic. It's desperately dependent on grant aid, and it relies on the permission of bureaucrats. Well grant aid doesn't hurt, as Merriman is quick to acknowledge, but it does tend to put a damper on things. "you have to ask, where are the channels for spontaneous creativity that bring about change?"

Conley adds "It seems impossible that the Festival can be free of an agenda. Merriman replies in a heartbeat "There is a political agenda and I make no apology for it! I've always believed art is politics, and art is a tremendous way to change people's hearts and minds in a non-threatening way. And people don't have to make a decision – it's not vote for me or against me. We can create a courteous environment and people can take from the message, without being barracked or persuaded that is the way they should think". "The Irish used theatre to define themselves when they were oppressed and to be honest with you, I'm playing them at their own game. I'm using gay theatre to define ourselves, because we too, have been oppressed".

The first five years marked up a significant evolution of a concept nurtured and grown in Dublin. The quality of that programme was so diverse and of such an innovative standard that it would prove difficult to follow in later years. But the Festival's reputation was growing abroad and this would yield a harvest of theatre to allow us to reach out towards a decade of gay theatre in Dublin.

chapter 7

The First Five Years

The Radiant Youth was, to be sure, the very opposite of Wilde's bad hero; but such was the author's love of paradox that this antithesis of character was just the thing to fascinate his poet's mind, from which the following pages grew

Basil Hallward introduction to 'The Picture of Dorian Gray'.

I am very grateful to David Cregan of the University of Villenova who asked me to contribute to a series of essay of gay culture in Ireland some years ago. The book was not published, but his excellent record keeping meant that I could access this mid-term review of our work done to date then. I also gratefully acknowledge David's editing. I often write as I speak and tussled with him over the web, as he generously imposed some form of discipline on my ramblings! Here is the end product, now published for the first time, without update hence there is bound to be some repetition and I beg my reader's indulgence in order to preserve the integrity of the original article:

The idea of the International Dublin Gay Theatre Festival had been germinating throughout my Master's in Equality Studies Thesis (UCD) process, as a new direction for a theatrical career that had both elements, theatre and equality at its core. When an unexpected gap came in my theatre schedule, I established the Dublin Gay Theatre Festival in January 2004.

My first calls were to promoter John Pickering and performer Eddie Devoy to come on board and they did. Later we formed a 'not for profit' company limited by guarantee and built a highly talented and committed volunteer base. I am now the Artistic and Managing Director of the International Dublin Gay Theatre Festival Ltd. Within 3 months of those first phonecalls in 2004, we staged 11 productions in May of that year (including one from the UK) and extended the Festival to 16 companies the following year (including 2 from the UK). In 2006 we decided to expand substantially and go fully international and 66% of our programme came from abroad and we have never looked back.

The political, artistic and social importance of what we want to achieve through theatre in Ireland and abroad, is deliberately planned. That is using the true cultural dynamic of theatre as an essential dynamic for change in society. The recognition of gay theatre as an art form motivates us, in conjunction with our premiere desire, to identify, develop and encourage gay art and artistry through theatre as an art from in Ireland and abroad.

We launched the third festival in the Mansion House in 2006 - the home of the Lord Mayor of Dublin. We were next door to the meeting place of the first Dail (Irish Parliament) in the month of the celebration of the 90th anniversary of the 1916 Rising – a revolutionary event which had at its core, equality for all citizens. Padraig Pearse, one of the Proclamation's signatories, as historians' debate, was probably gay, as was the martyred Sir Roger Casement. As a new Republic we still had kept some of the cherished traditions of the regime we then sought to overthrow, close to our newly liberated hearts. Ours was a degree of republicanism. The progression of a full Republic for all citizens has never exorcised those who have done many diverse things to protest their true Republican spirit and conviction. Convenient or selective republicanism is at best, a more generous description of what we have been put through as a nation, for the past ninety years.

One of the reasons we have an International Dublin Gay Theatre Festival is to unwrap the seclusion and exclusion of gay life, which has remained obscured from public view for centuries in Ireland. Ireland has long been constructed as a society that conceals it difference or its 'sins'. One such ongoing exclusion accommodates the notion, that prohibiting loving couples from formalising their natural relationships, in some way enriches a democratic society or underpins the moral or religious values that sustains heterosexuality and protects the family. If marriage relies on the behaviour of others for its validation or sustainability, then it truly is in a very rocky place. Straight people's marriages are constantly portrayed through that lense and they don't object to that. This narrow and flawed perspective ensures that differences are created and maintained in order to diminish the value of specific lifestyles and cultures.

Irish theatre challenged this effectively in the past, when being Irish was accorded a lesser status of citizenship by our then Imperial masters. Gay theatre hopefully can contribute something similar in the liberation of gay people today.

As always the pressure on gay people to defend themselves in public, in order to bring about a broader perspective of human rights, is seemingly never ending. It is timely that we continue to challenge this demeaning and false negative stereotype. We must not allow the negative stereotypes, developed at a time when it was essential to justify a difference in treatment, by creating a difference in status, to continue to prevail in our society.

The International Dublin Gay Theatre Festival presents our life and culture for what it is, to the widest possible audience, in the most accessible way, in a variety of programmes accessible to many. Let us not do what has been done before – there is space for truth in the arts – so we must strive for a complete perspective on gay life that shows the whole gamut of gay life, not as dictated by the negative stereotypes created by others, but by the emotional and intellectual richness of this community and those who know and respect us. It may not always be high art, but it is important art for a diversity blind society and an exclusionary arts regime.

When citizens are perceived as being different, then society can utilise this difference to discriminate. When such difference is deliberately constructed, what chances have the discriminated? One must take on those who insist on the negative stereotype and exploit that fear of difference to the advantage of the truth. One must present the 'feared' culture with confidence, professionalism and skill. Theatre enriches a civilized society. It is a forum where life can be portrayed and understood, from its many diverse perspectives. It is a forum that informs and creates a space which allows the audience to make up its own mind.

Society too can enable validation by offering the supports granted to the mainstream, to those who operate, to the same standards, outside, what is perceived to be, the mainstream. The role of national arts and cultural funding bodies is crucial if citizenship, diversity, freedom to express, communicate and human rights are to be embedded in the core of a society – especially one which seeks to follow the values and human rights so eloquently and fairly set out in the Proclamation - that to cherish and treat all its citizens equally. The only principle should be the merit principle – the bedrock of equal opportunity.

The International Dublin Gay Theatre Festival has looked to national arts and cultural funding bodies to assist us in fulfilling our art, our citizenship and our valid cultural expression to little avail. In 2006 in the anniversary month of 1916, I was very pleased however to acknowledge the only partnership we got from the arts and cultural institutions operating in Ireland that year and that was the generous support received from... the British Council. This is not surprising, as it was the British Council who helped establish the international reputation of the Edwards and Mac Liammoir Productions by funding its European tours before World War Two. The Festival honours their contribution today by awarding the best male performance and best aspect of a production in their distinguished names.

Our task in this artistic visibility endeavour is not only to honour Wilde, Hilton Edwards, Michael Mac Liammoir, Eva Gore Booth, Patrick Murray, Aiden Rogers and others, but to create a channel where new artistic endeavour can thrive, inspire and enlighten. We look at works by gay authors, or that have a gay character, theme or relevance. We examine issues of gender identity, masculinity and feminism to name a few.

The Festival is inclusive, accessible and great value. Men, women, regardless of their sexual orientation are taking part. Young people do. Older people do. The audience is local, national and international. 64 different nationalities attended Festival 2008. Difference enriches us. With this Festival we seek to build bridges between Irish and international theatre practitioners and locally between gay people and mainstream audiences. We place ourselves firmly in the context of artistic value. Our founding 'catchcry' has been 'don't attend because it is gay theatre - attend because it is good theatre'.

This Festival is for anyone who wants to see, or be part of a modern, pluralist and accessible event. We endeavour not only add to the already rich cultural arts landscape in Ireland, but hopefully we will entertain and help more people realise that difference enriches and fulfils the arts and a democratic society. A truly functioning arts sector in any democracy, is one where all citizens can realise their human right and responsibility to participate openly, freely and generously. Our presence helps give a meaning to that noble concept too often consigned to print but rarely realised in national artistic planning.

The context for the fifth Festival was very clear - the President of Ireland very kindly sent us a message of support. President McAleese said 'The Festival since its establishment in 2004 has served to build important bridges of cultural understanding across Irish society and to offer a fuller picture of cultural life on our island'. We are honoured, grateful and inspired for her insight and kindness.

The contribution this event made to the European Year of Intercultural Dialogue in 2008 is also unique. The Festival will continue to facilitate and to inform the dialogue by gay people within Irish society. It will not censor or inhibit the freedom of expression, which when respectfully presented in good theatre, is so necessary to build understanding, and to open the closed minds, who so often condemn without ever listening, hearing or knowing what is being said.

The European Year of Intercultural Dialogue was a valid context for the Fifth International Dublin Gay Theatre Festival – one that embraces the challenge, along with many others, to dialogue with wider society and to explain who we are. It was appropriate that The European Year of Intercultural Dialogue is not narrowly defined or confined to visible diversity such as race or ethnic origin. It was an opportunity to give space to many diverse aspects of the cultures that co-exist on this Island. That is what this Festival does well. In Dublin City Council we met a willing partner.

We engage mainstream Ireland in a standards' driven arts dialogue which presents our culture and explores and discusses its characteristics, value and relevance through theatre as an art form. We have made a significant breakthrough in defining ourselves in 2008. Those who fault the standards of the Festival are usually those who have cut off or contributed to the denial of the Festival's access to the resources necessary, to access and secure the very best of international gay theatre for inclusion in this unique event. The fact that they are gay and straight doesn't gall half as much as they fact that they claim to be arts centred in their commentary. It is merely protection of the 'cake' by those who already have a slice and can't or won't share.

At the 2008 Festival launch, I spoke about our common culture – an argument made much more profoundly by Harry Hay as far back as the 1950s. The first Government Minister to launch our event, Eamon Ryan TD contributed to this affirmation as did Dublin City Council. With its modest resources Dublin

City Council's arts policy is the driving dynamic of accessible theatre in Ireland. Dublin City Council went on to present a storytelling theatre production (The Intercultural Kitchen) to celebrate the year and included my own short work 'The Gentleman Caller' in the programme – the first time sexual orientation was included in their intercultural dialogue. They also significantly sponsored a new Intercultural dialogue award which was won by 108 Productions from Los Angeles for their production of Terrence Mac Nally's 'Corpus Christi' – which provoked an interesting religious dialogue during the Festival.

Gay people are often defined as just and only that – gay. If Tiger Woods was gay, we would be told little of his American / Thai heritage, his academic brilliance, his childhood prodigy, his good looks, his incredible talent – he would be just that 'the gay golfer'. We, as people, apparently have no other significant attributes other than the negative stereotyping of our sexuality. In the Festival we use the term gay as part of the concept of completing the whole identity of the artist.

I am fully aware that there are gay artists, administrators and people who don't like, or are not comfortable with what we do – emphasising the whole identity of the valuable contribution gay and lesbian people make to arts and society – clearly in the cultural context here, through theatre as an art form. They don't want to be included under that identifiable tag. Internalised and externalised homophobia, developed as a result of witnessing discrimination, is ongoing and deeply felt in Ireland.

The quality and richness of the art presented, I hope, will help combat that barren homophobia, while hugely entertaining and informing and challenging our diverse and growing audience. I hope too the great success of brilliant artists who are also gay, might act as a positive role model for young people, who may yet live to see gay members of Aosdana's complete identity, being included and recognised in the deserved laudatory acclamations and honours bestowed on them. It is not acceptable for society to laud the art and 'loath' the artist. This is the ongoing challenge of gay theatre.

This Festival and many other great gay community initiatives, are the best response to such learned negativity. I also run Mr Gay Ireland and Mr Gay Northern Ireland competitions as the Theatre Festival's charitable / civic / social initiative. This has been internally controversial and often dismissed as trivial. There are no positive visual images of young gay Irish people. This event is a HIV / Aids awareness and gay rights awareness raising initiative amongst a generation that never had a youth or educational service tailored for the needs of their emerging sexuality. It is a brief event so not hugely earth shattering. It has raised over 50,000 euros to date for gay and HIV causes and brings urban and rural communities together North and South, to present positive and attractive images and voices of young gay men, out and active in Irish society. Local newspapers like the 'Sligo Advertiser' and the 'Monaghan Post' have given their local Mr Gay great support by running ads and positive newspaper articles on the winners. Young gay isolated men and boys in rural communities read these positive articles which may help in replacing, even one of the obituary notices of happy young men, who inexplicably go missing or take their own lives far too often, especially though not exclusively, in rural Ireland.

The Mr Gay Irelands and Mr Gay Northern Ireland's have gone on to achieve a spectacular record of success in Mr Gay Europe and Mr Gay International in the USA. These young men confidently represent gay Ireland abroad often to disbelieving audiences about how much Ireland has actually changed! The fun event is a novel and lucrative way (for the charities) to engage this generation in gay rights and of course to raise significant sums (and awareness) for HIV / Aids. There are very few unmasked images of gay Ireland – even in visual art exhibitions of gay culture. Many of our masks as gay men are feminised by drag or colour. The Theatre Festival is clearly unmasked (happily including the drag and the colour!).

The International Dublin Gay Theatre Festival has something some other art activities do not – a passion and a necessity to succeed. As many non-theatre people as theatre people have stepped up to volunteer their services to run this huge event – 216 performances over 16 days in 2008, by companies from four continents. Change is controlled by the denial of resources, when 'permission' is vested in the chosen few. We challenge that denial by replacing the financial resource with the power and passion of those who are determined that change will triumph. The 100% volunteer element of the Festival has been the biggest earthquake for the 100% grant-aided sector to contend with, as our talent and commitment overcomes all obstacles put in our way – even deliberately by those threatened on two fronts – we challenge the societal norms in presenting our culture and the arts norms in presenting our art.

The Festival is treated differently by the Arts Council. On our 897th performance, a senior member of the Arts Council finally accepted the invitation (of a friend) and attended one of our events. Up to that moment, their Council members had relied on 'insightful recommendations' on where taxpayers' money should be wisely spent, from those who refused our invitations to attend. Gays and Lesbians are the most highly taxed in our community, as we are entitled to fewer pension or welfare benefits than straight people get for the same tax contributions. Civil partnership will 'cost' the Exchequer the most conservative minimum of 25,000,000 euros a year – there is no mention or compensation for us having been forced to absorb that cost for the past century.

The arts continually help define the Irish as a nation and a race. Gay arts can do likewise. Theatre has a wonderful capacity to educate, inform and discuss issues, raising the veils on cherished taboos or unexplained norms, and enriching pluralism and diversity within society. Theatre as an art form is a key to liberating silenced voices, to encouraging emerging voices, to recognise the capacity we have to contribute and the value of the contribution in a civilised society. It's a challenge that oils the wheels and drives forward our actions in this unique Festival of world theatre.

Our priority - new writing - this Festival's core value - is a major contribution to the art form, to informed debate and an important statement from which we may be able to assess and identify the true characteristics and qualities of gay theatre and gay culture – that is a significant cultural contribution.

It is not always economically sensible – presenting 35 Irish premiers but we have made it work. Each year we find a space for new playwrights – we have prioritised women writers/contributors here too. Katherine O Donnell from UCD had presented wonderfully at our Seminar on Lesbianism as something that exists in the shadows of our society. The Festival, thanks to contributions from Katherine, Sonja Tiernan, Naoise O Reilly, Vickey Curtis, Suzanne Lakes and American's Carolyn Gage, Kerric Harvey and Kathleen Warnock, is willing to help turn the lights on for this important, but still inaudible voice. Lesbian theatre has the additional hurdle to overcome – one which keeps women artists down, and the other which keeps gay artists down. We are proud of the work and effort we put in to encouraging new writing and of course in staging new works. All but one of the 35 plays staged in Festival 2008 had never been seen before in Ireland.

In 2008, if we had the resources, and if we had accepted all submissions, we would actually be bigger than the great programme presented each year by our good friends in the Dublin Fringe Festival. I stopped counting after receiving the 130th submission for 2008. We had submissions from Ireland, the UK, the USA – practically every major city - Canada, Brazil, Mexico, Estonia, Germany, Italy, Netherlands, Senegal, Republic of South Africa, Israel, Cyprus and Australia. This is staggering for an event so young and so badly financially resourced. This is wonderful for theatre, gay theatre and its audiences in Ireland.

Within a month of the end of Festival '08, we had already received our first submissions from Japan, Germany and the Czech Republic amongst the 36 submissions to arrive within ten weeks, immediately following, before we had even launched our submissions campaign for 2009. Hundreds of authors and actors from around the world join in this discourse here in Dublin or across the worldwide web. All make great sacrifices to come to Dublin and present their works…the number of repeat applications is most encouraging. They, along with our growing audience, are our shareholders – they are this Festival.

The Festival has prompted great new theatrical activity in Ireland. Outhouse, the gay and lesbian resource centre proudly unveiled and we commissioned their new performance space in 105 Capel Street for this year's Festival. We are delighted to have helped them drive this initiative at a time when performance space is at a premium in the city.

In celebrating five years – we were also celebrating our essence - that in these very self-centred times, there are still people who will volunteer, or write and work passionately to create a better understanding of the true diversity that makes up the arts and every society. That is active citizenship. Many of us might and do achieve good things on our own, but we are truly great when we do it together, with and for our community, contributing to respect for all cultures and lifestyles in our wider pluralist society. In that, the contribution of straight people to this Festival is one of the healthiest dynamics that fuels the passion for this event and allows the full exploration of issues like sexuality, feminism, masculinity and gender identity.

This Festival was never conceived as only a gay event – it was and has succeeded in becoming a mainstream event in the Irish arts calendar. The Festival and its hugely gifted artists reach out and welcome all who want to hear our voice and who might value the incredible, but often invisible contribution, of gay artists to the arts and to society, past and present.

It is from that acknowledgement that role models will emerge giving much needed guidance, inspiration and purpose to the future generations of young gay people – replacing the damage of homophobia in behaviour and policy, with a goal, purpose and acknowledgement of the special gift that every individual's sexuality and ability to love brings, when expressed fully and without fear, and acknowledged and respected equally in and by every person. It is from that, that new voices will be encouraged, heard and new art presented.

The Festival and our artists will continue to work on and to challenge those who won't listen. Our mere presence does that, but the quality of the work presented is the key to getting the attention of narrowed minds. We will continue to create the space for gay people and our many friends to express themselves in the arts, because we all are entitled to ownership of, and to contribute to, theatre as an art form. In that, the contribution of straight people is one of the healthiest dynamics that fuels the passion for this event and allows the fuller exploration of issues like sexuality, feminism, masculinity and gender identity.

We will continue to encourage new writing, new companies, new stories, new performances and new voices – gay and straight, on subjects important and relevant to us and to society. We will continue to insist on playing our role as full and equal citizens and by doing so, will challenge those who actively undermine our human rights and our citizenship. This is still necessary in a country that in many ways is a shining beacon of growing respect for gay people, but which still struggles with our right to love, cherish and honour our chosen partner and to care, nurture and provide decent, safe, healthy and loving environments for our children.

The President of Ireland has said the Festival has served to build important bridges of cultural understanding across Irish society. It is our determination in building those bridges, that we now encourage everyone to join us in crossing those bridges, to participate and benefit from what the President has so generously described as, our 'offer of 'a fuller picture of cultural life on our Island'.

The International Dublin Gay Theatre Festival has modestly reached out across five continents to give a space to a voice that has struggled to be heard in many countries and is still not heard in many others today. The fact that we in Ireland can hear that voice further contributes to the real meaning of diversity in expression, perspective and experience in the arts in Ireland.

The Festival not only entertains our audiences, but may also inform them and equip them to contribute knowledgeably to the rights debate, so frequently staged by the media, between us and the remnants of extremism who learned their views from some outdated and failed moral code. They apparently represent middle Ireland when it is clear middle Ireland supports equality of rights to marriage and parenting. In sections of the media, it is apparently an 'extreme' to want to get married in Ireland and one whose opinion can only be 'balanced' in a debate, by those who believe gay people should be prohibited from marrying and should endure discrimination in legal rights, status and respect, in our pluralist democracy.

There are those who wish to continue to conceal our existence with the trite remark 'you are all legal now' what's the problem? That problem is even presented to us by gay artists, who have not yet the confidence to place their total and complete identity in their work. I hope this event also assists in the self esteem and confidence building, necessary to overcome this internalised homophobia, still evident in the Irish, gay and artistic community.

If you asked many people what are the 'gay careers' they would possibly answer hairdressing, 'trolley dollies' and the theatre. Yet our gay theatrical history is almost invisible. If gay artists were excellent, and many are, then they were claimed as only 'Irish' not as inclusively gay. Wilde is still box office magic especially at tourist times. Did an Irish play pack 'The Abbey' all summer or did a gay play…or is it an Irish gay play? Didn't women have to be excellent in order to be equal? As the rights struggle continues, standards driven cultural expression enriches and progresses the rights debate.

Hilton Edwards and Michael Mc Liammoir are also honoured in our in our few awards. They certainly brought the notion of male partnership into Irish discourse, though in those days, it was the business element of their joint work that primarily allowed people to give their lifelong relationship some (though not legal) recognition. The absence, or the difficulty to trace, other gay contributions to the Irish arts scene, is a symptom of the Ireland of concealment that so suited religious and political agendas in the previous centuries.

The Festival is trying to identify these contributors, such as the late great Set Designer and dance advocate from Cork, Patrick Murray and the late Shakesperian expert and professor of Drama at St Patrick's Teacher Training College, Dr Aiden Rogers and scion of the revolutionary Gore Booth family in

Sligo – Eva, sister of Countess Marciewicz. We would like very much to hear of gay artists, living and long forgotten, so that we can affirm them and their contribution to the arts today, in some small way.

Theatre allows you to present what you wish, an audience can choose to attend, we dim the lights and you can take in what you want, uninterrupted, for an hour or two. You will be entertained, you may learn, enjoy, connect, relax, laugh, cry, be reassured, enlightened or just survive it! Your thoughts are your own and you have the freedom to bring as much or as little as you wish, from the theatre into your own life. This International Gay Theatre Festival is as liberating as that. It is not happening elsewhere in the world in such a specific internationalised format. It is driven by strong artistic standards ambitions and goals. Its increasing and diverse audiences ensure that this emerging space is sustained for the continuation of the opportunity to address and contribute to meeting the full challenge of the identification and recognition of gay culture and of its value to the arts and society.

The exclusionary 'vision' of the arts has allowed all arts spaces to fall to developers of apartment blocks, switched off audiences, insurance to triumph over accessibility, as artists have to become successful and skilful grant applicants, rather than new productive artists. It would be incurable but for the few brilliant people who see the dynamic of arts administration as the enabling dynamic of a struggling sector, despite all the obstacles put in their way by those who seek 'value' only through a monetary lens. Happily, we have been encouraged and inspired by some of these 'enablers' whose role in the arts world is invaluable and greatly appreciated by novice grant applicants like ourselves.

A key to the lack of challenge to this discretionary based policy is that many arts decision makers are all from the same class and the same circle. Ireland is a lot more than the view from the front room of the opulent Merrion Square. Those set up to develop the arts and to protect it, are presiding over a decline of huge proportions, particularly in Dublin. They need to get out from their Georgian surroundings and accelerate their thought processes into the multicultural, diverse community that is Ireland today.

The job is to identify new forms of artistic expression that reflect Ireland, a step beyond the old repertoire, done by the heavily long term grant aided institutions and to secure resources for them. The protection of the many meritorious, grant aided, arts producers is also essential, but the future is also with the new voices in our changing, dynamic, new multicultural society. No matter how many times that door is closed – Festivals like ours are a constant reminder to the blind eyes and closed doors, that we will be heard and we need to be heard if the arts in Ireland are to have a new sustainable dynamic.

The International Dublin Gay Theatre Festival fulfils the standards and criteria for arts funding – it's about time we got it in a meaningful and enabling way. Our experience to date with the Arts Council has been distasteful. Criteria were ignored, policies ignored and the process anything but transparent. No one attended the first 896 performances in this unique Festival. Here is my brief understanding of how we have been treated to date. We were told in our third year that we were 'too new' to get funding. When we pointed out their (alleged) 'homophobia' they funded a new gay company in a different genre less than three months in existence!

The IDGTF ticks many of their policy boxes, we create new audiences, we have a new vibrant volunteer base, we encourage and develop new writers, we create new space for new voices, all our companies are paid from the box office creating real employment, we network nationally and internationally. We didn't get the grants or the attention. Why – one word – gay.

In 2007, we had another long, good meeting with them and they agreed it was in order to apply for revenue funding. The subsequent 'recommendation' to Council was on the lines that we were not suitable for revenue funding, but that we were being funded under another scheme. The recommendation was that they should meet us and explore this! We had done the meetings – followed the advice and had not been previously funded. Nothing could have been further from the truth…which they subsequently grudgingly acknowledged with a minimal grant…not apparently because we merited it, but because we uncovered the flaw in the recommendation and in the process.

Our Arts Council funding, got on foot of an inaccurate report to the Council in 2007, is 5,000 euros. The obligations, accounts, policies, administratively to get the 5,000 euros are almost identical to the obligations if we were to receive 5million euros – hence I consider the current 'grant' to be a form of 'negative' funding – it cost us 5k to meet their accounting requirements in the first year!

There has been some 'regime change' in this body and we hope for a fair hearing as we enter our second five years. It is important to note the consistent support received from Dublin City Council and Failte Ireland through Dublin Tourism since our inception – in fact I think we have been instrumental in encouraging Dublin Tourism to have a gay specific page on their website! One or two people from the Arts Council did attend the launch this year, but it is unclear whether they attended any of the productions. The support of the Theatre Forum, the Dublin Theatre and Fringe Festivals, the Project Arts Centre, Smock Alley, The INTO and our other venues has been very encouraging.

We are being heard in 5 continents, in the embassies (Isreal, Italy) and arts organisations (Governor of Illinois Arts Fund, British Council) in 5 continents, in production companies in 5 continents, in the output of playwrights in 5 continents, in our own city, just... not in the national arts funding organisation.

Happily this lack of perspective, as to who makes up this nation does not exist elsewhere. Our participating companies have been aided by their own cultural institutions in every country, except Ireland. These institutions examine our track record and our output, our standards and recognise its value. They offer financial support to people in their own country to travel to Ireland to participate in this unique event in the birthplace of Oscar Wilde. They clearly see the value of this event...even from such a distance, many even travel to attend and learn more, and we gratefully acknowledge that. Such interaction enriches our work in so many ways.

But we can't criticise too much – it's a tight closed circle where grace and favour are as legitimate a currency as artistic value. In finding ourselves continually without meaningful State assistance, this has impacted on our ability to present even higher standards of work from more diverse regions. We had five applications from Australia in 2007 and even with modest support, some would be on our programme. I say modest, because the commitment of all the participating companies is the main driving force for their participation in this unique event. They see the dynamic, appreciate the standards, are excited by the intercultural learning and networking, are open to new perspectives, are inspired by new writing, informed by our educational programme, and appreciated by our audiences – hence they make a financial sacrifice to participate too.

Every year, men, women, of all ages and cultures, straight and gay tell me the Festival is valid and worthwhile. Every year they come back in increased numbers. We survey our audience and over 3,500 forms have been filled in each year giving the Festival productions an 87% excellent rating (5/5). It is, in their defence, that I reject the exclusionary attitudes of those who look into their own hearts and see Ireland – none of us can afford that today. In this Festival we open our eyes and our minds and see Ireland and all who make a contribution to it including the gay community and through this event their vigorous and inspiring partnership with the arts community.

Most importantly, we are here and are here to stay. We will drive forward this event because we have something of value to give to the arts, to our living, diverse democracy, to our own community, to the society in which we contribute an enormous amount to, and to you. We do so out of a passion, a commitment and a drive that would infuse and reenergise many an arts event.

We have reached out way beyond our country and our community and we have inspired an international response to which we have spared no physical effort to accommodate. That is art. This is a living culture. The International Dublin Gay Theatre Festival is a cultural event that will bring people together to define and to present Irish and international gay theatre in the years to come, which will inform debate and assist those who strive to change cold hearts and closed minds. Join us for the first fortnight in May every year in Dublin. www.gaytheatre.ie

The Festival was exploding with growth. The commitment of everyone in the team was extraordinary and generous. The challenges to ego began to grow as mimicking the arts mainstream, some administrative roles became artistic commentators. The potential was now obvious. I saw it as artistic potential, others saw it as personal and financial. That clash was unfortunately to emerge horribly in 2009 as the seeds of doubt were being sowed for a later harvest. The impact though of what we were achieving artistically and in the arts field was important and remained something we could rely upon in many areas, when the opportunity came to attack us, sadly from within. Festival 2009 was to herald unwelcome change and was to draw our energies over this period away from transformative theatre into the corporate battlefield of protecting a successful entity from commercial and personal exploitation which would use the integrity of the festival for things far from its original purpose and ambition. We were about to become a victim of our own success.

An Absolute Disgrace

There is no such thing as a moral or an immoral book. Books are well written, or badly written. That is all.

Oscar Wilde

Five years is a term of government in Ireland. A lot had been achieved since 2004, so that every single person who worked on or contributed to, or attended the Festival could be justly proud. No one person can attempt to do work on this scale – it takes a team and a shared vision.

Tony award winning actress, Anna Manahan sat with me in the wings of the Theatre Royal Waterford (by special permission) and she discussed with me how things happen in theatre. Her view of people like Mac Liammoir and Edwards whom she had worked with, or indeed the prolific Garry Hynes of the Druid in Galway, that even though everyone made their vital contribution, one person often was "the flame" to which they were drawn. She generously credited me with being "the flame" for the use of theatre and art to celebrate the Millennium that New Year's Eve in Waterford. I remembered the lesson rather than the compliment.

I had been aware of it in DAYMS. I had tried to move away from the Chairman's role five years in and designated another member to take over. I liked his ethos and ethics of inclusiveness. Out of the blue, this Dubliner was transferred down the country from work and I had to remain on. Again at the end of the second five year term, a Northside Dublin company had ousted their formidable Chair and I asked her to succeed me but she wanted to return to her own group which she did, in a 'counter coup' the following year.

I had been involved in politics in my youth and in a later interview with the

'Waterford News and Star' (where I had briefly worked as a journalist) when asked about politics and theatre I said " Being at a political party meeting is like being at a 'Legion of Mary' meeting compared to the goings on of theatre groups!" I was about to revisit that lesson.

I ended the fifth year with what had been an excellent Festival.

I realised that everyone had worked hard and was moved by how personal the event had come to be for them. They were entitled to that shared ownership. I also tried to convey that acknowledgement of ownership to those who did not see it reflected in the theatre produced, but in their own status in the gay community and indeed as they reflected their own, with mine.

I was only there for the theatre and began to hugely miss my own professional output. I was facilitating playwrights and other people to perform at my own creative cost. No one had ever offered me the supports the Festival gave to many. My own career had no more space for personal projects. My letterbox was full and there was no end to the Festival cycle, as we already had submissions for the following year, before the present year ended. I was on a cycle and could not get off. I had analysed over 130 plays on paper the previous year as well as attending and noting a further 50.

In the absence of any form of financial support for an administrator, who could have maintained records, applied for grants, secured the contracts etc. that witholding of support was a crucial brake on our progress and a dreadful personal strain. The Gay Film Festival happily received 20,000 euros for a three day, one centre event. We got 5,000 euros for a 35 play, 42 event, sixteen nights of over 220 performances, giving employment. Just like my Festival colleagues, I too was under pressure and was actively looking to ease the burden. I desperately wanted the Festival to survive me and wanted to hand the mantle over to people I trusted, whose theatre skills would enhance and develop our core ethos. No successor was obvious, especially with the sparse resources and the amount of work required.

I had still failed in my own governance guidelines and more 'blank' cheques had to be signed by me, because of pressure including time. I hated that practice. My home was the office and the archive. It contained tons of paper from plays to contracts. I noticed something in the programme of 2008. My address was the registered office and any letters that arrived were distributed at each Wednesday meeting – in that way I could at least have a good knowledge of what was going on, in the growing company I chaired. We had a central email which all correspondence should emanate. This was not happening. In the programme of 2008 I read a notice amending the official company address by adding an 'administrative address' and publishing its details in the programme – there were now to be two addresses and no one would have access to both. The question arose, just how much business was being done on behalf of the Festival 'off record' and why?

On a much more positive note, I decided to particularly reward the spirit of volunteerism through the Patrick Murray Award that year. The only other person who ever knew the awards in advance was the Administrative Director. They were confidential and I invited many people to present them on stage. I let him know the name of the Patrick Murray Award and the certificate was printed. That year in the Temple Bar Music Centre, we had all the nominee names appear on screen. The Murray award 'for an outstanding contribution to Irish gay theatre' was a direct award with no nominees. The Administrative Director usually joined me on stage for awards, some sponsored by Tipperary Crystal.

I had also arranged for the Lord Mayor of Dublin, Cllr Paddy Bourke, to call in to present this award. He was late, so late that I had to run from back stage to front of house to check on progress and to push forward my concert running order. At the last second the Lord Mayor arrived, we rolled down the screen and I announced that the Administrative Director had won the award as he represented the volunteer effort. Presented by the Lord Mayor it was a great moment. It was a complete surprise and I described him as 'the first volunteer'. I hoped it would reassure any insecurity of tenure and allow us to move onto the second term. I was naive.

The Festival did well financially in a 'Celtic Tiger' year but costs were high and we were putting nothing aside for a rainy day. We went to Edinburgh and the letterbox began to fill again all winter. In December my workplace hit the national headlines and the changes there meant that senior executives like myself, who had been limited in their scope to contribute to the workplace, were now in the spotlight in a very nasty political environment. Workplace pressure increased. Efforts to promote to managerial status or director level the Executive Committee members who had worked tirelessly, were strongly resisted. As we met to discuss the future, I pushed for a succession plan for both of us and the promotion of our younger colleagues. The Administrative Director pushed to be 'promoted' to Joint Managing Director.

In February, the Festival programme was burgeoning. We got unexpected word on the Executive that one of our minor sponsors now wanted to play a major role in sponsoring the Festival. The sponsor was a client of Mark Banchansky who had a senior retail position in the Dublin Airport Authority. It did not come as a surprise to either the Administrative side or the Fundraiser. The Fundraiser who had lodged in my house happily for many years, and who had been blocked from becoming a director, moved out within four weeks.

Absolut Vodka had just bought the rights to the iconic rainbow flag from its originator Charles Brown – the symbol of gay pride. What followed was an aggressive worldwide campaign to replace the recognition the LGBT community got from this Pride flag in people's minds, with thinking of a vodka brand. No international gay event of merit was immune to a contact from Absolut and an offer of 'support'. We all need support. I was concerned by the suddenness and indeed advancement of this offer. I went to meet them with the Administrative Director, on my insistence, and got them to engage at least with our ethos and my core issue of the positive gay identity. I was happy to collaborate with them in a mutual arrangement of support, but our identity was not to be compromised. I had worked too hard for the word 'gay' to be prominent, to sell it to the nearest shot of alcohol, to be cloaked in the Pride flag of the 1960s.

A very modest two year 'heads of agreement' was sent to me and it was accepted with the Administrative Director taking on the project management from our side. They would give us 10,000 euros in return for a name change to the Absolut Dublin Gay Theatre Festival. I wasn't happy and was uneasy at the how this interest had come about and the relationships involved. But it was the most hectic time in my schedule with contracts being finalised and weekly preparatory meetings delivering results. I suppose I had my 'eye off the ball'.

I advised that the Administrative Director consult the friendly advice available from 'Business to Arts' who do a lot of good work to assist such partnerships on the basis of mutual benefit. The report back was that the arrangement got the all clear. This later resulted in not being the case. Firstly 'Business to Arts' offered advice that in order to change a name we should look for ten times what we got, but secondly it was reported that when they subsequently met with the company, they allegedly claimed the investment was five times what it actually was. I speculated how that was conveyed, as in addition to the cash deal, the brand would undertake an advertising campaign which ultimately obliterated our identity and bullied us off the stage.

The 'deal' went ahead and the Administrative Director, who was also our Company Secretary, was to protect our corporate entity and my approval was needed at all stages. I heard very little. We all worked on in our fractious way but less and less post arrived at our official company address. Very little information was being transmitted in what was a hectic year, with the additional demands of a salacious sponsor to be satisfied. At the first launch of the programme we duly lauded our new sponsor. The Administrative Director also acted as host to introduce the speakers. The Minister for Arts had agreed to the launch but didn't show at the last minute. Normally as I had programmed the event, I would explain the programme and I was happy to have the sponsor speak. This year instead of introducing me, the Administrative Director announced the programme – off the top of his head. I'm good on my feet, but that was one extraordinary event that would be followed by many more!

On the week the public advertising campaign was due, I still had not signed off on the final artwork. I insisted to the Administrative Director and the Fundraiser that I approve it. To my horror, I was shown a poster featuring two large vodka bottles striped with a pride flag and the other resembling a tent but actually it was theatre curtains. Our tag was the last line at the bottom of the poster. The Festival logo was the size of the lid of one of the vodka bottles – we were obliterated. A row ensued and I insisted this be changed to equally reflect both brands. I asked that this be conveyed by my project manager to the brand on the Thursday. It wasn't. Having waited the weekend, on the encouragement of the Administrative Director who claimed he had gotten some minor amendments, I sent them a blaster of an email condemning their obliteration of our identity. In one way it played right into the hand of this 'coup' group. I was working on little or no information and I demanded a meeting with the brand and the two directors of IDGTF. It was granted. It was cool and cordial. To be fair, they had been given the go-ahead from our side. I also thanked them for putting the Festival logo beside the bottle cap now taking up about 8% of the poster. They assured me no changes had been made – so what exactly had I been shown in the first place? It was frosty and significantly our Administrative Director did not show up to the meeting. I never met with them again.

I had maintained our contact with Terrence Mc Nally and in an act of great generosity, he and husband Tom Kirdahy arrived in Dublin a few days before the event and helped us launch it early at a heavily branded vodka party. We had lots of press there. I made a short opening speech and was never heard of again. I remained in a corner as my Admin team did a photocall. Good on them! At the end of the night an enquiry was made as to where I was, by a senior female brand manager and she introduced herself to me. Essentially I, or the theatre event I represented, was swamped.

This continued to be as the Press launch/photo opportunity was held without my input. We had again been unable to meet four weeks before the start of the Festival due to acrimony at the committee meetings. Any enquiry as to our finances or any agreed branding with the vodka company was greeted aggressively and defensively, accusing me of micro managing – a catch phrase that caught on – I never knew less about any Festival as I did in 2009. Somebody obviously did not want me to know what was really happening.

As the Festival opening drew closer, I then went to welcome the volunteers briefly to their first workshop in Outhouse. I spoke positively to this group to audibly hear once I finished 'Thank God that's over now we can get on with it'! I left the workshop and met Connell Kennedy on his way to the workshop, and told him that relationships were at an all time low and I could not wait to be shut of it. There was now a 'committee within the committee' which excluded most of the committee members. My board was oblivious, but intact.

For the first time ever, throughout the Festival, I never received a box office report. I had sent a respected colleague, who had managed two major theatre box offices for theatres in Dublin in, to assess what was happening. She left in a week, confiding in me that it was 'a train crash' and an expensive one! I was now being airbrushed out of the Festival and with that, the theatre and gay identity was vanishing under a vodka brand. That was 'boring' and I was painted as some arty crazy guy who hadn't a clue how to run an event.

During the Festival the 'coup group' began to resign. I was under personal attack and dissention was being spread. The Gala night was a dreadful affair behind the scenes. Absolut also invested a reported 25,000 euros into our Gala night, including an opening dvd promoting their brand. I discovered, on entering the venue, that they had constructed a three sided stage with no entrances or exits, and had fixed a seat on stage right, a giant inflated vodka bottle pride striped, stage left, and fixed a permanent podium in centre stage – where 30 pieces of diverse theatre were about to perform live. I eventually, with the help of stage manager Oran Ostinelli, fixed this bizarre set up and we were able for the show to proceed with one entrance in use all night.

At the Gala night very few words were exchanged between the two directors, except once he noted a resigned committee member in the front row and described him to me as 'a complete idiot (he was to be his co-director of his new company a few days later). We had a two years 'heads of agreement' with the vodka company and when their manager spoke at the Gala night, he pointedly said wished the Dublin Gay Theatre Festival well. I corrected him in public and noted it was the 'Absolut Dublin Gay Theatre Festival' – the dye was cast, but I did not know how it would run. Obviously there was some alternative agenda playing out all season and only very few were privy to that.

Once again, as a result of no communication, I was forced to sign 27 blank cheques for the immediately departing companies. Then a rather bizarre occurrence happened when the Administrative Director reported that his 'night had been ruined' as money had been 'stolen' from his briefcase in the box office. Though never cleared up, it appears to have been a false alarm, though I did feel for him. Obviously there was a lot on his shoulders.

On the Gala night I suffered the ignomy of having to present my 'identity theatre awards' under a ten foot inflated striped vodka bottle. I had invited the gracious Lord Mayor of Dublin Cllr Eibhlin Byrne whom I knew and you could see the faces of the vodka people visibly change when speaker after speaker, including the Lord Mayor and our Ambassadors paid tribute to my own work and vision for the event – that was not as scripted. The following day our PRO sent me a draft press release with a photo caption showing the two directors with the Lord Mayor for release – I wrote back saying that was not possible as I had not been included in any of the photocalls that night. I never saw the photograph. I was also not included in any of the thanks on stage. We were in for a battle royal at a time when I had hoped to move on.

I had no idea how the Festival had done financially. When I enquired I was told we were 'doing fine'. I was the Managing Director! I moved to regularise the corporate governance immediately. I contacted our legal advisor and prepared to hold an EGM on governance matters. Something was up and I did not know what, but I was determined to be fair. I created some breathing space by setting out the issues of corporate governance in writing but convening the meeting on July 7th 2009 – six weeks hence. I hoped that would create space to sort matters out. I contacted Mark Banchansky to appeal to him to mediate between the sides, as I felt it was his professional standing and contacts that brought the vodka brand to us, he would be a fair and honest broker. He agreed to meet with me. I went on holiday to recover from the incredible stress of it all and what must be regarded outwardly as a very successful Festival. Beware what success can breed. I contacted Mark on my return in mid June and I called the Administrative Director to see if matters could be sorted agreeably. He said he would consider it. The 'micro-manager' still had not one shred of information on the Festival's outturn. At least I knew no cheques other than those designated for the companies, had been signed. Wrong!

On June 29th when I asked our legal advisor to progress matters but to ensure fairness in what had been set out in the written notice, he rang me back and asked who was the 'Absolut Dublin Gay Theatre Festival LTD'? I replied that had been our licenced trading name as per our sponsorship agreement, but as it contained a registered trademark, we could not register it as ours, of course. He replied that a company of that name had been registered immediately following the end of our Festival. It had four directors. Obviously, I was not one of them. I was sick to my stomach.

I got a hunch in the panic to check something out. We had waited years to get a centrally located hotel in Edinburgh for the Festival there. We booked it in advance from year to year. I don't fully understand why, but I rang the hotel and asked them were our two rooms still securely booked. I was told that the Administrative Director had cancelled one of the rooms three weeks earlier! I asked the clerk to check that he was sure he had cancelled the room and he confirmed. I then said that I could not impose on him to secure my room for me as he had used his credit card and that would be an imposition, and I secured the remaining room on my own credit card. I was apparently to be left stranded in Edinburgh but I gazumped him. I realised that I was weeks behind in this game, but game on!

I made some more enquiries and found that all our venues had already been booked by this 'new entity' for the weeks of our scheduled Festival in 2010. Some had been told I had resigned. A new web page was under construction with our logo as its screen saver. I still had no accounts. Our data base had been accessed for four weeks without us knowing of any risk. The four directors were the administrative director and in this instance his partner (not his daughter) Connell Kennedy, Mark Banchanksy and former fundraiser Gary Tiernan. No wonder Mark had never kept his appointment with me and no wonder Absolut had appeared to 'jump ship'.

I contacted Absolut. They said they had not given permission for the registration of their trademark to any other entity. A later correspondence was a letter confirming their' ongoing' association with an entity that hadn't existed. Most sinisterly, this major company included the line 'we no longer have any association with Mr Brian Merriman'. They never had had an association in any form with me personally, but it seemed they were collaborating with this new entity, as it attempted to pose as the Festival I founded and shared. It was also clear that no other long standing, loyal and hard working committee members were aware of this plan either. Everyone was excluded by the 'gang of four'. Here is the report of the previous year's meeting, upon which I now called to EGM to report on progress:

2008 Chairman's Report

1.0 Welcome. I have called this EGM to improve the governance of the International Dublin Gay Theatre Festival Ltd. Some improvements have been introduced to comply with company law. The AGM approved the accounts for 2006 and 2007 (note 1 attached). Resolutions (which) were passed about the 'director's loan' and this has been acted upon. The (previous) AGM elected Brian Merriman as Chairman and Managing Director and John Pickering as Director/Company Secretary. Both are the cheque signatories.

1.1 The process of signing blank cheques in advance, for administrative purposes, has been a cause for concern. In 2008, though this practice continued, cheque requests were accompanied or in the context of very detailed accounts of the income situation of the IDGTF (almost daily) from the box office. Financial management was therefore enabled to some degree. The proposals agreed were to further improve the transparency of our systems.

1.2 A series of meeting was held between the two directors after the 5th Festival and the Chair/MD put forward a plan first to the directors and then to the Executive Committee, outlining key governance issues: Budgeting, Financial accountability, Transparency, Mentoring, Succession Planning, Board Membership, Communication

1.3 It was agreed that:

1.3.1. A Budget was to be produced for the first time for Festival 2009. This would involve a 10% reduction on expenditure for 2008 in light of the recession and to take into account the ticket prices were to be set at a reduced flat rate of 15e incl. booking fees.

1.3.2. The practice of signing blank cheques would be replaced by a system where all payments would be accompanied by a chit or form briefly outlining their purpose to be signed off by the directors. A facility to do this weekly before Executive Committee meetings was outlined.

1.3.3. The head of sponsorship was to have access to budgets and financial information to target specific expenditure items with a sponsorship response to give effect to the budgetary process. John (Pickering) was appointed to liaise with Absolut our new sponsors. Gareth (Hurley) was to take notes of Executive Committee agreed actions.

1.3.4. All business would be done through the central email account. A new gmail account was set up to facilitate this. In exceptional sensitive circumstances the two directors would decide to maintain confidential correspondence in an appropriate account. The ambition was set out to have a central archive of all contacts and procedures.

2. The above was designed to begin a process of mentoring new directors and successors. Two members of the executive were identified initially as being suitable and crucially willing, for directorship status, Gareth Hurley and Gary Tiernan, with a view to including more members of the Executive into this process in the short term. The succession process had begun.

2.1 Gareth Hurley and Gary Tiernan were given the titles of Directors on the Executive Committee, as was Chris Nugent. Connell Kennedy assumed an equally pivotal role as PRO. The process of up-skilling and appointing members of the Executive Committee to the Board had begun. I had also discussed their ongoing membership with existing members of the Board and am grateful to those who indicated a willingness at anytime to facilitate the appointment of members of the Executive to the Board, in their place.

2.2 The Chair indicated his desire to rebalance the current company membership structure in favour of the Executive Committee taking on new responsibility, i.e. appointing two members of the Executive to the Board while maintaining membership at its current level of 7. Initial moves to progress this were made in April but put on hold pending the outcome of the review of the effectiveness of the new governance procedures and their implementation.

2.3 The Company Secretary indicated a strong desire to be given the title Joint Managing Director – the Chair agreed to review this issue positively at the conclusion of the successful implementation of the new governance process in May 2009. The Chair began the process of moving towards this and played a more Chairman like role this year facilitating the individual members to take (more) personal responsibility for their new briefs.

3. In order to maintain respect and to improve relations it was agreed that any dispute or decision would be resolved at face to face meetings and the communication with each other over controversial matters by email was prohibited.

The EGM was held on July 7th 2009 and my Chairman's Report went as follows:

4. I regret to inform the meeting that my attempts to improve the transparency of our governance have failed and hence the necessity to call an EGM.

4.1. Various new (unauthorised) procedures were introduced which centralised the access to our administrative processes and financial management to the exclusion of all other responsible officers.

4.1.2. A draft budget was produced based on initial outcomes from the 2008 accounts. No accounts have been lodged with the Auditors or made available to other Directors though they have been in a state of finalisation since January. The planned reduction of expenditure by 10% could not therefore be implemented or monitored by the Executive or the Directors.

4.1.3. The process of signing blank cheques proceeded without any accompanying documentation. Meetings were cancelled and no essential corporate or financial information was provided by email as had been the case in previous years.

5. No information about the income from the box office was provided at all during Festival 2009. Direct questions were met with vague non- specific answers like we are within 200 euros of last year (but no 2008 figures were available for comparison). Remedial steps in relation to any emerging loss were rendered impossible. No indication has been given to date on any less favourable outcome for the Festival in 2009 as against 2008.

5.1. The only indication of a financial outcome to date was given by the Company Secretary in an email from his private email address not copied to the IDGTF. On June 21st he wrote to a participating company who contrary to contract was not paid by the final night. The email informed our client company that 'the Festival has run out of money'. No such information had been given to any member of the Board or the Executive Committee. It was stated that an EGM was to be held and that I would be in touch with the company afterwards. (see appendix 2).

5.1.1. I trust the reference in the email to the awaiting 'final funding from the Arts Council and DCC' is incorrect. I think DCC has paid in full but the Failte Ireland/Dublin Tourism grant may not be paid in full. I note the reference that I would be in touch after the EGM. I remain unaware as to the amount yet to be paid. Decisions as to who and what should be paid remained in the exclusive and exclusionary domain of the Company Secretary contrary to agreed policy. On June 9th the CS sought the address to send a cheque to – on June 21st he pleaded inability to pay. On July 6th it was brought to my attention by the client. I haven't signed any company cheques for weeks, so the limited stock provided by me during the Festival, was obviously used to meet the selected obligations to date.

5.1.2. This is a matter of grave concern to me as Chair and Managing

Director for the proper governance of, and for the meeting of the legal responsibilities of this organisation.

5.1.3 The IDGTF can verify ticket sales by reconciling its accounts with the receipts for bookings through 'Ticketsolve' and the signed nightly sales returns from volunteers. Gareth Hurley reports that our access to our 'Ticketsolve' records has been blocked, despite the IDGTF being the registered client. The decision to block this verification service was not authorised by any known individual and is a matter of concern.

5.1.4. Cheques were received apparently made out to the Absolut Dublin Gay Theatre Festival – a title we held on licence from Absolut Vodka for two years only. A request was made to change the company name to facilitate the changing of such cheques but I thought it unwise as a) we hold a temporary licence to use that title, b) there is no guarantee that Absolut will renew their 10,000e contribution plus marketing campaign beyond next year. The Chair has no knowledge as to what happened to these cheques whether they were reissued in our favour or remain to be cashed. The Chair has no account as to the cash sums received from nightly venue based ticket sales (variable from 400e to 1,000e per night 2008) or programme sales (1,300e 2008).

6. A theft was reported to the Chair of X thousands of euros on the final night. No figure was given and no one has had any access this year to payments made to companies. The Company Secretary was convinced he filled an envelope with cash for the play 'Walnuts Remind Me of my Mother' and left it unsupervised in the Button Factory Box Office. On his return, he reported the envelope was there and the cash gone. He reported it to the Button Factory. He described it as 'destroying my night'. On enquiry a few days later, the Secretary informed the Chair that the event didn't happen as he had paid the company the previous week. Had an envelope been filled with cash and deposited in the Box Office on the Gala night? Was it empty or gone by the end of the night which prompted the actions outlined above?

7. As Chair all my correspondence for the year was either conducted through or copied to the central email account. I was the only director to honour this process. Negative and personalised email correspondence was conducted

through email despite being strictly prohibited, with the Committee members with regrettable consequences for inter-personal relationships and subsequent meetings. A leadership disaster.

8. The function of the Company Secretary is to ensure compliance with legislation and to protect the interests of the Company and its brand. That is a fair test of the proper functioning of the office. Certain actions have come to light which require an explanation as to whether they have been taken in the best interests of the IDGTF. There is also an issue about the business names registered to the IDGTF, which the Chair was assured were done and it transpires was not done.

9. The absence of data, correspondence, assets, all publications and materials produced by, donated to and purchased by the IDGTF from a central archive is of concern. These include but are not exhaustive, all records, contacts, agreements, licences, audience response forms, brochures, programmes, banners, Excalibur stands, printed matter, posters, a donated painting, media cuttings and archives. Any use by any other entity of any material generated or pertaining to represent in any way, the work of the IDGTF to date in its 6 Festivals must be legally challenged and publicly exposed.

10. Under the Data Protection Acts we have collected information, which if used by any other entity is a violation of this Act. The data collected by the Festival this year is not in a central or accessible archive. Any unauthorised use of contacts or data held or collected by the IDGTF, by any personnel for any other entity, who gained access to this data by virtue of their involvement with the IDGTF, is against the law and we must report any such misuse immediately to the Data Protection Commissioner. I authorised the changing of passwords on our email accounts recently to ensure we were not open to an allegation of breaching the Data Protection Acts.

11. In effect the resolutions today are being presented to bring proper governance to the IDGTF in relation to financial responsibility, budgetary matters, transparency and financial management. They are a reasonable template for the ethical management and protection of our business interests, obliged by the proper carrying out of our legal and corporate responsibilities.

12. The resolutions are in line with the outcome of the meetings between the

two directors in January 2009 and are an implementation of the strategy set out at those meetings which has failed in its implementation to date. The resolutions were sent in advance to the Company Secretary before any EGM was called, and followed up by phone and in writing with offers of meetings to establish whether the EGM was necessary or to facilitate an alternative view as to how the Festival would proceed in the future. All such offers were declined and eventually confirmed as declined in writing to Board members.

12.1 The resolutions as indicated are open to amendment and presented for discussion and approval.

Brian Merriman, Executive Chairman, July 7th 2009

That the Extraordinary General Meeting of the International Dublin Gay Theatre Festival Ltd approve the following resolutions:

1. That all matters and finances arising from the 2009 Festival are accounted for and presented to the membership within four weeks of the date of this resolution.

2. That members note the commitment of Brian Merriman and John Pickering to donate the account item known as 'directors loan' to the Festival for inclusion in the 2008 accounts or the 2009 accounts as administratively appropriate. The Festival thanks Brian Merriman and John Pickering for informing Plunkett Cooke and Company of this commitment, as agreed to, at a meeting of the Executive Committee last February.

3. That all documents, assets and records pertaining to the Festival are lodged in a central archive in the registered office.

4. That the registered office is the only address sanctioned for use to transact any business on behalf of the Festival.

5. That the EGM will appoint the two company directors from the date of the meeting to redevelop the structures of the company for Festival 2010 and that this matter will be considered again by the members at their AGM. These two company directors will be the only signatories on all bank accounts.

6. That Gareth Hurley be appointed Company Secretary (not a member of the Board) with immediate effect and the members record their thanks to John Pickering for his work in that area to date.

7. That as Chairman, Brian Merriman is mandated to appoint a new Executive Committee to properly administer the Festival on behalf of the members. As Chairman he may appoint a number of people with specific responsibility operating under the title of 'Director' or 'Manager' to indicate their area of responsibility.

8. That company membership will be immediately reviewed with the intent of including new members of the Executive Committee as members of the company, on the nomination of the Chairman, with company membership to remain at the maximum of seven persons. Proposals for changes in personnel will be dealt with at the EGM.

9. A simple majority of members will suffice in each instance to give effect to these resolutions.

The Administrative director was still our Company Secretary and yet was the Managing Director of this 'rival' entity that had registered our trading name as his own. His daughter who has never attended the Board, resigned minutes before the meeting started, in a letter to her father as Company Secretary. He stormed into the room, screamed and roared and threw papers on the table and left. I managed to ask him one thing. "Are you satisfied that at all times you have served as our Company Secretary you have always acted in the best interests of the company and protected its entity"? " I am" he replied that was a difference and a chasm of governance, I could not bridge – ever.

I perused with my fellow board members present, the papers scattered on the table. They indicated that two cheques had been cashed for large amounts of money each week and the companies had been paid in cash. The other 25 cheques had been selectively used to pay bills, especially of suppliers that he had already booked for his own 'event'. Critically we had a dance piece that agreed to donate the proceeds of their show, if I included them in the programme, to a nominated charity. I nominated the New Fill Project at St James Hospital HIV Clinic and fitted in their short performances in our schedule. I also agreed the Festival would waive its box office percentage in favour of the charity. It had not been paid. The charity money, though paid into the box office had not been paid over and there were no funds remaining in the account. I immediately wrote a personal cheque, contacted the performers and the charity and honoured that debt. I then discovered that the only venue not paid had been the gay community centre 'Outhouse' which the new event had not booked for 2010. I contacted then and assured them I would honour the debt and we did.

This was the one Festival I had not run 'my way'. The 'their way' had left us starved of cash and with strong evidence that the extensive Vodka advertising campaign resulted in our first recorded fall in our box office since we began. It was clear we would not be at a loss without them – that was good at least.

The campaign by the new event to claim our identity and history got dirtier and dirtier and others who wished us ill were of course thrilled at this development. The spin emanated that there had been a 'split'. There had been no split – we knew nothing at all about it. How can you split when the conversation never took place?

I consulted a leading corporate lawyer while on holidays with my parents in Wexford. He indicated there were issues of serious concern to be addressed and that I would need 15,000 euros up front, to begin that process. I went back to where I was staying and was lying awake at 4am when my mobile phone rang. My Mother was calling from downstairs – my Father was having a heart attack. He was rushed to hospital and I accompanied him in the ambulance at 5am – he also had pneumonia. Happily he later recovered.

Having become aware on the evening of July 7th of the full extent of the financial crisis we were left with, I then set out to regroup. I had lined up our long standing volunteers Gareth Hurley and Chris Nugent to instantly replace the resigned Pickerings. I immediately contacted 'Outhouse' and others whose contracts had been breached. We set about trying to catch up on what had been done in our name with all our contacts. The calling card left by the Marquis of. Queensbury for Oscar Wilde at his club when he wrote that Wilde was 'posing as a somdomite' rang in my ears. For the past six weeks another entity had been 'posing' as us and continued to do so for some time.

The volunteers holiday weekend had been hijacked when this group attended and addressed them and told them the Festival had left me. In fact most people showed remarkable restraint and stayed with the IDGTF. However they exacted a social consequence if you stayed and none if you left. Each member was contacted and many either left both groups to avoid the campaign or stayed put. We were six weeks behind in this well planned campaign. A dinner was held for key members on the night of the EGM by our former Company Secretary and to his eternal integrity, despite his personal friendship with one of the new event's 'directors', long standing committee member Gareth Hurley walked out of the dinner and told them what they were doing was morally wrong. Gareth at a most difficult time assumed the crucial role of Company Secretary of the IDGT and we have never had a worry again about transparent governance. He has grown and blossomed into this vital role of trust.

The media were thrilled with the controversy. It was national news and has convenienced all those who want to relegate our significant work for theatre with 'handbags at dawn and drama queen' headlines! Gay Community News who had the vodka brand as one of their advertisers, also did an article on it. When they called, I opened our entire library of correspondence – even what I regretted writing, to them. It was not reciprocated on the other side. In difficult circumstances GCN wrote a balanced article. Once it was published, I was contacted by the author whom I had not met previously, but who had unlimited access to our records, and he volunteered for our Festival!

The atmosphere in our own event changed. Yes some people were feeling exposed or ostracised but an instant change was that Committee meetings became as they should be. Discussion was open, transparent and welcome. Not all offers of help were sincere. We designated one committee member who had worked in the area to look out for our grant application deadlines. When I finally pressed him, we had missed it by five weeks and even the Lord Mayor could not assist us. The new member wasn't seen again. Some showed up at volunteers meetings to listen and report back. We had made a rule that we would never refer to the other event in public and we would not carry out our work in the context set by them. We would continue to do what we did well and for the right reasons.

All my committee and Board signed a letter to be issued on behalf of IDGTF to parties who had been contacted by the other group posing as us. Everyone studied its content in great detail and made up their own mind whether to sign it or not. We immediately set about recovering our identity and I announced the first ever Winter Festival of the International Dublin Gay Theatre Festival in October. It was good to be concentrating on gay theatre and we needed to pay our debts.

After much deliberation and legal advice we issued the following letters. The first was to Producers in Edinburgh, where I had successfully secured my accommodation. We wrote:

BE ALERT!

Congratulations on your participation in the Edinburgh festival. We have been organising the International Dublin Gay Theatre Festival since 2004 (check www.gaytheatre.ie). Last year we had 140 submissions worldwide and surpassed our 1200th performance in Dublin. Our patrons include multi Tony Award winning playwright Terrence Mc Nally.

In 2009 (May 4th to 17th) we were sponsored by Absolut Vodka for one year and titled ourselves the 'Absolut Dublin Gay Theatre Festival'. Unbeknownst to us in June 2009, after our Festival concluded, one member of our Board, John H Pickering has registered the title of the 'Absolut Dublin Gay Theatre Festival' in his name and the name of three other (non IDGTF Board members), Connell Kennedy (his domestic partner) Mark Banchansky and Gary Tiernan. John Pickering did not alert us to his actions or resign from our company until July 7th. This new company has represented themselves as being our long established event and has used our materials and our intellectual property. This matter is subject to legal action by the International Dublin Gay Theatre Festival Ltd and complaints and actions from various State agencies including the Data Protection Commissioner, the Companies Registration Office and the Office of the Director of Corporate Enforcement.

I am alerting you, that you may be approached by these individuals who are posing as our highly regarded festival. This company has never held a festival. They are not and have no claim on the track record, intellectual property, logo, programmes etc of any event presented by us. They have no background in theatre as an art form. As a fellow producer, we are embarrassed but duty bound to protect you and your company from misrepresentation, hopes or contracts that may not be fulfilled.

The International Dublin Gay Theatre Festival has a vibrant committee and Board of professionals who have volunteered their services to develop this unique art form. Our volunteer corps is also working on our winter programme this October and our seventh unique festival in Dublin in 2010. Please do make a submission to either event on www. gaytheatre.ie.

You are free to make your own choices but the established, not for profit, limited by guarantee company that is the International Dublin Gay Theatre Festival Ltd is taking whatever legal remedies that are open to us to prevent this group from assuming our legitimate business or from presenting any such festival in Dublin in 2010.

Yours sincerely,
Brian Merriman, Executive Chairman,

Artistic Director IDGTF Ltd estb. 2004 August 6th 2009

IDGTF Executive Committee: Brian Merriman (Artistic Director), Gareth Hurley (Volunteers and Web), Chris Nugent (Production Manager) , Eddie Devoy, Derek Mc Cauley (Funding), Francis Larrigan, John O Driscoll (Public Relations), Peter Mc Loughlin, Vickey Curtis (Assistant Technical Manager) Eoin Whelan (Accountant).

I didn't like signing these necessary letters but was fully conscious of the negative personalised campaign being waged against me and the need to protect all our volunteer members for such personal vitriol. We then had to try to unravel the deliberate misrepresentation by this new event to our existing contacts. We wrote:

Dear

The developments over the past few months in relation to the Gay Theatre Festival founded by myself and vested in the good colleagues who make up the International Dublin Gay Theatre Festival LTD have been a source of distress, sadness and embarrassment to us all.

Unbeknownst to the Board or Executive Committee, one Director of our company, with his domestic partner, two people who served as volunteers during this year's festival and our designer, formed a company titled with the trading name we used for 2009 and secretly entered into negotiations with one of our 2009 sponsors to 'replicate' the event which we have been running since 2004. This is most regrettable.

Their legal representatives have copied us with a letter you have received from these five people all claiming to have served as 'Directors and Executive Committee members' of the IDGTF LTD. Four have never served in that capacity. The only one to do so is John Pickering – none of the others were ever members of our Board. We are at a loss to understand when writing to you to clarify matters, why they still 'pose' as such. None served as a service provider, committee member or volunteer in the festival in any arts or theatrical capacity, as none have an established background in producing, participating in or presenting theatre – the core service provided by IDGTF Ltd.

The long established 'Dublin Gay Theatre Festival' is being replicated in name, in the venues we hire and at the exact same time of year. Some of you were even under the impression that I had resigned from the IDGTF or that everyone else had. IDGTF Ltd is fully intact and enjoying very high levels of support, including financial, from the arts and gay communities during this stressful time for which we are very grateful.

To date, the IDGTF has received 2 resignations from its Board – John Pickering as Company Secretary – many weeks after he had set up his new entity, and his daughter Roshene as company member. They were immediately replaced at Board level by our long serving Volunteers and Internal Communications Manager Gareth Hurley as Company Secretary and Chris Nugent our highly qualified Production/Technical Manager as a company member. The Executive Committee is operating at full capacity and includes many people of excellent standing in the theatre, the gay community and in the professions such as accountancy – some have served since its foundation in 2004.

We have tried to limit our communication with you as one of the critical issues we had to deal with was the unilateral dispersal of our income for 2009 by our former Company Secretary, without the knowledge or direction of the Board or Executive, leaving one production company (Fitzgerald & Stapleton) and one venue (Theatre @ Outhouse) unpaid, despite our binding contract in 2009. These matters were satisfactorily addressed within hours of them coming to light in July by the Board. An entirely new transparent system of financial management and accountability has been put in place to ensure that no one person can compromise our contractual relationships in the future under the direction of a qualified professional accountant now a member of the Executive Committee.

We then, despite the personalised correspondence being circulated, set on a proper course of legal action to protect our identity and intellectual property. Some of you may have been under the impression that there was some dispute on the ownership of the IDGTF Ltd – there is not. We invoked a series of legally based actions and some have yielded an initial result which I hope may clarify some of your concerns.

We have received correspondence from this new group's legal representatives which now confirms what we had heard being stated in public, unfortunately it definitively implicates you in the undertaking of this new venture as follows:

Referring to the booking of your venue they state:

"In doing so, they persuaded venue owners and sponsors (including Irish Distillers/ Absolut) to come on board with them for this new and competing festival. The venue owners and sponsors did so in full knowledge that our client and individuals involved were operating a new festival, which had no relationship with the previous festival. In fact we are advised that this may well have been a key persuading factor for the owners and sponsors, i.e. it was precisely because our clients festival is to be distinct from your clients festival and the individuals involved in it that may have grounded their decision to support our client's festival. As such, it was absolutely not relevant to them what festival name or branding was initially used by our client. What was actually relevant to them was that they were dealing with our client's directors (these people they know and in whose festival organisation abilities they have confidence), knowing those directors to have ended their relationship with your client and now to be operating separately to your client's festival. "

Is this your, or a fair understanding of your dealings, with this group and your relationship with us? If you are of that opinion, could you please confirm to us and we will then consider our viability accordingly?

However we also note the additional paragraphs received:

'Entirely without prejudice, and due partly to requirements which are placed upon it by Absolut, we can clarify and confirm the following:

1. Our client has now applied to the Companies Registration Office to change its name to Gay Theatre Ireland Limited, and will obviously use this corporate name going forward in all its communications as required under company legislation.

2. Our client intends to change the name of its festival with immediate effect to 'Absolut Gay Theatre Festival, Dublin, and in the branding for its festival, will utilise rainbow colouring for each of the words "Absolut" (which Absolut/Irish Distillers requires to be presented in black), 'Gay' 'Theatre' Festival' and 'Dublin' instead of the previous block green colour. It will also utilise the word 'new' before the expression Absolut Gay Theatre Festival, Dublin.

3. In its branding it will not use the Oscar Wilde/Green Carnation logo, rather the standard "Comedy/Tragedy" or Janus Masks which commonly represent the theatrical arts.

4. Our client has taken the opportunity to send further clarification letters/emails to each venue and sponsors with whom it has had dealings thus far in relation to its festival in order to reiterate to them that it has nothing to do with your client's festival and instead is operating a new and competing festival. We enclose a copy of the standard communication which has been made with these venues and sponsors in this regard. Our client will also be making clear in any and all of its oral or written communications with the relevant public, including marketing material and on its website (once this is live).

End quote.

We continued our letter: *There are other matters which are still outstanding which we will have properly addressed. It is clear from this however, that had these matters been initiated at the beginning, that no confusion about our identity would have arisen, and none of you would have been put in the position of 'referee'. It is noted that Absolut have also required this group to initiate change and clarity. It is noted too that finally there is acknowledgement that they are 'a new and competing festival'. Was this your impression when they reserved the traditional dates for our festival with you?*

The Board and Executive Committee of the IDGTF are aware that the hiring of your venues is being used to 'legitimise' their structure and intent. The letter from their legal representatives fully confirms your alleged endorsement and this has been transmitted to sponsors and grant-aiding bodies. This is a serious matter if it is untrue.

We fully accept, that like ourselves, you were not in possession of such clarity that now exists, when you accepted a deposit from an entity that you knew only to be our festival. However as can be seen from above it is reasonable to deduce from their protestations that you are being publicly implicated in the 'negotiations' to 'replace' the IDGTF as Dublin's Gay Theatre festival by this other entity. As we have done nothing to place you in this position, we would appreciate an honourable clarification.

You now have a clear understanding and experience of the creativity and intellectual property that has created the IDGTF over the past six years. You are aware that involvement in the IDGTF has over the years been open to everyone in the arts, theatre, gay and mainstream communities. We respectfully ask, is it your company's policy, when you are now fully abreast of the facts, to honour our previous associations or not? We sincerely hope it is.

Alternatively, will you continue to accept these representations which were invoked with our long established contacts, unbeknownst to us, under an opaque guise that did not differentiate between this new company soon to be known as Gay Theatre Ireland ltd and the International Dublin Gay Theatre festival Ltd with whom you have had good relationships since 2004. We sincerely hope you will not – or will you facilitate them at any time span in advance of our previously announced Festival next May.

The Board and Executive Committee of the IDGTF Ltd ask you to honour previous arrangements and to confirm our booking of your premises for the Seventh International Dublin Gay Theatre Festival from May 3rd to 16th 2010 – dates publicly announced three weeks before this new company was incorporated.

In the future, it may be the case that this sorry situation could be best summarised by 'imitation is the best form of flattery' by this small group and their sole commercial sponsor. But the art form is what has motivated and driven the professionals, academics, patrons, artists and volunteers of the IDGTF to date and will continue to inspire their entirely voluntary labour, which has created good employment for artists, venues and an emerging dialogue of understanding between the gay community and mainstream society. This objective is not 'for sale' to any potential commercial sponsor.

IDGTF, like all other arts practitioners, are very conscious of the need to protect and stand over the creative property of an artist or groups of artists and we would not facilitate replication in any way. If new arts forms are to be produced, then this should be encouraged, but the minimum is that any differences should be clear at least in name and dates from established and original events. Registering our licensed trading name for 2009 as their own (which we could not do as it included a trademark), booking only our established venues for the actual same time scale, and sending letters of a personalised nature about former colleagues is not art, it is not fair and it does nothing to promote the inclusion of the voices of gay related art and artists in theatre as an art form – the sole aim of the IDGTF Ltd.

We have over 30 submissions to date for 2010 and are also presenting a winter programme of gay theatre for the first time from October 23rd to 31st. We are in negotiations to stage the premiers of a work by Terrence Mac Nally and the USA's pioneering gay playwright Doric Wilson in 2010 as well as encouraging submissions from Irish artists. We need clarity as to your intentions as to whether you will continue your association with our long established festival, or whether this new entity, now in the process of changing its company name, is to be given the facilities previously hired by the IDGTF Ltd. We need clarity in order to proceed with honouring our negotiations with the many applicants who hope to present their works under our banner in 2010. They need to be confident that all contracts entered into with IDGTF will be honoured in full.

We trust that you will honour our long established arrangements as we have always only dealt with you in good faith, and dedicated our work to the furtherance of theatre and gay theatre as a valid and vibrant art form. We regret the fact that you have been involved in this mess and have done our utmost to maintain our standards of clarity and good faith at all times. The Board and Executive Committee look forward to an early and positive reply so that this vibrant arts event can continue to flourish in 2010.

Yours sincerely, Brian Merriman, Executive Chairman, On behalf of the Board and Executive Committee of the IDGTF ltd – members listed below, presenting Dublin's gay theatre festival since 2004.

Each Board member read it, and each Executive Committee member read it and all agreed to sign it as a fair representation of these shabby outcomes. The chips were down and many people of integrity stood up for what was correct. It did demean us to have to do so, but in light of what was being circulated about us we had to respond. A letter from the other side emerged in an Equality Tribunal case I won, later as evidence against me. The Equality Officer described it as a 'castigation' in his findings. Enough said as to the tactics being employed. However I knew the effort being put in was designed to knock us out before we presented our 2010 programme. It was also highly personalised as the 'castigation' analysis confirmed.

After a lengthy correspondence, we managed to get outstanding records returned. I found them dumped without warning in black plastic sacks and in my front garden on the very busy South Circular Road – lucky I was coming home that day. Some of those documents were confidential and others, vital to claim the grants used by us for the 2009 event. The deadline to claim these vital funds had long passed due to incomplete records. We successfully appealed this situation and were awarded the monies owed many months later.

The tactics got dirtier as our efforts to affirm our own identity were established and dignified. Plays were suspected as being poached and only three of our hundreds of producers also jumped ship – suffering substantial losses as a result. All have since returned. During the 2012 Festival our posters were constantly ripped down and our brochures frequently and mysteriously removed from public venues. GCN ran a fundraiser in one of the gay bars and we asked could we distribute our brochures at the event. They said yes and we found that Absolut attired promotional staff were removing our literature – brochures that never referred to them in any way, in our own gay venues.

The worst instance occurred when our youngest ever playwright, 18 year old Aaron Rodgers reported that his posters for his first play were being ripped down in venues. We investigated and it was true. We could not keep a poster up – upon which the theatre companies were now depending for their revenues – for more than an hour. I went public on Facebook stating that we knew the staff were not ripping down our posters and appealing to those who were to cease. I penned the phrase 'An Absolute disgrace'. We got a lot of support, but not before it was reported maliciously by the perpetrators, that we had accused the staff of doing it to the venues. Another lie. We battled on, focussing on promoting good theatre and quality art.

We had gotten a response from Absolut's legal department and they ensured the other company's name was slightly amended not to be identical to the one used by us the previous year under licence. They denied the letter of agreement for two years was valid – but even though their senior manager involved was himself gay, his local knowledge would surely balance up our fears that they had themselves been duped by the 'coup' group. Common sense did not prevail and the Absolut brand launched an extensive advertising campaign using the identical ads from the previous year, in support of this new entity. It is astounding to think that such a major company would engage in this form of 'corporate bullying' of a small 'not for profit' voluntary group that had clearly been the originator of the concept and owner of the intellectual property of the Festival, established in 2004.

We had no resources except our morality to challenging these large bodies but we did pursue them through all legitimate channels. Despite the engagement of the Advertising Standards Authority the industry regulator – they found no 'confusion' in identical advertisements being used for two distinct events! In the Vodka company they defended themselves saying there was no confusion between the two events, but it was then discovered they had paid the last trench of our 2009 sponsorship to this new entity – even they were confused! They mischievously stated in press reports that they were 'continuing to support the event' but the reaction from many people was that despite this endorsement, their association was discrediting them. This sense of abuse of power and perceived collaboration to destroy the International Festival, though amusing to some of the gleeful, soon began to be viewed with concern and disgust in many fair minds. Our experience with the regulatory bodies left us with a much keener sense of how Ireland fell so far when recession caused by the collapse of standards in the banking sector, took hold. The powerful are listened to in corporate Ireland.

The Irish Times then did an article on two gay festivals and featured an interview with their MD. No comment was solicited from us and their spin was printed verbatim. It was astonishing and disgraceful journalism. Our years of work to establish a valid cultural identity was now demeaned again by pictures of ageing transvestite 'nuns' skipping up a street! When asked to define gay theatre in the newspaper, their MD repeated a truncated version of our own definition. When pressed on what it meant the reply was reported as 'that will suffice' – end of discourse! The reason for the division was cited by him as 'artistic differences' with no further comment. We were never invited to contribute, but then again we had no lucrative sponsor with a large advertising budget behind us!

The division between the entities was clear - It was about governance and control. Those who guffawed at our woes were in fact at risk of endorsing bad governance. My own technical director was approached and reported an offer that if he joined them 'there's a salary in this for us'. The vodka company was being viewed as an endless pit. The problem was they did not know how to create the theatre as our team clearly did. Their website recorded as their technical director a good friend of ours who wasn't even in the country and had no association with them! The bubble was deflating but gasping to get to opening night.

The vodka company appeared to pump in much more money into the alternative event, than previously to us and it was a theatrical, box office and financial disaster. A governance error in their online box office was discovered by one of our curious members who could log in every evening to order tickets and be told exactly how many were still available – in far too many cases, considering the ambitions of their artists, it was 90-100% capacity available within 30 minutes to curtain up! Their plays were selling by days into their run for 'two-for one' and many shows were cancelled. As had been proven from their vulgarly dominant vodka campaign, which saw the first dip in our box office, the previous year – this bigger campaign which now only draped that event's logo in the rainbow colours owned by the vodka brand', recorded a box office of less than 50% of the previous year. We in turn had 48 full houses!

They had booked our venues, taken and replicated our dates and produced performances back to back with our long established dates – ensuring that those who would really suffer were the participating companies in this ego driven battle. Box office was already dipping with the onslaught of recession, so to stage combined, the biggest amount of shows ever in the first fortnight in May was administratively stupid in the extreme. We had even suggested to them in writing that they stage their event at another time of the year and we would wish them well. In truth they probably would have erased us considering their resources, but then they would have to admit their campaign to pose as us was in fact falsely based. It was a game of poker and we would not blink because we had nothing on our conscience. For a major brand to associate with such a debacle is just reward.

A lengthy legal correspondence went on all year. We eventually retrieved our property including street banners and archive and full records on file. The Companies Office allowed them to register the similar name and the Data Protections Commissioner accepted their assurances not to use our data base. It was an incredible waste of time, designed only to bring down the event owned by everyone who had built it and not just a few. I got my clearest indication of their impending disaster when in another rambling email from their Managing Director, I was invited to join their Board three weeks before the start of our Festival. It gave me no pleasure, but I knew our concentration on our artform was heading for a victory and the viscous personal attacks had failed to sustain a group of volunteers who all left the entity shortly after.

The accounts showed that IDGTF ended their 2010 event which had begun for the first time, with no seed capital, with all bills paid and 12,000 euros in the bank to build the following year. This was the achievement of an open, transparent, voluntary process. Despite getting a much greater influx of capital from their sponsors, rumoured to be up to 20,000 euros in cash plus the 50 - 100,000 euros advertising campaign, the Absolut branded Festival lost all of this and 6,000 euros more. Absolut were not to be seen again and the vodka event folded immediately.

Maliciously though, the other event continued to pose as viable and suggested information to grant bodies, probably to ensure we would not get our previous allocation, even in the year they no longer would exist. The festival named after Absolut, with their full permission, did untold damage to gay theatre, turned off volunteers, economically damaged their participating companies, fed the gossip and ensured a theatrical experience that many companies in Edinburgh assured us, was one of the most negative they ever had endured.

Volunteers left, the media could once again describe our culture as 'handbags at dawn' and the millionaire driver of 'the split' abandoned all involvement immediately when his event registered a loss of 6,000 euros. As his track record demonstrated prior to my involving him in the IDGTF, he had rarely if ever darkened the doorstep of a theatre and once the Vodka bottle was empty – he was never seen again! Just as Absolut turned the Dublin Fringe Festival into an identity-less event, they had failed to do so with us. The Dublin Fringe is unique to our city and our artists. The Absolut Fringe could be held in any place in the world – to us identity is more important than vodka money. This is not partnership or support but a result of the restricted opportunities alcohol firms have to generally advertise. Jameson, a sister brand in Diageo know how to do it, as does Ulster Bank in supporting the arts, while positively associating their good brands with the arts identity. No such sophistication was available to us and those who went down the greedy road did their sponsors and their own reputation no favours. That is not what business supporting the arts or big companies helping voluntary effort is about. What we endured truly was an absolute disgrace!

The IDGTF 2010 atmosphere and box office success had returned to where it had been in the early days. We had showcased the greatest number of new Irish plays that year, and attracted many new volunteers previously reluctant to join our entity up to 2010.

We were back on track as a team of positively motivated and focussed volunteers. We were, bruised, but holding all our meetings up until the Festival opened, united, poorer but loyal to each other and our shared ambition. We had all saved the Dublin Gay Theatre Festival! We had done so by staying committed to the core ethos that inspired so many people to give of their time and talents since 2004. That was my personal motivation. I had resisted all temptation to even check online what they were doing and programmed as always, with one thing in mind – showcasing the best in gay theatre.

Our friends at home and abroad rallied with many famous playwrights donating to a fundraiser in New York City to assist the Festival, organised by Ambassador Kathleen Warnock. Our volunteers worked hard with much less resources to create good theatre, but strikingly a wonderful atmosphere, long since missing, was restored. On the packed Gala night which attracted over 200 guests, I was presented by the volunteers with a bottle of Smirnoff! Everyone got the message and the absolute disgrace of corporate collusion with internal gay deception, had failed completely.

Why it is necessary for voluntary effort to go through this is a debate others can contribute to, but it is astonishing that we were the subject of such negative action. The end result was equally astonishing as David proved more than a match for the branded negative Goliath!

scene 6
2009

Love that's fresh and still unspoiled, love that's only slightly soiled, love for sale

Cole Porter lyric.

At the beginning of 2009 I tried once again to tackle some of the untidiness of the original company formation. As part of the transfer from a limited company, to the not for profit company in 2006, the entire residue from one Festival was transferred via a 'director's loan to the successor company. I did not like seeing myself in the accounts as being a debtor of this new company, especially as I only held these monies in trust from the collaborative effort that was the previous entity. All attempts to address this were resisted by the other director. I was particularly concerned as the accounts also showed that these monies were accumulating 'interest'. I consulted the auditors and confirmed that we could in fact 'donate' this money to the not for profit entity now in operation. I tried to get agreement for this and failed and eventually brought the matter to the attention of the Executive Committee. I was also irritated by the fact that if I paid a bill for the Festival, the refund was appearing as a payment to me rather than payment for the service provided e.g our Edinburgh visits. I did receive a donation towards expenses for my 12 months of the year service, set by the Administrative Director on a par with his, despite the huge difference in the costs involved. However I had never sought anything from this voluntary effort and only accepted a contribution when funds allowed. That ceased after 2009 when we got back control of our company.

The Executive were dismayed at the resistance to donate these 'loans' to the company and at a heated meeting the other Director eventually agreed to do so but suggested that the interest recorded in the accounts go to him. This too rightly angered the group and eventually the agreement given was honoured many weeks later. This event turned out to be a fortunate equivalent to 'De Valera getting back control of the Irish ports in 1938 on the eve of the outbreak of war'. Had we not succeeded in getting back these 'loans' we may not have been able to survive the 'war' that was about to break out!

Festival 2009 was a very good programme initially branded as the Sixth International Dublin Gay Theatre Festival. Frank Mc Guinness the celebrated Irish playwright attended the performance of his rarely seen play 'The Bird Sanctuary' by the Actor's Circle, London. He gave Mark Pollard's direction a high honour when he proclaimed 'You got it right!'. We had made huge efforts to get a play from Zimbabwe called 'Loupe'. Africa is a hostile environment for the expression of any facet of same sex culture. We worked hard to facilitate the Imdlalo Productions involvement but despite the best efforts, we went dark in 'The Project' for one session in our opening week. I was very disappointed.

Bright Heights Theatre Company from the UK made up a lot for this when they staged the Irish Premiere of 'A Dog Called Redemption' in 'The Project'. Mark Pollard had submitted this dramatic and dark tale of homelessness to me previously. Written by Matthew Landers, I liked the work but such was its content that nothing less than a superb production would pull it off on stage. I said no to featuring it in 2008, because I wanted to see it in Edinburgh that August. As my crazy schedule there clashed, I was sending someone else to see it instead of me and Mark rightly persisted as he is known to do, until I rearranged everything to see it myself. It was set in one of those damp and dingy tunnels only Edinburgh can call a performance space. Mark stood at the back of the venue seeing me writing furiously all throughout the production. At the end he told me when I stood up to approach him, he was ready for what he thought would be an avalanche of criticism because I had written so much. My first words were 'welcome to Dublin!' He was gobsmacked. He asked what had I written? I said from two minutes in I knew it was a great production. I then spent my time pouring out venue ideas, marketing plans etc for its appearance next year. In the end, Matthew deservedly won the best writer that year and his co-star Graham Elwell the best actor!

'Silenciados' was a wonderful piece of theatre from Sudham Teatro, Madrid. Almost entirely choreographic with few words, this was a compilation of five different stories of gay oppression ranging from an Auschwitz prisoner to

Octavio Acuna a gay activist killed in a small town in 2004. At the end of this powerful and breathtaking performance, I asked to keep a small prop – a sign held up during the show painted 'No Intoleranca' – I still have it.

Our previous short from Imogen Brodie had now evolved into a full play and 'The Iron Eyelashes – After the Wall' returned to acclaim. I had been recommended from a visit to the USA, a production of the well known play "Two Boys in a Bed On a Cold Winter's Night" Bed' by James Edwin Parker and Adam Weinstock's 'Creative Concept Productions'. This was a little 'old hat' on face value, but I couldn't help being curious to note that it was first produced about 17 years after decriminalisation in the USA. We were at the exact same stage of our development and I wondered what relevance it would have to us? My Technical Director, Chris Nugent did trojan work building a raked bed and with the added attraction of a former porn star in a leading role, the play sold out!

David Wray was at this stage the Honorary Musical Director of the Festival. His company produced 'Listen To My Heart' the music of David Friedman starring amongst others Ben Morris who went on to win the TV show for the cast of 'Fame'. I found the setting disappointing and it had failed in particular to deal with the live acoustic of the hard surrounding of Smock Alley. But the show was musically so strong and succeeded in making unfamiliar repertoire familiar.

New Thematical Dance Theatre, Berlin, Germany, presented a Russian dance collaboration called 'Tchaikovsky's Wife'. I was delighted and relieved our audience supported this tale of the appearance at the gay composer's funeral of his wife and her mental torment all explained through dance and atmospheric setting. The Russian dance temperament did not suit our ethos and I discovered their aggressive stage manager shoving my crew around during the fast changeover. I intervened immediately and stopped the change-over until the behaviour changed. Luckily our diversity meant we had our own technical volunteer that year who could speak Russian. After the drama was over, both stage manager and bullied volunteer appeared before me the best of friends!

Suzanne Lakes too evolved her earlier short into a full length play called 'Goodnight Alice'. Lakes writes in the old style Dublin wit and she and Ciara Mc Guinness are masters of their traditional craft. A wonderful period piece came to us from Theatre North 'Lord Arthur's Bed' told the story of a gay couple moving into an old house and discovering under the floorboards a calling card of previous occupants in 1868. The precursor to Oscar Wilde's trials in 1895 was the trial of cross dressing couple Ernest (Stella) and Fred (Fanny) who are celebrating Stella's marriage to Lord Arthur Clinton. This terrific piece was greatly assisted by a fine cast including Spencer Charles Noll as the crossdressing lead – another nominated performance of note.

Bash'd was anarchic and alternative rap tribute performed by two gay hip-hop artists 'Feminem' and 'T-Bag'. It was high energy and unexpected theatre from 'The Gay4pay Co-op', Alberta, Canada that played to strong and appreciative houses – even pleasing the Irish Times!

A beautiful three hander of 'The Picture' (of Doran Gray) came to us from Neal Utterbuck's pen in Indiana USA. Three equally good performances teased out gender, sexuality and morality on a treatment that had evolved through our own dramaturg process –ending with a fine piece of theatre. The team also contributed a hilarious mimed short by using only their 'thumbs' in the shorts programme – called 'hand job' – very clever theatre.

'Three To A Room Theatre Company' travelled from Victoria, Australia with a gripping internet based one man show called 'I Love You, Bro'. This macabre tale was powerfully portrayed in a tight script by Adam Cass, inspired by real events in a teenage chatroom.

With our Kildare youth team going on to other things, we met with Independent Youth Theatre Dublin who presented Shaun Dunne's 'Killed by Curriculum'. This was extraordinary good writing from our youngest playwright, where he told five stories interspersing them with the poetry curriculum of the Leaving Certificate Examinations in Ireland. Good performance and clever structure earned this 19 year old a playwrighting nomination and began a good association between this talented stable of young artists and the Festival. I split this run between the youth group and another young playwright from the USA. Dan Bernitt had never been outside the USA before and his first passport led him to Ireland. His complex text of a fraternity 'Phi Alpha Gamma', could easily have been played by fours actors (and I would like to see that treatment) but instead the energetic Bernitt played them all himself with success.

Truant theatre Company from Manchester delved into the role of teachers challenged by homophobic bullying in schools in 'Care Takers'. Written by Billy Cowan, we meet an ambitious headmistress and new teacher Ms Lawson who believes her young student 'Jamie Harrow' is being bullied because he is gay. The battle between protocol and the instincts that brought the young teacher to her vocation are played out to dramatic outcome. Two great parts for women, in a highly relevant piece of theatre.

TOSOS returned to us from New York with a comedy 'Pig tale' by Chris Weikel. Directed by Mark Finlay, this comedy took a turn when Johnny's (Patrick Porter) boyfriend 'Dave' (Jesse May) wakes up and he has been turned into a pig! Add to that a stoner 'Kyle' (Tim Deitrich) and a 'Cuban Trannie' (the return of Moe Bertram) and you have 'an urban fairie tale'. As previously referred to, Artscape presented their final play (for a while) with 'Careful' by Fiona Coyne, TV presenter of South Africa's 'The Weakest Link', inspired by the Festival itself and producing two first class performances by Diane Wilson and Deirdre Woulhouter.

Wiczy Theatre from Torun, Poland created another first in their presentation of 'Broken Nails' in English. We meet Marlene Deitrich and her dresser. Deitrich is a puppet masterfully controlled by the puppeteer and tells the demanding story of the final 13 years of her life as an ageing beauty and icon. This was a thrilling and an athletic performance of great skill.

John Arthur Pinckard Productions squeezed in their production of 'Minor Gods' into the space at Outhouse. Set in a confined apartment this tale of 'Henry' a prominent geneticist and 'Felix' a rent boy, revealed an unexpected connection between these two men. Strong acting and direction made Pinckard's play a perfect fit for this intimate venue.

We had a plethora of one man shows apply again, especially from America. I chose Jeffrey Solomon's multi part show 'Santa Clause is Coming out' for the 2009 programme. Yes even Santa is 'gay' and this hilarious tale had a strong underscore, well presented by the versatile Solomon. Elizabeth Whitney is a pint sized powerhouse who presented 'Wonder Woman – The Musical'. This hilarious tour de force immediately grew her own cult following and I was delighted to note even my hard working committee loose themselves in the cheesiness and mirth of this impactful show.

I always like to have Oscar Wilde feature in the programme if possible and this year the contrast between 'The Picture' and 'More Lives Than One' helped tell his story and make it relevant to modern times. Originally inspired by Micheal

Mac Liammoir's 'The Importance of being Oscar' Leslie Clack gave us a swift tour of Wildean highlights in true Oscariana in a one man show in the Cobalt Café. The Focus Theatre was back with us in association with writer Elizabeth Moynihan and her play 'Walnuts Remind Me of My Mother'. This play though a little too dependent on angst was a worthy debut from Moynihan as a writer. Its Irish setting made it particularly relevant to the Festival's intent on encouraging new Irish writing.

The Shorts, including Neal Utterbuck's 'Hand Job' continued our plan of encouragement with the hilarious 'Adventures of..' possibly writer Kathleen Warnock's best piece in the Festival to date. A 12 year old discovers who she is when her sci-fi adventure TV heroes comes to life! Rachel Devlin MC'd , enthralled and intimated the shorts audience with her charismatic German fraulein chanteuse. J Stephen Brantley's 'Break' from New York, dealt with a young junkie withdrawing from a heroin addiction squatting in a house when the owner turns up – with a powerful role from Hunter Gilmore. Mark Yeates play brought us to heaven where 'George' was to be sent back but this time as a gay man. Yeates was another who first volunteered with us and ended up as a shorts playwright with 'Seamus,Seamus'. I wrote my piece bringing together Pope Benedict's anti-gay Christmas message with the teachings he learned as a boy in 'Hitler Youth', with Kenny Moynihan, Rian Corrigan and Keith Willis playing in 'Seventy'. 'Singing Out Six' became just that with six performers. The stress of the 2009 Festival took its toll on my sinuses and the audience were instead treated to a great night of music and theatre with six performers, all roped in at short notice, who tore the house down each night in the Cobalt Café, to my eternal appreciation.

I finished off my Wildean programme by scheduling five performances of The Peculius Stage Company's joyous treatment of Oscar Wilde's 'The Happy Prince'. I had written a song of that title for 'A Chelsea Affair' which was later performed in the National Concert Hall. I was charmed by this interpretation when I saw it in a cramped hotel room stage in Edinburgh. It began an interesting and valuable association between myself and its young 'Prince', Callum Cheatle – who was already showing all the signs of a deep theatrical intelligence and a capacity to bring people together to do good theatre – could the baton be passed on? I was hopeful. I coincidentally got an email from two young parents enquiring was there any show suitable for children in the Festival? The father said he was determined to bring his 6 year old up, with a perspective of diversity. I had failed to make an association between the Festival and the National Children's Theatre at the Ark in Temple Bar. Each approach was politely turned down as they always programed at least 18 months ahead. 'The Happy Prince' proved a ground breaker in that one matinee attracted 12 children and their parents – finally making us truly inclusive!

 I have already discussed the charitable contribution made by Emma Fitzgerald and Aine Stapleton in donating the proceeds of 'A Dog of All Creation' an uneven contemporary dance piece of varying duration, that too broke new ground in presenting naked women performers for the first time in the Festival.

I hope sometime that the true value and accomplishment of the 2009 Festival will be appreciated. The nasty and relentless atmosphere of closeted coup destroyed a very accomplished year of gay theatre for many who worked truly hard to make it a success. In retrospect, it is important that that success is celebrated too! Perhaps our survival and further evolution was its greatest legacy!

Just when I thought I would be winding down, we were faced with a new opportunity to change the Festival for the better. Gone was the resistance to change and we moved very fast. For the first time members of the Executive made up the majority of company members with Gareth Hurley as Company Secretary and Chris Nugent accepting membership. Secondly we sorted the mess of our accounts out and immediately circulated copies of all our financial dealings to the Executive Committee. A representative of the committee Dominik Brzeski and later Joe Duggan both qualified accountants were given full access to our bank account and indeed took over some financial management. No more blank cheques were ever signed and no cash payments were made to companies. Each participating company now provided their bank details and their box office grant was transferred directly into their account by electronic transfer online.

More women joined the committee and everyone had a clear role. Emma Weafer, Siobhan Killen, Ciara Nolan, Rachel Fayne, Annick Thijs and Jen Butler took up Executive positions. Box office calculations were now done by a troika Gareth Hurley, Dominik or Joe and chaired by Board member, Francis Larrigan. The few 'spies' who offered help quickly went away as they clearly saw our sole motivation was our own ambition to present gay theatre – nothing else. A lot of work was put into getting our audit working well. We had no money, no venues, no sponsor, no successive trading name, all we had was lots of people interested in gay theatre and an ambition that nothing would stop us.

Excessive spending was curtailed. Gone was the costly train crash of a box office system – the following year the box office cost was reduced by 99%. No more dress suit hiring for Gala nights, no hiring of photographers or media monitoring agencies to tell our sponsor what they already knew from their own media tracking. All the wasteful vanity projects were gone. We then set out to re-establish our own identity and within weeks announced on October 14th the programme of the International Dublin Gay Theatre Festival's first winter programme, in the presence of the Lord Mayor Cllr Emer Costello who hosted us magnificently! She was the fourth successive occupant of the office to do so.

We sent a clear message from our launch:

"We are very proud citizens of Dublin – a city that embraces inclusiveness and diversity. We are very proud to invite artists from all over the world to come to Dublin each year for our unique event. Since I established this theatre festival in 2004 and vested its ownership in the gay and arts community, we have had 1100 performances staged in Dublin from across five continents".

"Volunteerism is a finite resource especially with the high standards of delivery required for such a unique international event. This year following our May Festival, one of our directors resigned and I would like to acknowledge the many good works John Pickering did for the Festival during his tenure. He has been ably replaced by our long serving Executive Committee member Gareth Hurley as Company Secretary. With John went one of our sponsors, but happily as we lost the alcohol, we fully retained the artform. Theatre is the only reason we undertake this endeavour. We strive to give a voice, a space, a benchmark and a recognition to gay art and artists through theatre as an acknowledged artform in a changing Ireland. That's what motivates us, it's a valid artistic endeavour, shared by our growing audiences and one which we continue to commit ourselves to achieving to the best standard possible"

"Looking to the future we have 70 submissions already from five continents this year and we have two and a half months to go before the submissions deadline. The art is there, the artists are willing to travel and we must rely on you to ensure our viability for 2010 and beyond. With these changes also comes a very generous and active response from the gay community. 'Outhouse' the gay community centre has supported us in this winter festival and there has been an influx of professional expertise onto our Executive and Board. Joining the long serving stalwarths are PRO, RTE's John O Driscoll, Accountant Eoin Whelan, Dublin City Council's Derek Mc Auley, former Manager of The George, Peter Mc Loughlin and Dublin Devil's Francis Larrigan."

The address went on to contextualise the new work ahead. Boyzone singer Stephen Gately had just died but his husband Andrew Cowles was excluded from many expressions of sympathy on this tragic death. Civil partnership was still a live issue.

I also addressed another issue. Most young people were being defined in a commercial environment mainly owned by straight people. I wondered how to break into that environment and present a slight alternative. I invented Mr Gay Dublin first of all and then Mr Gay Ireland with the support of Scene City Magazine, to try to mobilise a civic spirit in young people to take their roles as young gays into their community. The Mr Gay title was a suitable incentive to get them to engage with us. Also most of my theatre work had been done to support HIV and AIDS, with the Festival never going to make a profit, I needed another HIV fundraiser initiative –so Mr Gay Ireland and Mr Gay Northern Ireland was invented and I associated the Festival with it in order to broaden its appeal to younger people. By 2011 we had raised over 110,000 euros for gay and HIV charities. We had supported the HIV housing charity Round Tower, BelongTo youth services, the KAL case, Dublin Gay Switchboard, the Festival and very largely the New Fill HIV restoration Project at St James Hospital. Young gay men were coming out in their own local media – like the 'Newry Democrat', the 'Belfast Telegraph' and local radio. The 'Sligo Advertiser' had run an ad campaign to vote for Mr Gay Sligo in our webvote. The 'Monaghan Post' even rang Hollywood for the result of Mr Gay International. As part of their participation, the heat winners had to organise a fundraiser in their own community for HIV. 100% of the funds raised went directly to the charity. In Gorey, County Wexford, a grandfather accompanied his grandson Mr Gay Wexford on his HIV charity walk in the small town.

In Moate Co Westmeath another HIV walk was held, this time led by the contestants entire family. One father brought sponsorship cards into his workplace for another contestant. A 22 year old contestant came out as HIV positive during the stage show, having expressed an interest to me to be in the competition 'because you are fundraising for me'. The finalists then had to raise their visibility in their local town (plagued by the high rate of young male suicide). Finally we brought them to Dublin for a weekend where they were introduced to many of the community groups for discussion on gay rights, safe sex and HIV prevention with Doctors, community advocates and the Gardai.

I had not much interest in the main prize, which was representing Ireland in the Mr Gay competitions internationally. The Festival's then Administrative Director was flown to the USA, Palm Springs and West Hollywood, twice at Mr Gay Ireland's expense, to accompany the winning Irish delegate. One year the delegate insisted I go too and as such I brought my human rights agenda to the international events with success.

I later became a Director of Mr Gay World (with responsibility for rules and policy, Africa and Europe), which was established at what became known as the 'Dublin Summit'. The Irish Final was always adjudicated on the basis of fundraising, an interview before a panel of peers and international representatives, the webvote and five Judges , two gay, two straight women and a straight man. One year, the then Administrative Director nominated his daughter's partner as a judge and he enthused greatly about his experience. Suddenly this charitable activity became something apparently 'unsavoury' in his mind. There was indeed an unsavoury element of it, but I was the victim. The former Administrative Director wrote letters to Festival sponsors alleging amongst other things, that MGI was demeaning to the Festival and citing it as one reason for his exit.

Later I began to receive threats personally and to my home arising from a deal made by a volunteer with a company with an association with the Administrative Director. The threats were of such a serious and sexual nature that I called the Gardai and eventually took the company trading as Read's of Nassau Street to the Equality Tribunal in the absence of any apology. There is no point in advocating people to stand up to such behaviour if I wasn't willing to do so myself. The case was heard in the middle of the 2011 Festival run! In their defence, John Pickering not only provided a 'character reference' for the perpetrator, but also an unredacted copy of the letter he had sent about me to third parties, which they now subsequently tried to use to demean my good name, in front of the Tribunal. The impartial Equality Officer in finding in my favour, referred to the letter as a 'castigation' of my character. I won the first ever same sex harassment case under Irish equality legislation involving two men and was awarded financial compensation. Other members of the gay community also offered character references to the guilty party, many of these also supported the vodka festival. The full outcome of the case is available on www.equalitytribunal.ie – key in my surname. It is truly dangerous when people lose sight of the real issues of commonality to that extent, but perhaps some were not fully aware of the details being investigated.

I had to address this personalised letter writing at the winter launch: "One of the issues we also face is homophobia and that can be internalised. Writing to straight sponsors, grant aiding bodies or supporters about my involvement in a charity event as being inappropriate for the Festival is something I totally reject. To identify the recipients, those good people, as those who might entertain such homophobia, is incredibly insulting to them. There is nothing inappropriate about raising the profile of young gay people in rural Ireland, even in a fun way. Our young male suicide rate is evidence enough that the freedoms prevailing, sometimes just through anonymity, in urban centres, are not as common place in rural or isolated communities. This prejudice causes anguish and isolation for young gay men sometimes resulting in tragic circumstances. Positive young role models are essential in rural Ireland. We do not take ourselves that seriously in being afraid to add to the fun of gay life in Ireland too, to our charitable endeavours."

"Whatever we do to generate positivity is fine by me. Whatever we do to raise funds for excellent charities is fine by me too. It helps young people embrace whatever gift of love and sexuality they have been given, to live their life to the full. To attempt to discredit this is internalised homophobia at its worst". In the meantime Max Krzyzanowski, Mr Gay Ireland, won the first ever Mr Gay World contest in Vancouver that year and went on to be a strong advocate for gay rights through his leadership of LGBT Noise. That year also Mr Gay Ireland had not funded a trip for the Administrative Director to join the delegation.

Our launch was the last official function of our kind supporter, Jack Gilligan who retired that week as Dublin City Arts Officer. We presented him with some gay theatre memorabilia and invited him to speak. The Winter Festival finally got 'Loupe' to Ireland from Zimbabwe. Joe Steiff's 'Golden Corral' was a last minute cancellation but 'Verity Alicia Mavenawitz' and actor Eimear Morrissey presented a new production of 'And The There Was Me'. We heralded another Festival first - the Irish Traveller community is harsh in its treatment of its gay members.

Playwright Rosaleen Mac Donagh with the assistance of 'Upstate Theatre Company' staged a play reading of her gay Traveller play 'John and Josie' to huge acclaim. The audience were spellbound at the depth of the piece and it ranks as one of the best play readings ever in the history of the Festival. The ambition to see it fully staged remains elusive. I was joined as a playwright by Suzanne Lakes, Gina Costigan and Sharon Sexton in an all Irish Theatre Shorts programme in the Cobalt Café where Irish stand-up comedian Gearoid Farrelly also made an appearance. I collated some of my other work including my 12 minute short film 'No Evidence' and my two plays 'The Gentleman Caller' and 'Tumbling Down' into another programme of retrospective Irish gay stories in Outhouse. It was to be an 'annus horribulus' but we were on our way doing what we do best.

The Winter Festival put the International Dublin Gay Theatre Festival identity back clearly on the map. It was made possible by many Irish artists who this time donated the entire box office to help the Festival get back on its feet. So many actors do that – they help so many good causes with their time and talents and are often not fully appreciated when it needs to be reciprocated so that they can earn an honest living through the arts. It ran from October 24-31st and gave a great boost of confidence to our battered volunteers and reminded them what gay theatre is really about. We were financially clear of all debts within three months and determined to fulfil our 2010 Festival programme.

2010

Since we can not change reality, let us change the eyes that see reality

Nikos Kazantzakis, author of 'Zorba the Greek'

Two gay Festivals was the chant of 2010 in the media and the chattering classes as Wilde would say. Ours remained a curated programme. We also had a new sponsor in Google and made proud new flags to be flown on the Quays! 'RTE supporting the Arts' sponsorship gave us free radio prime time ads – an impossibility with any alcohol in the title. Our Website had a bright new image thanks to the endless generosity and talent of our new designer Gerry Cleary. Gerry an artist and graphic designer is an old friend and he completely revitalised our images and printing and made a previously tiresome activity a pleasure.

We were being taken on night by night with a programme that accepted all entries. We didn't care. The quality of the 2010 Festival programme was sufficient to demonstrate what we were about. We cut our cloth to suit our measure. We no longer offered free accommodation. We lowered our ticket prices as recession bit, and we, through Mark O Donoghue, Alan Jacobs, Derek Cosgrave and their technical team fitted out empty spaces and turned them into venues. The production companies flocked to us! Regardless of the outcome, I had structured this Festival so that all the bills were paid in full by opening day. The survival of the Festival into the future would be determined by the robustness of the box office. We were fully prepared to wind it up if it had no financial future. The programme was very strong out of the 148 submissions received, we were presenting 173 performances, 124 performers, 27 plays over 16 nights with tickets from 8-15 euros. It was sink or swim!

We began a new association with the magnificent support of the James Joyce Cultural Centre in North Great Georges Street. It was wonderful to house a programme featuring Tennessee Williams (Auto Da fe), Joyce's only play

'Exiles', the story of Joe Orton ('Noel Road, 25') , 'Oh What A Wilde Wardrobe' by Martin Williamson, and the works of AE Houseman in such an auspicious premises over a fortnight. Joyce's portrait hung to the right of the stage area and one felt its expressions change with each performance! Mansel David's 'Take Desire Away' was a master class in this solo theatrical form. His sensitive and insightful portrayal of AE Houseman's works was positively received on RTE televisions arts programme 'The View' reviewed by Professor Diarmuid Ferriter.

'Noel Road,25' was performed in Spanish and once again with subtitles allowed us to entice the deaf gay community into the Festival. The dialogue was passionate and rapid and the subtitles flew by at a dizzying speed! 'Exiles' was reviewed by the Festival reviewers as follows: "It was Joyce's stated desire to have his play sit on the shelf beside the works of Ibsen et al – this will only happen if the plays are stacked alphabetically'. The original script which was rather 'Cowardian' arrived full of menacing glottal screaming and posing that made a nonsense of the piece but…it sold!

Bottom Dog Theatre Company from Limerick treated us to a rare autobiographical piece from Limerick Actor, Myles Breen. Breen had worked with me in the Olympia previously and gave a very strong performance as an ageing drag queen in 'Language Unbecoming A Lady'. Callum Cheatle (The Happy Prince) returned to do his own play 'The Photographer' and study and deliver his final university exams all through the night with colleagues Steffan Griffiths and Paul Thorpe – they all still graduated with impressive honours! As they had a shorter run, I included a community group with their production of 'Beyond Therapy' by Christopher Durang, directed by Diane O Keeffe, for two performances only.

We had new and refreshing visitors from South Africa. Irish child abuse whistle blower Andrew Madden as previously referenced, introduced Peter Hayes's wonderful performance as an abuse survivor facing his elderly nemesis in 'The Tricky Part'. Hayes also wrote and directed the charming and riveting Pam Ngwabeni in the true account of lesbian corrective rape in South Africa 'Ncamisa – Kiss the Women! – a true highlight in storytelling. Both artists collaboration here was near theatre perfection. The latter play thankfully lifting the sales of this worthy joint offering. I was later contacted by an arts correspondent of 'The Guardian' newspaper who tackled Hayes, as a man, for writing a women's story! He referred the journalist to me and a glowing endorsement article followed!

Vanessa Fielding has a long track record in creating theatre in Dublin. She knows the success, failures, trial and tribulations all too well. She and a cooperative of artists were opening a premises in the rejuvenated market area of Smithfield in Dublin – it was the gutted ground floor of an apartment building. We hired it. Director Michael Scott generously came to our aid with drapes and a rig and Vanessa worked hard to install toilets etc. We took over two spaces, a huge area with the most uncontrollable natural acoustic I have ever encountered. All the hard surfaces and a furrowed metal roof made even a breath seem like thunder. It had a dreadful effect on the smaller venue where strangely, the toilets were also located. Our valiant crew did amazing work rigging it out and the front of house people marshalled four shows a night with great efficiency. It would be great to house the Festival in multi-venue premises, a possibility originally intended for the development of Smock Alley.

I got a call from the manager of a bar to ask were we using The Complex in Smithfield as he had just seen the 'vodka committee' peering in its windows – one of their lot was an architect. Days before we were due to house four plays there, coincidentally and anonymously, reported 'planning objections' were presented to the owners. Thankfully all could be answered and we opened unhindered. No stone was to be left unturned in this battle allegedly arising as the' Irish Times' reported out of 'artistic differences'!

Joseph C Walsh began his connection with us that year with a strong production of 'The Laramie Project'. The previous production had only been associated with us, so I was happy to have it. After a slow start and the RTE radio campaign it built up to good audiences. Shakespeare is as 'Naked Will' and Wilde explore, rumoured to be gay. Anton Dudley took a treatment of rival Christopher Marlowe's play on the gay King 'Edward II' and Kaolin Bass brought his talented and large US team to Dublin. I loved it in concept and delivery. A mixture of puppetry and some very talented performers contributed to creative theatre. We are unlike the English and are not as exposed to Shakespeare and Marlowe as we should be. It was a cruelly tough sell, but the company were a treat. We had encountered Australian drag troupe 'Drags Aloud' at Edinburgh and their finest show 'At the Movies' came to the Complex. If they had only a seat sold in the morning, they spent the day in drag on the street and packed out at night. The movie spoofs were funny and the costumes were as loud as the soundtrack!

Next door we had a feast of new and exciting Irish writing that sold out. Patrick

Kinsella's 'Chalks' dealt with a repressed artist's desire for his young student with a macabre ending. The staging of this play was a challenge for this company and the actors were inhibited, which never let Kinsella's script fly. Jennifer English's comedy saved the day and having dramaturged this work with Patrick, I still believe there is more in this show than we saw in its premiere production. Rebecca Walsh's 'Working Late' set in a small company facing recession in Dublin and the interactions of the three worried colleagues, actors Walsh, Kathryn O'Hart and Thomas Mc Loughlin supported by Marc Mc Cabe treated us to a real comedy gem. This was a real step up for Irish writing and was a sell out show.

I read a play by a young playwright and never connected that he had in fact worked as a volunteer at the previous Festival. Alan Flanagan has a remarkable creative talent. His ingenious play 'Billy Redden' is a fine example of how a play doesn't have to be about being gay to be a gay play! Billy Redden is thirteen and one night his later self comes crashing through his wardrobe each 13 years older than the last. Underlying this plot is not a save him from a miserable gay life – it is finding a cure for Huntington's disease. It is remarkably clever and was well played by a talented cast of six men. It was my fault that it was programmed opposite 'Drags Aloud'. Even with their soundtrack on low, the crazy acoustic drowned out 'Billy Redden' causing me great angst that this wonderful piece was not being presented by the Festival at its best. The entire production team were amazing in their tolerance. The moment young Billy is told he is gay, neighbouring 'Drags Aloud' soundtrack booms through the wall with 'Somewhere Over The Rainbow' – you couldn't have planned it, but it was tough going. The last 20 minutes of Billy Redden were played in blissful silence as the Drags show was over. Flanagan produced possibly the most original Irish gay play the Festival has ever had the honour to stage and it won three awards for outstanding contribution to Irish gay theatre, Flanagan's writing and actor Geoff O Keeffe – a feat not repeated.

Standing proud in this line up of Irish talent was Elliot Ramon Potts gripping HIV drama, 'Loaded', where guys advertise they are HIV+ and then engage in unsafe sex – so who is responsible? Here we had a straight and gay actor, directed by a woman, do the most plausible and realistic bed scenes seen on the Festival stages. Joel T Bauer and Rik Walter were superb in unpeeling every layer of Potts gripping script.

Following a tradition which the Festival structure can create works through play reading and/or short to full length production – one of our biggest successes was the return of Sharon Sexton in 'Somewhere Under the Rainbow' by Cillian O Donnachdha. This was superb theatre and earned wide praise. Her live study of Liza Minnelli was flawless and her singing powerful. O Donnachdha's script which began life as our theatre short, evolved into a full length play of music and biography. This production later went on a national tour having filled the Olympia Theatre in Dublin. I rarely go to see shows twice – I've seen this four times!

Our youngest playwright ever came from the Independent Youth Theatre stable and is now graduating from Mountview Academy in London, to no surprise. Aaron Rogers 'Fragile' was a contemporary three hander played by Fergus Mc Carthy, Janna Kemperman and Denis Grindel and was a creditable debut in a Festival brimming with new Irish writing talent. Mark Power, Chris Nugent and David Wray joined me in 'Singing Out Seven' at the Cobalt which also hosted our regular shorts programme. Dorothy Parker's 'The Sexes' had a relevant same sex adaptation by Sandra Lee Villegas. 'How to Murder Your Mother' was great fun from the pen of volunteer Hugh Cardiff, directed by Emma Weafer with comic playing by Siobhan O Brien and Brian Talbot. Emma also directed Gina Costigan and Amy Redmond in Lisa Saleh's comedy 'Confessions Of A Bridesmaid'. A short play that longed to be a full length was 'The Middle Distance' by Dubliner, Mark Ward. Set in a male sauna where an unlikely conversation strikes up. My own short 'Pieter's Coming Out' inspired by a true incident on Facebook in South Africa was postponed until the following year as my actors were very unprepared. I had enough on my plate!

Storytelling theatre had been a bit of a blind side by me. Thanks to the dogged determination of Kimberly Dark, her work 'Dykeotomy' made it to the Festival in 2010 and what a charming and accessible study of gender it was. It played in 'Pantibar' with Peter Van der Merwe's autobiographical story about growing up in South Africa 'In The Arms Of A Lion' which continued to show the diversity of South African theatre that refreshed this programme.

We had 48 sell-outs, a final committee meeting for the first time in three years where we all celebrated and looked forward with optimism. We worked hard, kept replacing our posters and brochures and certainly deserved our Gala celebration in the Complex. Lidl and Aldi were emptied of treats and chocolate, the Dice Man bar brought in a keg and 'Convoi Exceptional' a three drum, one saxophone band from the Netherlands, drummed all our emotions out until the early hours in The Complex. So much so, the Gardai were called as they thought we were having a rock concert which was booming around Smithfield. They were amazed to find there were no microphones or speakers – the insane acoustic of The Complex made its mark again, but we sure did party and we deserved it!

We had run our business wisely, we had unbelievable support at home and abroad and nothing could dent what we were about. We did not set out to win or lose, to drown in vodka or our sorrows. We just continued to do what we do well, to create a space and support for new voices celebrating the gay cultural identity through theatre as an artform. The applications began to flood in for 2011!

2011

Same-sex couples should have the right to civil marriage. Our time on this Earth is limited, I know that better than most. Life comes down to who you love and who loves you back- government has no place in the middle

Republican Senator Mark Kirk USA.

2011 was hardly a brand new dawn but we had survived in style. It was clear to us that there was no longer going to be a 'competing' event, but the myth was perpetuated for as long as it could be. Even though the vodka event's volunteers had been told it was no more, within six weeks of its last day, 'new dates' were announced to compete with 'Queer Notions' the occasional event staged by 'This is Popbaby' for its small stable of creative writers. We continued with our 'business as usual' plan and now were fearful of the deep recession that was engulfing Irish society. Previous recessions had inspired renewed volunteerism and a surge in (low priced) theatrical activity. There was little evidence that this recession would mirror previous ones, as the spoiling of expectations of the' Celtic Tiger' generation had only bred a sense of failure, as VIP queues dispersed and instant 'celebrity' is a poor replacement for actually investing in learning your chosen craft.

We battled on with our work and international interest was as strong as ever. At this time too, I was to be approached by Innbrook Entertainment – a US producer of note of 135 productions at the Edinburgh Fringe. Calvin Wynter, their Executive Producer asked to see me at Edinburgh and suggested a partnership with a view to touring gay theatre between Ireland, the US and

Australia. I was pleased, but told him we were 'too small' for his venture. He replied "I have been monitoring your Festival. I have sent shows there. It is the biggest and the best event of its kind in the world".

Our discussions were ongoing. It is no surprise that having endured the assault of the previous few years, I too wanted an exit strategy, so I set about rebuilding and refreshing the Festival. My core team of volunteers were still a bit 'shell shocked' and it was time to re-invigorate them and the event, as it planned for its future. I went to see Willie White in the Project who greeted me with "it's the law of the jungle and the strongest man is still standing"! He immediately renewed our use of 'The Cube' for the Festival, true to his word. I could not bring myself to contact Smock Alley, or to a lesser extent the New Theatre – I probably could not afford them anyway! Prices now were to be kept deliberately low to combat this recession.

Gerry Cleary our inspired designer came up with a new treatment of the logo to celebrate year eight. The Dublin Film Qlub showed 'Carravaggio' by David Jarman which I introduced in 'The Exchange' as one of our free events, along with a play reading of new Irish writer Paul O' Beirne's 'Moving On' in the 'Front Lounge' which was well received. 'The Project' hosted four plays. "The Little Dog Laughed" by Douglas Carter Beane, was a light comedy directed by Mark Pollard which packed the house, set in the drama of Hollywood agents and a closet star. The Irish media took to the good looking stars and kept asking them what it was like 'playing gay'. In fact they were real life partners, who had just broken up, and that was the 'real' story! 'The Project' box office staff also confided that it gave them their first full house that year!

I had seen Grant Smeaton's production of a verbatim transcript of Bette Davis's 1971 TV interview on the Dick Cavett show, in Edinburgh. It was well presented and though Bette was a bit burly, it captured the theme brilliantly, including a 1970s TV ad break promoting chocolates called AIDS! Once again, because the Festival does so much to interact with the companies, some tend to look on us as employees and absolve themselves of working on their own show's promotion. We pushed 'Bette/Cavett' strongly and it is striking how these gay icons no longer live in the memory of the younger generation. On the fourth day, when their producer asked the box office, 'what have you done for us today?', finally the ever helpful Gareth Hurley replied 'I will reverse the question – what have you done for you today'? They finally got promoting and it deservedly sold well in the end.

There is a tendency in commissioning scripts to constrain theatre 'by committee'. It is a dangerous phenomenon. I had a discussion with a producer in 2012 who said next time he would give the writer a much tighter brief, as it had not turned out as he had wanted it to – in fact it had been a considerable success. I asked what about the writer and the story s/he has to tell. They do not write to second guess a concept you have in your mind, which you can not impart yourself through playwrighting.

Another example of script dictation, was a most appealing proposal from director, Michael Scott. Michael wanted to write a trilogy called One, Two and Three. This was a personal story, beautifully constructed and giving an insight into Irish gay love, rarely seen. I liked the script. Michael is prolific and always madly busy. He is always pushed to meet deadlines and I was thrilled we facilitated his return to 'The Project' for the first time since he had been its Artistic Director a decade previously. Michael handed the 80 minute piece to 'an editor' and despite Patrick Byrne's strong performance, the 45 minute edited piece ripped the heart out of the original writing, baffling the audience with its unexplained introversion and ensuring 'Two' and 'Three' sadly remain unwritten. What should have been my Irish headline act, which did inspire some great media coverage, where Michael explained the concepts of the play beautifully, also had a knock on effect on the play 'Righteous Money' which followed it in 'The Project'. There was too poor an audience for the early show to pass onto the following show.

'Righteous Money' written and energetically performed by Michael Yates Crowley, was an edgy one man show dealing with greed and the collapse of the banking system as 'CJ' is heroically 'outed' on live TV, by his male assistant and lover. It was a tremendous performance and so appropriate to the time of the financial collapse in Ireland, and 'The Project's' ethos. But once again 'The Project' audience did not respond. Gay writers, who are voters apparently mustn't do 'politics' in the broader perception? Just as Jeff Key's anti-war play had not attracted them, 'Righteous Money' did not either. It should have and if it had not been in the Gay Theatre Festival, it probably could have packed 'The Project Cube'? We continue to have mountains to climb, but in this instance it was most unfair, as Ireland needed to see this avarous piece of monetary lust and corruption, as we 1.8 million workers were burdened with a 134billion euro burden of bank debt overnight.

Ricardo Melendez is a passionate performer. His award winning performance as 'Nijinsky' had packed 'The Project'. He returned in a transgender piece where a prince was concealed by his Mother, from the warlords who murdered his father, and raised the male heir, as 'Sofia', to become 'Queen'. Melendez was magnificent as his lavish costumes in the Renaissance piece. But the box office appeal was not there and as a true professional, regardless of the size of the audience, the performance quality never flinched in the 'Back Loft'. This space gave us a huge welcome but exhausted our volunteers, who literally had to equip it from scratch. Much more appealing to a section of our community, was Joseph Mercier's 'Giselle, or I'm too Horny to be a Prince' – an autobiographical tale about Mercier's late start in ballet, with added leather fetishes and some serious naked dance exertion.

As always we had our disappointments. The signs were not good when we contacted the prolific 'Belt Up Productions' in Edinburgh. This talented company had produced a site specific piece 'Lorca Is Dead' about Lorca and Picasso and the surrealist movement. The audience sits in amongst the action and indeed deliver lines in this frantically paced production. I spent months bringing them to Ireland and indeed hired and equipped 'The Back Loft' to accommodate their production specifically. Once the programme was published, a Jethro Compton emerged, for the first time, as a producer and confided in me that they were in serious financial difficulties and it was a large cast show. I broke every personal rule I had, and eventually offered to accommodate the cast of nine in my own home for eight days, in order to facilitate their performance. Communication was sparse and I was aware that they were doing a run of a show in London. They advertised their Dublin show on their website. By the middle Saturday, the day they were due in Dublin, we began to get a series of calls. The starting time was wrong, the turn around time was too slow – but the other company on in 'The Back Loft' were fully accommodating. Their get-in was due to begin in a matter of hours. Try as I may, I could not establish if they were coming. By 2am on the Sunday morning, I called it quits. They had not booked their air tickets to Dublin and obviously were in a lot of internal dispute. We had had a waiting list that year and as always, it is the loss to the other company who wanted to perform, that cuts the deepest. The conduct of 'Belt Up' was astonishing but not unique. They continue to produce theatre. 'Lorca is Dead' proved to be true.

'Bang Shoot Blast' by Karl Watson not only maintained our youth drama contribution excellently, but were a compensating joy in 'The Back Loft'. 'Come as Soon As You Hear' Productions from Ireland delivered a play for anyone who is in love, or has been, or will be one day, for boys and girls who love boys and girls. It was a strong piece well delivered by six great young actors. As I left the play one night a man from the audience approached me, to say his son was in the play. At the awards night I informed the audience and the young cast, that this man had in fact been a very handsome 'twink' in my young directing days. I don't know who got the biggest cheers, the son or the Dad – but it made me feel old!

I had seen 'Mysterious Skin', the stage adaptation of Scott Heim's novel (and movie) in Edinburgh, performed on a stage the size of a letterbox! Young directors are under pressure especially when they bring a professional cast to a new Festival in a different country! You could see the pressure on director Peter Darney's face. He was a young man who took risks to enhance the quality of his work. He arrived in Dublin with an entirely new cast and was not the best communicator. There were times in this play about a boy who feels he was inducted by aliens, which in fact is his method to block out a shared boyhood trauma, where you could not take a breath. I remember meeting the stressed Peter on the street, about to go to do a radio interview. He enquired as to what I thought of the production. "Peter, I had seen this in Edinburgh and was glad to invite it, but if it hadn't come, I would have moved on. Having seen your new cast, I would have sacrificed a limb to ensure this was in the Festival – it is truly powerful". Peter gloom was no more and I lived up to my accolades by awarding best actor to Oliver Walker and best actress to Julie Addy from his great cast, that year.

Steven Dawson of 'Outcast Theatre' is a hard working, accomplished playwright, producer and director from Australia. I had read and seen his work and it took us three years to get his internet comedy 'Buttboy and Tigger' to Dublin. By that time, gay internet plays had moved to their second phase of newness, but the comedy and the wonderful playing made this a great Festival favourite. Some companies learn by visiting us and together we grow. Joe C Walsh's 'Laramie Project' had initially and undeservedly struggled previously for early audience. Matt Ian Kelly had been with us in 'Gaydar Diaries'. These artists came together with Greenwich Theatre and set their sights on our Festival. It was to be of benefit to us. I had once been flatteringly likened to Harry Hay, the true pioneer of gay rights in the hostile USA of the 1940s. He set up 'The Mattachine Society' and this amalgamation of theatre companies submitted a play about this to the Festival. I knew about Hay, but not about his associate designer Rudi Gerneich – I was thrilled to see this new formation and to get this play. One of the original members of the Mattachine's, Darrell Calvin actually flew in from New York to see the play and to introduce himself to us. It was an inspiring and uplifting quality piece of theatre, beautifully directed and acted. It remains a true Festival dramatic highlight.

The youngest star of 'Billy Redden', Blayne Kelly was inspired by his Festival involvement to write his first play and 'Interrogating My Mother' was premiered. This play deals with a meeting between an estranged Mother and her gay son, with a very dramatic twist at the end. The work grew considerably in writing and performance from its submission date and merited selection in the programme.

Another play from a previous Edinburgh proved timely at last and 'Kipper Tie' productions from the UK presented the story of the bisexual Lord Byron in the James Joyce Centre. Harper Ray shone in the title role of Bernie Byrne's production of 'My Dearest Byron' which challenged the capacity of an old Georgian building to cope with the electrical demands of a production, but all went well, for this was a finely crafted piece of storytelling theatre. David Wray, Eoin Cannon and Paul Monaghan made history by being the only production ever invited back. It was a good choice. This two man, hour long show tune epic, presents classic musical theatre through a gay male lens in 'Memoirs of a Gayshow'! It still produced one of the Festival's most memorable poster images and the quality of these Irish, West End stars performance of Wray's challenging, humorous and innovative arrangements, made it one of the best musical shows ever to be programmed.

Graham Elwell, the award winning actor from 'A Dog Called Redemption' contacted me about "An Actress Prepares" the verbatim performance of Marilyn Monroe's final magazine interview. It is an extraordinary theatre piece in that the interview reads like a script. It suffered somewhat from Irina Diva's strong eastern European pronunciation, but the phraseology of the icon shone through in a show that attracted a mainstream audience. 'Sean Gilligan Productions' presented our first Irish female singer Amy Fidgeon in 'Amy Sings The Icons". Set on the last night of an NYC nightclub, this one hour of female classics packed out and was one of our highest selling shows. 'Sticks and Stones' a two hander play presented by 'On The Reel Productions' from Australia was a gripping claustrophobic drama of two guys stuck in the limbo of a waiting room. How they got there and how they were connected unfolds in this powerful drama that packed the theatre at 'Outhouse'.

Each night we go to a different gay venue to host our Festival club and to get some performance opportunities for our shows. The Club particularly suits singers or drag acts. It is a challenge to be big in your own country and then for just one week, to try to break into the Irish scene, which is tightly controlled by our own headline drag acts. They are very generous in allowing our drag shows to share their stages and that is appreciated. What happens when the visiting acts won't co-operate – they don't sell. 'The Screw You Review' by 'Dewey Chaffee Enterprises' was fun. It is clever, inappropriate and well performed. 'Dee Dee and Dewey' (a Statler and Waldorf type crank) have great fun with the audience each night and I even got Alan Amsby, Ireland's first drag queen (Mr Pussy) to attend. But 'Dewey' did not appear to be comfortable in touting for an audience at the clubs. Whenever 'Dee Dee' was allowed to, it did boost the numbers. Australia's 'The Girly Side of Butch' and 'Drags Aloud' had proven that if you work the Irish audience – and it is hard work – you will be repaid at the box office. Their US counterparts did not embrace that method and sadly a good show did not do so well.

One actor shows, especially autobiographical ones, are submitted in abundance and are also a tough sell. There are so many similarities, especially in the 'coming out' story, that they are often left languishing at the bottom of our sales figures. Now and again, a new treatment is submitted and in 'Watson Arts' US production of 'Brazil Nuts' we had a real hit. I actually contacted the producer to see how large the cast was, as I could see at least four essential players. I had to be strongly reassured that this could be carried off by one actor and it was in style. This hilarious multifaceted tale of a US lesbian trying to marry her Brazilian partner was terrific. It was a play to appeal to anyone but once again our female audience yo-yoed and she went from small houses to deserved ovations in a tour de force performance by Susan Jeremy.

The guy who really got the Festival right was a young Canadian producer Rob Salerno. His play 'Big In Germany' is not very strong and his casting of the straight actor as the gay guy and the gay actor as the straight character did not pass the plausibility test. However when it comes to producing, Salerno knows his trade. He seemed to appear at every queue to promote his play each night and was justly rewarded with great houses, all who were warmed by this light comedy. His was a masterclass in production commitment and loyalty to his cast and show.

It was time for Burlesque and thanks to the UK's 'Lashings of Ginger Beer ', we got it in bizarre abundance. It was odd, great, funny, dreadful – all the things that make up good burlesque and queer feminist cabaret was ideal for our 'Cobalt Café' audiences. Canada's 'Squid Ink's' production of 'Funny In the Head' was another classic one actor tale. With the double disadvantage of trying to deal with the very pertinent issue of mental health, Jan Derbyshire's autobiographical tale was excellent storytelling theatre. But where was the audience and especially the women? It was even more pertinent when on the night she packed out – the audience were on their feet, before the last letter of the final word had been delivered. She was a joyous performer with a skilfully crafted message. "Let's Pretend We are Having Coffee Thirty Years Later' is not a catchy title to sell for a one man show, but 'Circulo Vertical' from Venezuela gave us our first South American offering. This autobiographical story runs the gamut of gay crises and is performed naked. This caught the imagination of Brenda Donoghue from the supportive 'Mooney Show' on RTE Radio One who attended and recorded a great piece for broadcast on national radio. It is great to see that when we engaged the media, how more 'mainstream' our programme became, but without that, we remained a niche event.

The 'Theatre Shorts' fulfilled the Cobalt programme and taught me another lesson. My own work has always had the lowest priority, even from my own volunteer corps. This time I had written a short play about a young guy who faked a gay youth suicide on Facebook. It prompted huge responses especially from an older generation who had seen so many of their young friends perish in this way. I wrote it for stage especially when I discovered that the South African hoaxer had used a picture from the Compton Model Agency in Dublin. My two young actors did not learn the script and I pulled the production, to do not a lot better the following year, when lack of commitment meant one actor didn't show for his tech or dress rehearsals, despite the potential I had discovered in the other actor, the charming David Flynn. The real cost of running the Festival for me is that I miss directing and performing, as the workload has completely swallowed up my personal production capacity. This tussle is what remains the biggest incentive for me to leave the Festival to pursue my own creativity, rather than putting all my efforts into showcasing and mentoring, in some cases the work of talented others.

So the shorts programme for the first time a completely Irish programme, was in the skilful hands of Mark Ward's 'Saliva' directed by Emma Weafer. This dark occult piece based on a Greek myth was well played, followed by the premieres of 'The Arrival' a gay surrogacy comedy devised by Kenny Moynihan, Lynn Rafferty and Shay Griffin, later made into a short film. I'm not convinced that the same hilarious script was ever delivered twice! The comedy accolade went to Siobhan O' Brien and starring 'Chalk's comedienne Jennifer English in Patrick Kinsella's hilarious 'Patty Cake' co- starring 'Working Late's author Rebecca Walsh. You will never look at chocolate cake in the same way again – hilarious comedy from this talented collaborative team.

We have had a great connection with local media. Anna Livia and Near FM opened their airways to us and our shows from the start. Dublin Community TV a terrific service, worked on a joint project with us where a Festival programme was broadcast three times a week. The companies were thrilled with the exposure and I suggested our young PR team host it, making instant stars of Jan Schneider and Judi Blax our voluntary PR team. It is important to me that our volunteers get something for their CV from their generous work with us.

The celebrations at the Final night were great. We had protected what we had created with dignity. Sure we had given some fodder to the enemies of innovation, but we had not only held our own, but focussed in an undeniable way on what was important – the presentation of quality and diverse gay theatre.

The box office pattern went into spasm this year and did not reflect any previous pattern, reducing the average booking of earlier years from five plays to 1.5 plays per audience member. The recession really hit the buying power of our audience. We had high visibility from our tiny budget. By the Thursday morning of the first performance week, we were 40% behind on the previous competitive year. It was implausible. Suddenly the box office shot up and we ended up, despite the recession with the overall box office take up 7%. It was heart stopping stuff and very uneven with early week performances not doing well. However the loyalty of the audience was sincere and once on a Thursday they had any extra cash, they headed to the Theatre Festival. Our walk-ups (sales at the door) jumped dramatically to unprecedented rates. Normally it would top up a pre-booked house by 10-20%. The recession audience could be trebled with at the door sales. The first ever Festival held exclusively on Dublin's northside, a point noted by the

Lord Mayor Emer Costello in her generous hosting and support for the event, all ended happily.

During the previous years, Company Secretary, Gareth Hurley and I had fronted a series of meetings with funders assuring them that we were financially sound and under good governance. There is a considerable burden on 'not for profit' companies. State aid only goes to companies that are limited by guarantee. This means you have to have audited accounts annually. Bearing in mind the Festival's finances were now fully transparent and we had the benefit of qualified accountants in our volunteer corps, the added burden of raising funds for an audit was felt. The cost was equivalent to a theatre rental for a fortnight. As grants reduced hugely, our grant aid was now being eaten up by audit and membership costs to the tune of 50% of what was granted.

It was then discovered that, despite the effort Gareth and I had put into governance, and the fact that we had audited accounts signed off on time, the auditor's company never filed the accounts. It meant that while we were assuring people of our bona fides, the Company Registration Office files told a different story – our accounts had not been lodged. We were furious and in disbelief. Our accountant found out that in fact we were a few weeks from being struck off for failure to lodge two years accounts. We had paid for them. I decided to handle this mess myself and eventually brought it all back in good order. I was about to take my first short holiday after two stressful years and I summoned three senior volunteers to share a task. I would sort out the accounts mess – which despite having paid fees and complied fully, the CRO said it was still our corporate responsibility to have the accounts lodged and there was no recourse on the auditor. It is no wonder there is such a crisis in standards in Ireland.

I alerted the senior volunteers to the practice the strapped Arts Council had of shifting deadlines, especially close to holiday times. We had barely made the Sept 23rd grant deadline for 2010. I said I would do the accounts, if they ensured our application to the Arts Council went in on time. I left the country and was a little surprised not to get any query about the grant form. By Sept 23rd 2011 I was anxious and I emailed the trio. There was a silence and later I was told the closing date had been brought forward again to September 9th and we had missed it. I was speechless. No sooner had we turned one corner when another self-inflicted wound happened. A brave rallying call charged us four with raising a quarter of the anticipated loss each. I raised my quarter by getting the raffle at the Mr Gay

Ireland final for the Festival and by returning with David Wray, Eoin Cannon and Ranae Von Meding in 'Singing Out 7&8' in 'The Cobalt Café' in March.

Events like ours, dealing with bureaucratic requirements and as big as our Festival really do need administrative supports. We have no office, phone, computer or even a chair and yet we had presented over 1,500 performances of gay theatre in Dublin. We are invited to some training courses but they are always scheduled for events that have a staff free for daytime courses. Volunteers who already give up a month to the Festival from mid-April to mid-May can not do these courses.

The starving of funds to such an event ensures administrative lapses and excludes us from the network of shared knowledge and experience. I addressed this while in Edinburgh. I had identified the skills of a young Durham University graduate Callum Cheatle (The Happy Prince / The Photographer) who had managed the Durham Arts Festival, and made him a proposal. He had graduated from university and was doing a six month tour of Asia, the Solomon Islands and Australia. I asked would he intern with the Festival afterwards? By Christmas, he had signed up and he injected a much needed boost of organisation and enthusiasm into our ninth Festival. It is amazing how positive a response can be had when someone new asks the same question. Callum was to prove invaluable in getting us through a year – our ninth which is always a challenge, as you move towards a bigger anniversary.

I was also fortunate to be approached by a young accountant from Galway, Joe Duggan. He volunteered his services and proved invaluable. I immediately identified him as a potential vice chairman for the Festival and he took the initiative in so many areas from sourcing prizes to online banking. It was a good strong team to make progress. The flow of submissions continued, and many returned to us, as we planned our ninth Festival in relative peace in 2012.

It was not all peaceful as later that year, we got a letter, out of the blue, from the Revenue Commissioners enquiring into a matter, covering the Festival's business from its inception. If true, it would have closed down the Festival. Joe was fortunate to have access to top class advice and when he showed the letter to an expert, he commented 'Someone has reported you. This is not a standard action by the Commissioners. Someone has contacted them'. Here we go again! We knew our business was in order and produced a strong and clear defence of the matter. Revenue was excellent to deal with and sent the matter for legal advice. The outcome was not only 100% satisfactory, but we received a clear undertaking in writing, that the matter had been sorted in perpetuity, which was most helpful and reassuring, when planning our future. It was clear that we were still under attack, but yet again, because of our good governance, we proved robust and transparent, on all matters.

scene 9

2012

Mohamed Ali Baashi ,18 years old gay boy, was buried in a hole up to his chest and then pelted with rocks by fighters from the rebel ALQAEDA Link group ALshabaab on Friday 15th march 2013 in barawe somalia, about 50 miles from the capital, Mogadishu

I needed to take heed of the recession but I also don't like cutting back. I decided to reshape the programme in order to sustain the employment of participating companies. 2011 had sell out houses and some empty ones – at 34 events, we had too many draws on our struggling box office and if not addressed, the viability of the event for professional companies, would threaten its future.

There was a change of regime in 'The Project' and an openly gay Director took office. I had paid the bill in full and attached a letter enquiring about booking the 2012 dates to the cheque after the previous year's Festival as was standard practice. The letter was apparently not received, but the cheque was cashed! Also inexplicably we were told by 'The Project' that the Dublin Dance Festival had moved their dates forward now clashing with our event, which had been held on the same dates for the previous eight years. With the failure to apply for the Arts Council grant, in truth we probably would have been pushed to afford the venue anyway. I set out over two days and began to hunt for free venues. In the 1960s Dublin boasted more theatre seats than any other city in Europe per head of population. Times were changing and a political ideology in Government at the time, did not value these 'British' Georgian or Victorian buildings and many fell into disuse. This and the advent of television, more transport and cinema, meant that many theatres closed down. Twenty first century Ireland was not so well provided as the decade of my birth.

I walked the streets, especially around the 'gay village' area and tried to identify spaces that would not need much rigging, as we had no funds for that either. 'The George' and 'The Dragon' bars were in financial trouble and they became separate entities. The Bank took over 'The George'. This had been one of Dublin's most profitable pubs, but a recent regime had completely lost touch with its core clientele. My generation moved out. In November 2008 it was 4.70 euros for a pint in the George after 11pm. One year later it was 6.10euros. On top of that, long time customers were being asked 'do you have a membership card' as well as the decibel level increasing, reminding me of my middle age! The Bank was now in control and happily many familiar faces returned to run the 'historic' premises. The same company also owned 'Speakeasy' opposite the 'George'. Thanks to Stevie Devine and Derbhal Leavy, they allowed us free use of their basement performance space for the fortnight, just as Shane Harte and Rory O Neill kindly did in 'Pantibar' in Capel Street. This saved our lives and knocked out most of the ill effects of the volunteers' failure to apply for the Arts Council support.

I did not replace 'The Project' as a venue but was welcomed and well facilitated in a previous venue, the refurbished 'Players Theatre' in Trinity College – Wilde's alma mater. Our northside loyalists with Tadhg Mac Phaidin and staff in the 'Teachers Club', Jamie and the Kenny family in the 'Cobalt Café' and Mark Tierney and staff in the 'James Joyce Cultural Centre' at the behest of Senator David Norris, meant that we were intact and still viable.

January is the month when contracts fly across the internet and indeed across the world. I decided to also reduce the number of second shows at 9.30pm too, to consolidate audiences and to maximise and boost the box office take for companies. Gerry Cleary our designer once again created a new logo and we were off.

We boosted the number of female members on the committee to its highest ever level with Emma Weafer, Siobhan Killen, Ciara Nolan, Annick Thijs and Jen Butler taking senior roles. There was a difference between those who had survived the vodka debacle and the many smiling and new enthusiastic faces around the committee table, which brought much needed new life to the event. Committee meetings are held in my home every Wednesday at 8.00pm and we were getting them streamlined and more productive. The Irish habit of always occupying a committee's mouth with tea and nice treats, certainly diffuses tension, as does an occasional sojourn in the local bar, 'Leonard's Corner' on the South Circular Road, for a post meeting drink and further discussion. It is vital that volunteers are rewarded with what Joe Duggan turned into a catch cry 'When does the fun start Brian'? It was fun again at last. It is a good reminder for any voluntary group – the work must be done, but it also must be fun and sociable for those who give so much to the event.

The slimmed down programme was shaping up well. It was launched in the Arlington Hotel, Temple Bar by Ireland's first openly lesbian and married politician, Senator Katherine Zappone, who spoke generously and eloquently about gay life and culture. At that launch, I publically indicated my intention to stand down after year ten. I hoped this announcement would flush out commitment and herald the longed for succession plan I had for the event, to live long and well, after me.

One of the first plays in the mailbox was 'Live, Love Laugh' an autobiographical story of actress Eilish O'Carroll. Eilish was the daughter of the first female Labour party and non-dynastic TD. She played 'Winnie' in the BBC TV smash hit comedy series 'Mrs Brown's Boys'. Her niece Fiona O Carroll had been in my pantomime at the' Olympia' and her brother Brendan O'Carroll, had appeared in my charity shows 'Euro Vision For Asia' in the 'Olympia' and the 'Ray of Hope' show at Vicar Street. Brendan's agent Rory Cowan had always been a kind supporter. None of these reasons drove me to accept the play. Here was an insight into Catholic Ireland in the 1950s and beyond and how eventually Eilish discovered her own identity in the smog of instructed teachings. It was funny, personal and revealing. I snapped it up and it became the biggest selling show we had in years, packing 'Players Theatre' before it set off on a national tour. Eilish got tremendous support from the lesbian community, but that still did not transfer to our other similar programmed shows, remaining a final frontier for us to engage women in our diverse programme.

We also welcomed the return of Artscape from Cape Town. Previously I had invited our then ambassador Roy Sargeant to deliver a lecture on his friend author Mary Renault at our seminar. Juliet Jenkin author of the 'Boy Who fell from the Roof' wrote an imagining of her life through a meeting in the afterlife of Mary and Alexander the Great and their relationships with both of their lovers. Sargeant had been estranged from us for a while and then had published a book of plays claiming that all had been produced at the Dublin Gay Theatre Festival – that description was untrue as one of the plays, though accepted, had never been presented at our Festival, to our hurt and annoyance.

Michael Mears the CEO of Artscape and I had met in Dublin that year and it was most helpful. I first entrusted him with my plan to slim down the event to sustain it and he gave good advice and encouragement. I later visited South Africa on holiday. Now Roy was to return and Gareth Hurley corresponded with Roy and clearly set out the issues that had divided us, with his support for the vodka event. It helped to bring about a genuine apology and a greater understanding. I was pleased to welcome them back again. Juliet Jenkin wrote another great part for actress Antoinette Pearce and Diane Wilson (Careful) returned as Mary. It was a good piece ,well executed, but I wonder how sympathetic Jenkin was to the central character? This limited Wilson's considerable skills and left us in a bit of a dilemma about Renault. All her papers were destroyed on her insistence after her death and we had high hopes this play might fill in the gaps. However many questions remained sadly unanswered.

'Bottom Dog Theatre' company are an interesting and ambitious group based in Limerick. They proposed a production of 'Elegies for Angels, Punks and Raging Queens' – a dated musical treatment of the plague of AIDS in the US. Liam O Brien and I had an animated discourse about the capacity of the venue. It is harder to sell sometimes in the context of a Gay Theatre Festival and in the end 'Players Theatre' was a fine setting for this well sung piece and its large and talented company. They were followed by the return of the depleted 'Drags Aloud' - Australia's 'Kris del Vayse' and 'Jessica James' travelled with their glittering, new two hander, 'Les Coques Ups' and it did not disappoint. Once again, their work ethic in drawing in audiences proved a winner and drag is a particularly accessible artform for attracting straight people.

'Speakeasy' on South Great Georges Street, hosted a new Irish play by Hazel Quinn called 'Half A Person', dealing with depression and relationships. Despite obscure images on the poster which made it hard to sell, the play was well received and a worthy debut from this new writer and her team. One of the best solo shows ever to hit the Festival was one of our most difficult sells. We can not understand why? Michael Lynch is black, from the Bronx, effeminate and one hell of a singer. The originality and performance of his one man musical show was breathtaking in its delivery, but fell on largely deaf ears in our wider audience appeal. Stage manager Chris Nugent made it his business to promote this wonderful jazzy storytelling show of 1970s NYC. I rarely get the chance to see a show twice – I did this one out of pure choice and hunger for seeing two accomplished musicians on stage.

'Pantibar' hosted Andrea Alton and her 'World According to Molly'. Molly is a lesbian poet security guard of little finesse, that plays wonderfully well in the USA. It did not transfer as well to Irish audiences who struggled to get on the same humorous wavelength, despite the power of the performance. It was followed by Tim Paul's 'bear play'. Bears are usually hairy and heavy gay men and Paul's autobiographical internet play attracted another new cohort of audience, who were charmed by his delivery and the risqué-ness of his funny and complex storyline.

Greenwich Theatre returned with a play long residing on my wish list. They initially proposed 'Gross Indecency' the Oscar Wilde trial play in their submission. We later had the gay community theatre group 'Acting Out' include this in our free play reading session this year to great acclaim. Then Greenwich floated Michel Marc Buchard's play 'Lilies'. 'Lilies' is one of my all-time favourite plays. It is set in Canada in 1912 and deals with young love, religion, murder, prison life and the reuniting of the alleged murderer with the Bishop who loved him as a young man. It's a wonderful movie and if any group could stage it, this collaborative one could. Joe C Walsh's direction and a smashing talented all male cast, produced a tidy and intense production. One night at the end of the performance in the 'Teachers Club', they were approached by an audience member, Tony award winner Brent Carver, star of the movie, who had travelled over from the US, especially to see this production! It was clear from our box office records we were attracting more and more theatre tourists.

'My Funny Valentine' by Canadian David Devoe is based on a true story where a 15 year old high school boy sent another boy a valentine card. The other boy shot him dead. Devoe's script introduces seven witnesses and could easily fall into the 'Laramie Project' mix. It doesn't. It is original in concept and Jay Whitehead's solo performance was superb. He represented a rich tapestry of seven small town characters of both genders flawlessly. This was a fine example of director, author and actor working seamlessly in communicating a piece of modern storytelling, through theatre as an artform and earned Whitehead the acting award in a hugely contested field this year.

Irish actress Ranae Von Meding approached me with a play by Diane Son 'Stop Kiss' about two women drawn together as victims of a homophobic assault. Von Meding and Sarah Griffin's performances lived up to the quality demanded by the script, directed by Simon Manahan.

The 'James Joyce Cultural Centre' was to resound to the tunes of 'Memoirs of a Gay Show – the Sequin' – a clever sequel to the hit show by David Wray, Eoin Cannon and Paul Monaghan – with a title suggested by myself. The latter's sudden hospitalisation cancelled the show without replacement and proved yet again, we still were not immune to cancellation. 'The Queen Bees', Barbra, Bette and Billie, from vocalist Amy Fidgeon and pianist Sean Gilligan transferred to the Cobalt and entertained royally. 'Rock N Wrestle' by Colin Clay Chase was an energised autobiographical play dealing with everything from mental health issues to a Justin Bieber crush. Clay Chase endeared himself to the Festival team and played the demanding script with passion, energy and commitment. The 'Theatre Shorts' programme included Peter Tate's one man story of isolation and homelessness 'Odd Man Out', which was well acted. Lisa Saleh, an American playwright who had a success with 'Confessions of a Bridesmaid' returned with her short about artificial insemination 'Womb Service'. This derived from a longer play and didn't quite work as an independent piece. Stalwarths, Kenny Moynihan, Lynn Raftery and Vicky Curtis (Director) returned with a hilarious comedy 'Don't Press Pause'. Combining a few ideas I had seen before in 'Two Girls, One Ring', this fast paced story of a couple with different ambitions did exactly what you want short plays to do – leave you wanting more!

Kathleen Warnock presented a four hander all female fairy tale called 'Outlook', demonstrating her continued growth as a playwright. Kathleen's personality is in her plays and she likes positive outcomes. This play and its every well balanced, talented cast did so well in the James Joyce Centre and finally engaged the US embassy in our work after years of ignored invitations. 'Between' was the sexiest play of the season! A trilogy blended into a 50 minute comedy about boys growing up, a drama teacher/student relationship all rolled into one fast paced. moving, funny and skilful play by Oskar Brown from Germany via South Africa, which sold really well and deservedly. Handsome, Boss model, Nicolas Campbell proved he was more than good looking when he bagged a nomination as Best Actor in 'Between'.

'Aul Divina and Me / I was a world premiere from the pen of Cillian O'Donnachdha. This clever two hander starring Geoff O'Keeffe and James Butler was set in Ireland in the cash trapped home of a former drag queen, who had to seek a new lodger. A young man, born in a time free of criminalisation replies and moves in. The 'referee' is this clash of age and experience, is a portrait of Maria Callas and O Donnachdha's research unfolded into a strong and believable script, which won him the Oscar Wilde award for new writing.

Callum Cheatle moved over to Dublin in March and his work as our first intern Festival manager, began to achieve many positive things for the Festival. He was well liked, committed and creative. Callum was passionate about the success of the event and challenging to me in a constructive way. It was great to see young blood infuse the event. I had written yet again to the Embassies of our visiting companies. The Festival does so much to positively portray foreign culture in Ireland to little acknowledgement or support. Callum, combined with Kathleen Warnock, worked diplomatic magic. The British Ambassador attended 'Lilies', the US embassy offered some travel support to 'Outlook' and the Australian embassy put forward a proposal for future support. Contact was also had from the German and South African embassies – strangely only Canada did not respond.

Though I often consider myself fortunate, I am not necessarily a lucky person. My Mother's health had been deteriorating over the Spring. She was immobilised by arthritis and though mentally totally alert, was confined to bed and could not move. On the Thursday before the Festival opened, the word came from Waterford that her life journey was coming to an end. On the Saturday, the companies began to arrive, I travelled home to break the news to my 90 year old father, with my brother, and returned to Dublin jumping at every phonecall or text. There were many, as our volunteer force was at full and effective steam. A whole pile of artists had arrived and all were busily making new friends and doing multiple 'get-ins'. I remained with the Festival until we opened on Bank Holiday Monday, and then I had to engage with the certainty of her passing and went to Waterford on the Tuesday of our opening week. She died on the Thursday May 10th at 5.30 PM. Gareth, Joe, Ciara and Callum led the entire crew in maintaining the Festival. Friends stepped up and volunteered assistance to them. I was experiencing something I had no reference points for and far from being able to take over and lead, I was very much exhausted. The Festival usually wears me out anyway and the trauma of this was too much to bear. On the day I got news of her imminent departure, I also started getting emails from a contracted artist. Theatre has no mercy.

Ty Jeffries ' Miss Hope Springs' is the son of screen actor Lionel Jeffries (Chitty, Chitty, Bang, Bang) and does a live singing drag show. He was signed up for the Cobalt Café. As is our wont, the emails began to arrive telling us what an honour he was doing for us by appearing in our Festival and demanding new things. We treat everyone equally and once the threats had died down, we got a sudden doctors certificate saying he was unfit to travel. Yet another space that could have gone to a willing company, lost. When I appealed to him to understand my Mother's illness he retorted with 'if she is so ill, why are you not by her bedside'? I couldn't win. It's a cruel business and my sense of commitment to this voluntary work, coupled with the merciless discipline required for good theatre, was a huge strain. My mother was buried on her 83rd birthday on May 12th.

I returned dazed and empty for the Festival's second week. The funeral had been held in her home in the great community that is Ferrybank, Waterford, but I had only lived there for six years before going to College. It was a very strange experience going through that without the support of friends from my life in Dublin, as many were valiantly keeping the Festival going. Many people did not know what had happened – those that did were very supportive. I was relieved to sit in the quiet of darkened theatres in the evening, suspending my grief in the stories of theatre. I continued my assessment of the awards with Callum's and Gareth's input.

I am a strong believer in seeing through the continuum of the artistic direction of the Festival. I accept and analyse the submissions, programme the event and then reveal my own analyses of the productions in public at the Gala night, where we present Oscar Wilde statuettes to our winners - our Oscars! Callum, out of concern, wanted me not to host the Gala, but I insisted. Meghan Carry the lovely and talented singer/songwriter who played the lead in 'Outlook' took the stage in 'The Workman's Club'. It's a tiny stage and has a tiny wing. I was offstage and about 3 feet away from her and she dedicated a song to me in my loss. I was deeply moved and sent a message to David Wray that I could not sing myself that night, after all. Megan had said it all for me. However the theatrical family lifted my spirits and we celebrated the ninth Festival, despite its cruel personal toll.

The celebration of what had yet again been achieved by all who contributed, was roof raising. The affirmation of artists who may have suffered at the box office but were lauded for their art, was complete. We always finish the concert with volunteers and artists onstage and an audience on their feet, as we look ahead singing 'Seasons of Love' from the Jonathan Larson's musical 'Rent'. "525,600 minutes…how do you measure a year in a life? How about Love?" It's a real anthem for this unique international cooperation and artistic sharing, inspired and delivered in Dublin, but shared worldwide by the emerging and distinct gay culture which unites us all.

Scene Ten

2013

Pope Francis is a conservative who is anti-gay marriage and anti-gay adoption. He has described same-sex marriage as the work of the devil and a "destructive attack on God's plan." He has also said that gay adoption is a form of discrimination against children

Huffington Post 13/03/2013

Making it to year ten was an achievement in itself. Making year ten a theatrical achievement was an even greater task, in the face of recession and no extra resources. Callum Cheatle, Joe Duggan, Alex Kennedy and other volunteers were all now in the UK, or studying and we started again to identify good workers who had the Festival's interests at heart. Dermot Devoy, Stephen Mc Connell, Louise Hales and later John James Hickey and Joe Kearney all came on board to help in what would be a challenging year.

We eventually got about ninety play applications. I wanted to have people who knew us and the Festival back with us to celebrate the ten years and still to find and present new talent. The scripts and proposals came flooding in regardless of the deadlines. They ranged as always from the brilliant to the bizarre. One person had a recording of his show but was 'loath to show it to me' and offered me no further information! Some proved hard to track down, some broke all the rules, and others dealt with subjects or styles we had featured previously. However the Irish were in good form and had some interesting proposals. The closing date for submissions is December 1st which means many a night spent reading over Christmas and offers being made in January. There are three stages in being accepted. We publish our details online and many do not read them and try to begin a 'negotiation' after they get an offer – they are soon dispensed with. We check up mid-way, is the submission still valid and even though confirmed, we discover later that is not the case. We then short list and finally make an offer, identify a suitable venue from our contracted list, and sign a contract.

The programming is a delicate balance, like building a house of cards. For example after the first round offers, three companies that previously confirmed could not accept their place – this resulted in ten offers being changed by dates or venue. Each week has to be balanced between drama, music, cabaret, Irish productions and specialist interests to ensure similar works appealing to one audience do not clash. It is possible to see every production in the Festival's diverse programme. We then give each company a further four weeks in February to get their house in order and to confirm flights etc.

On February 27th I offered an additional matinee to an American company and they accepted. One of their cast then wrote that evening and offered me an additional theatre short. On the following day, as the brochure was almost ready for print, I get an email from someone calling herself an 'Executive Producer' – note my earlier warning. What resulted was that this company of actors had made no preparations whatsoever to fulfil their contract and were not coming. I have no idea what their intentions were, but in this case this producer did honour their penalty clause in the contract and was mortified when one cancellation resulted in five changes to arrangements for other companies. One young Irish company threw a hissy fit on being given a bigger venue and withdrew in a tantrum – I now had two 'vacancies' as we were going to print. In short, I always have a reserve list and we managed to fill the gaps, but there appears to be no solutions to the incapacity of some in the arts to do business ethically. Then, two venues tried to change the agreements, but we had them in writing and all was well. By lovely contrast there are always others who will facilitate and accommodate a programmer's dilemma in every way they can. At least we got the programme out and a very good one, thanks to Gerry Cleary by the launch on March 19th.

I was very honoured to be present in the Hugh Lane Gallery to launch our tenth programme with the Lord Mayor's representative and former office holder, Cllr Andrew Montague. We like to make connections in Ireland and for us, not only to launch there, but to stage our first performances there in May, is a great link to the envied home of the Francis Bacon Studio. We host lunchtime opera in

'The Hugh Lane', with 'the Francis Bacon Opera' by composer/director Stephen Crowe, on Tuesday and Thursday May 7th/9th at 1.00pm. It's the transcript of the famous Melvyn Bragg TV interview (which plays there), set to music. I hope gallery supporters will recognise this as a must see in the home of Bacon's studio in the daytime and in the nearby 'James Joyce Centre' at night. I had seen this in Edinburgh and the singing of Christopher Killerby (Bacon) and Oliver Brignall (Bragg) is only rivalled by the fulsome playing of pianist, Elspeth Wilkes.

The Gallery, like ourselves is very grateful to Dublin City Council for supporting both organisations and it was great to see us linking our scarce resources together in times of economic challenge. Times changed in recession and more people were now open to sharing resources, as testified by the incredible welcome we got in the Gallery. As those of you who have read this know, I value shared citizenship very much. Bacon though his career was developed abroad, still valued his 'Irishness', perhaps part of his rebellious nature in England, and we too smile when some still consider our mainstream event as in some way, rebellious.

True, we didn't ask permission to put this biggest event of its kind worldwide, on in Dublin, but we didn't need to – art is for everyone and all our voices are valid and all our audiences valued. We like to feel connected. It's good to note not just the association with Francis Bacon, but with Hugh Lane, who's Aunt, Lady Augusta Gregory was a founder of the national theatre, which too gave a voice and a channel for it to be heard, in a time of oppression, through theatre as an artform.

Anniversaries can bring a new energy to any event. We established the Festival in the 150th anniversary year of the birth of Oscar Wilde in Dublin. We find ourselves in 2013, marking the 40th anniversary in June of the granting of the Freedom of the City of Dublin to the most famous same sex partnership, Hilton Edwards and Micheal Mac Liammoir in 1973 – a time when they were both criminals! We mark the twentieth year since decriminalisation in 1993 and we celebrate our tenth anniversary as we launch a programme, that will pass our 2,000th performance of gay theatre in Ireland, making Dublin the recognised home of this artform, worldwide. Not a bad record for a totally voluntary action by a few theatre professionals, that has had an impact worldwide.

Despite the recession, we still had almost 100 applications from five continents this year. The programme is packed with new writing, drama, comedy, music and events celebrating the positive gay identity today and making some amends for those whose history was never fully written, because it could not be.

Historical characters who feature, some because of the absence of history in an imagining, include Roger Casement and Padraig Pearse, Eva Gore Booth, Oscar Wilde, William Shakespeare, Benjamin Britten, Francis Bacon, George Frederic Handel, and even a character called Daniel Boone (no relation), and we will hear the music of gay icons, Judy Garland, Petula Clarke, Dusty Springfield, Lulu and even a gender interpretation of the music of Franz Liszt, Chopin and Clementini.

We have free events, a seminar on our ten years of gay theatre as discussed in this book, play readings by a Polish/Irish theatre company called 'Forbidden Love' in 'The Front Lounge' and of our Patron, Terrence Mc Nally's classic 'Lisbon Traviata' in the community centre 'Outhouse' directed by Joe Redmond. Director Michael Scott agreed to host free Sunday discussion sessions dealing with gay identity. Here we would tease out the impact of identity on established performers and professionals, with Alan Amsby (Mr Pussy), Chris Rowan (Bunny), playwright Gerry Stembridge, producer, Bill Hughes, Ambassador, Kathleen Warnock and others.

I hugely object to the stigmatisation of gay people when children are discussed, especially when it is led by the forces convicted of abusing and concealing such horrendous crimes and criminals. The ongoing fear to discuss child welfare continues to give plausibility to the very forces whose minority of adherents destroyed so many lives and taught an ignorant society to turn a blind eye. I want to welcome and include children in the audience of this event. We have a wonderful children's musical adaptation of 'The Happy Prince' by a musical family composer Sue Casson and her husband Tom Blackmore, starring their children. This is a must see for young and old alike who love Wilde's fairytales and the magic of good musical theatre.

We are issue driven too in our programming. Theatre is more relevant when it reflects society. We are relevant to society and have discovered that no matter what the country of origin, gay culture does not need translation. We all relate to it, as discrimination and the response to it, has a common resonance in the shared experience of LGBT worldwide. Small town attitudes are unpacked in a series of plays this year. 'American Western a new play by Neal Utterbuck produced by 'Gravity Partners' sees a welcome return from this American group. Utterbuck mixes the American worship of the military with the revelation of the diversity that includes heroes. Kathleen Warnock returns with a play about a man and a woman, childhood friends who meet again. Warnock's commentary on life is relevant to the exploration of our right for broader social commentary in 'That's her Way'. 'Fred' UK, collected real life LGBT experiences in contemporary Birmingham and the West Midlands. Writer Jonathan ap Emrys and Director Robert F Ball worked with a cast to shape 'Lasting Sense of Sudden' exploring contemporary issues like 'coming out' in religion and social acceptance in modern Britain.

As always gay plays have an advanced sense of body confidence. There is a distinct lack of a costume budget in 'Strip Search' by Peter Scott-Priesland, but it is much more than a voyeuristic delight. The raw story of a soldier stripper, played by Damalo Onadeko, cuts to the bone a life serving in Iraq and earning a living as a stripper after the war. 'Unsex'd' is the hilarious back stage story of boy actors playing Shakespeare's female leads, premiering from Canada. Award winning actor, Jay Whitehead stars as the ageing boy lead is faced with training in his pretty young successor (Adam Beauchesne), who now enjoys the favours of Mr Shakespeare. USA's 'Do Not Disturb' theatre company's production of Greg Turner's 'Role Play' which uncovers the world of internet liaisons and fetish roleplays in an adult presentation of a darker side of gay life.

'Theatre North' previously came to Dublin with 'Lord Arthur's Bed' as previously mentioned. Writer, Martin Lawton and director, Andrew Mc Kinnon are known for their cutting edge work in the UK gay theatre scene. Martin has a penchant for fetish exploration with nudity. I challenged him to write something new and told him of the speculation about Georg Frederic Handel's sexuality, as he declared his 'detestation' of women. Rising to the challenge, Lawton penned 'Handel's Cross', an imagining of the life of the composer who premiered his world famous 'Messiah' in Dublin. What I got was a tight, clever, fetish, naked imagining of his life which is bound to appeal and present an historical character even Handel might have found difficult to imagine! Handel's colleagues Liszt, Chopin and Clementini's music is examined by our French company 'Mise En Chant' as they compare the connection between gender identity and physics, in a night of classical music and singing in 'Ego Quantum' at the 'Cobalt Café'. The Netherlands is well represented with the return of writer/performer, Menno Kuijper and his hilarious cabaret 'the Undutchables' playing in 'Pantibar' and percussion group 'Convoi Exceptional' will star once again at our Gala Night and awards in 'The Sugar Club'.

The Irish contribution is very strong with Daniel Maguire, graduating from the children's chorus in my production of 'The King & I' in the Olympia starring Gemma Craven and Stephen Brennan. He is now producing with Stella Bass in 'Do R Die Productions' colourful 'Shout! – the mod musical' starring Stella, award winner Sharon Sexton, Laura Bella Griffin, Laura Kelly and Kelly-Marie Ni Cheallaigh in our newest venue, the Jig theatre on the top floor of the Powerscourt Townhouse Centre. Ranae Von Meding's 'Timador Productions' continues to grow and she presents Audrey Rooney's interpretation of 'Bash'd – Latterday Plays' a successful trilogy by Neil la Bute. A world premiere by Derek Masterson and produced by 'No Tears Productions' deals with an intimate conversation between an older married gay man and a younger man who have a chance meeting in a café one night. 'My Second Self' is a wonderful insight into the common ground that exists, but is often excluded, from the ageist commercial events that separate the generations on the commercial gay scene.

'Company D' productions tackle 'Once In a While the Odd Thing Happens' in this centenary year of the birth of British gay composer Benjamin Britten. Britten had a long relationship with singer Peter Pears and separately with W H Auden and runs for two nights in the James Joyce Centre. Young women also feature prominently with 'BRB' a teenage murder mystery by Kristen Stoddart and directed by Jessie Kirby. She joins Irish stand up comic Breda Larkin, from Ballinasloe, in a full week of Irish lesbian theatre in the James Joyce Centre. Across the street in 'The Cobalt Café' writers Sonya Mulligan's short about a daughter's final conversations with her dying Mother (A Dying Shame) and Vickey Curtis comedy starring Sean Meehan 'Title TBC' make a big contribution to the all 'Irish Theatre Shorts' programme. Joining these two shorts will be 'Bridal Bath' another comedy from the prolific Kenny Moynihan. My own works 'Poets' Cornered' about how Shakespeare, Wilde and Padraig Pearse conveyed same sex love in their poetry is done in limericks and is a total contrast to the Irish, black, gay soccer star short, inspired by and co-written with Peter Smith, called 'Half time' which completes this popular programme.

Award winning writer Alan Flanagan stages an imagined meeting between Eva Gore Booth and Sir Roger casement in another world premiere play. This came about as a result of a discussion Alan and I had in Edinburgh about Dr Sonja Tiernan's excellent biography of Eva Gore Booth published in 2012. 'I Run, I Sing, I Swim, I Dive' is directed by Cillian O Donnachdha, who also won the best writer award as did Flanagan. This exciting collaboration brings the best of young Irish theatre practitioners together with the key stories of our lesbian and gay heroes of the past. This strong Irish contingent is a big endorsement of the impact of the decade of gay theatre on Irish writers and production companies and is a fitting celebration in this anniversary year.

A musical play that originated in Argentina is being produced by 'Tilt Entertainment' from the US about a son who formed a relationship with his Dad through their joint devotion to Judy Garland. As Garland's career retracted so did the relationship. 'Judy, A Tribute', directed by Alejandra Ullua with original choreography by Gustavo Wons, this live music performance stars Domonique Evans, Tony Ponella, Christopher Poeshi, Ty Baumman, Joseph Spitale, Corey Thompson and Andy Collopy is at the piano.

Glamour and stars also feature in the behind the drag, solo premiere play by Australian 'Drags Aloud' star Kris del Vayse. I have often encouraged drag artists to find their voice. Kris is returning in the world premiere of her own solo show telling life as gay performer and drag artist in Australia and beyond, over the decades in 'Pantibar'. South Africa is well represented again in the drama element of the programme, despite our disappointment with the absence of 'Artscape' in our anniversary year. 'The Rust Co-operative's production of 'The View' has been nominated for a string of national drama awards. Written by Philip Rademeyer, with Ella Gabriel and Roelof Storm in the leading roles, this prison based drama presents a series of video conversations between the prisoner and the people from his past and is highly anticipated as being a dramatic highlight in a quality programme of theatre.

Short Plays are very popular. Bash'd is a trilogy and the Irish Shorts will sell well. 'Casa 010' wrote to us from the west coast of the USA and this energetic group have fundraised so hard to bring a big team to Dublin in 'Brown and Out' – six short comedy plays about being LGBT and Latino, produced by Miguel Garcia and directed by Martin Morales in another new work for the Festival. It will be interesting to include this distinct LGBT culture in the programme and to find an audience for this collection of six short plays.

In this diverse and broad based tenth year programme, we look at gay and lesbians, bisexuals, footballers, parents, sons and daughters, drag queens, fetish, friendship, ageism, women, prisoners, latinos, teenagers, comedians, musicians, poets, physicists, composers and straight people in 35 plays from Ireland, UK, USA, Canada, South Africa, Australia, the Netherlands, France and Argentina.

Our performances include 14 short plays, in three separate programmes making up 36 new plays and readings in the 2013 programme spread over two weeks, with a new programme each week. Despite rising costs we maintain our ticket prices at a very accessible ten euros for matinees rising to top price evening shows at fifteen euros. The enthusiasm of our volunteer crew who will each 'adopt' a play and promote it, is a great reassurance and welcome for companies who invest so much in making the journey to Dublin again or for the first time. We wish them well and early box office indications are showing we may yet survive to make it into our second decade.

If you are not careful newspapers will have you hating the people who are being oppressed and loving the people doing the oppressing

Malcolm X

The International Dublin Gay Theatre Festival has a theatre legitimacy, after ten years. We have had many a talented artists onstage and back stage. We have inspired, facilitated and helped new writers on their journey. Artists like Terrence Mc Nally, Emma Donoghue, Mark O Halloran and Adrian Dunbar have lent their active support. Tony award winner Brent Carver travelled to see a play from the US, so did Juliet Mills and Maxwell Caulfield, stage, screen and television actors, theatre tourists and many more distinguished practitioners have all attended.

We have had our citizenship over the years, acknowledged by the President, members of parliament, Senators including our first patron David Norris and Katherine Zappone who launched the event last year. Successive Lord Mayors, Paddy Bourke, Catherine Byrne, Eibhlin Byrne, Emer Costello, Andrew Montague and Government Ministers, Eamon Ryan and the Arts Minister Jimmy Deenihan TD, have all graced our launches and programmes. We are greatly honoured by all our audience support as our online ticket sales pass the quarter of a million euro mark this year.

We are delighted to be in The Hugh Lane Gallery, the James Joyce Centre, Oscar Wilde's alma mater in Players Theatre at Trinity College, the ever supportive Teacher's Club and Cobalt Café – with us from day one, the Sugar Club, the Front Lounge, Pantibar, the Exchange, Outhouse and the new Jig theatre in the Top floor of the Powerscourt Townhouse Centre. We look forward to filling even bigger venues in the future, fulfilling our policy of theatre, in the city, for all the citizens.

We are grateful for the support of many of these venues and indeed from the start, Dublin City Council Arts Section, Failte Ireland and later the Arts Council and our media partners, and commercial sponsors welcoming the return of drinks sponsors this year who have been a joy to work with, 'Bombay Sapphire', 'Darling Cocktails', 'Barefoot Wines', gay commercial premises, Harold's Cross Health Centre' and our accommodation hosts, the ever welcoming Arlington Hotels.

This recession has not mirrored the previous ones. There has been no big jump in volunteering as many of our skilled and valued volunteers have emigrated since the last Festival. We are still entirely dependent and grateful for those who volunteer to help us and are delighted at the skillsets and diversity of those who do so. We have volunteers travelling to the Festival from abroad from Malin our first intern from the Netherlands in 2009, to Callum Cheatle and Paul Moss from the UK and now Martin Pol Koob from Scotland and Richie Gary Samuel and Michael Anderson from the USA, to lend a much needed hand this year again. But they are young and on the move and it is great to see them return each year, even more accomplished in theatre!

The recession is hitting and we acknowledge in partnership, the huge investment the individual companies are making to come to Dublin. The plays need an audience. We have grown our audience base and have taken initiatives to encourage and facilitate arts tourism.

Each year we have a great technical team who help stage all these visiting plays with skill and creativity led over the years by Eddie Devoy, Alan Jacob, Derek Cosgrave, Chris Nugent, Mark Donoghue, Naoise O Reilly, Siobhan Killen and Ciara Nolan and their indefatigable crews. Each year the Board of seven members cedes the organisation of the event to an executive committee. We have benefitted from so many people who help with the organisation at the Executive level, including this year Gareth Hurley, Dermot Devoy, Louise Hales, Emma Weafer, Stephen Mc Connell, Ciara Nolan, Siobhan Killen, Annick Thijs, Dominic Brezski, Joe Duggan, John James Hickey, Joe Kearney and Jen Butler. Their innovation in fundraising, pr, volunteer co-ordination, marketing, front of house, distribution etc is complimented by professionals with specific talents like our generous designer Gerry Cleary. These talented people, past and present, taken a concept and turned it into a reality and sustained new theatre activity in the city for the past decade. They are the reason we have reached year ten!

I have had the honour of leading these teams and the artistic direction of the event I founded for the past ten years. I am exhausted, as we have brought this event thus far, with literally no resources at all. We have little assistance in meeting the demands and expectations of audience and companies when they see a Festival of this calibre and scale. It runs from my front room and I have been sitting in a chair since mid-November to today, six hours a night often seven days a week. We have 9 more weeks of intense work ahead. Even writing the book has been a solo effort, hence the absence of an essential good editor! Volunteer Vinny Ryder, like so many others, made the publication possible by responding at a volunteers meeting to my call for a designer. What an epic task in a tight time-table and how grateful I am for his work. It is important to record these ten years.

If the Festival, which is a roaring success, is to continue on, we need help and that is why this year, as announced last year, it is my final term as Chairman of the Organising Committee. There have been many that could take over, but most have emigrated, the others see the amount of work involved and have infinitely more sense than myself to take it on. If the Festival can find a new organiser or manager, or financial support to fund this, then I will remain as the Artistic Director in the short term. If not, despite the demand and its success, this could be the last one, which I would regret greatly.

This has always been a team effort led by my co-director Gareth Hurley, the Executive, Board and volunteer corps, but it needs a new manager. It is not and can not be a 'one man band'. I appeal to someone or to some resource to help us to carry the torch into a new decade of creativity and impact, that will keep our home in Dublin at the centre of this innovative and growing artform worldwide. My belief in the Festival remains undaunted and is constantly renewed when I encounter all who make such a contribution onstage and off each year. Thank you!

When trying to see why this was still important, I found myself in correspondence just this week with a very successful gay artist. An artist of high achievement, who has publically referred to their same sex partner and child on television, can change hearts and minds and recreate the new norms of a modern Ireland. I am going to be vague on detail because I don't want to breach a confidence, but I found these two emails less extraordinary, but reoccurring. They were prompted by an invitation to take part in the planned free event, an audience with key lgbt artists hosted by Michael Scott. I think this response to our invitation sums up the ongoing challenge we face internally and externally:

"I had thought I was being asked to talk about my production and women in the

Arts. I had not realised it was to discuss my sexuality and how that affects my work (which it doesn't in any way at all).

I'm afraid I'm the wrong person for your talk. I do not discuss my sexuality with anyone, in private or in public. As far as I am concerned all humans are equal, men ,women, black, white,gay, straight, bi, trans etc etc. Therefore, it goes against all my beliefs to discuss anything about sexuality and how it should in anyway affect the workplace or views of same. I am vehemently anti segregation, always have been and am very vocal about this. It angers me that in this day and age there is even reference to one's sexuality".

To which I replied: I have dedicated the past ten years counteracting the negative stereotype in a number of ways. Firstly asserting the right to citizenship of all people in the arts, secondly, if labels are being put on us, then at least we should define our own identity. We should then seize any opportunity to define the diversity of ourselves, through creating new opportunities for new voices in the arts and to recognise the artists from a time when that was impossible.

Hence we look to role models not only to encourage but to inform. The idea was to have three sessions on identity in the arts - no person has one identity and indeed our sexuality only completes our identity. I coined the phrase early on challenging society's attitude ' it is not acceptable to laud the art and loath the artist' - as art is based on truth, the artist is complete when there are no barriers imposed, accepted or defined by others. IDGTF rejects the negative stereotype and, at a cost, asserts our right to participate.

I want to have a discussion on identity in the arts. People who have had their contribution valued regardless of perceived labels. We need role models who will help others who accept homophobia as an inhibitor of their own truth, to find that truth and challenge the controlling norms. For example few women, never mind gay women, succeed in media? Many gay people that do, exploit the stereotype – 'Sean' in Coronation Street for example. However, just because we reject this, doesn't mean others do - in fact we are done down, not only by 'our own', but by those who insist on us occupying an artistic ghetto.

What would be the impact of Fox Channel wanting to fund your production in the US for example and then to discover it was by an artist whose identity is complete? Would they fund it - why should it be a consideration at all - it is, because of their right wing agenda?

There are lots of topics and identity issues to be explored that cross over into many other areas. Why don't women write plays is a question Emma Donoghue and I have discussed, especially as we have so many gifted women novelists. Where are their stories in theatre and on the screen ? How are women constructed on stage and screen and to whose norms? Why do so many talented women get less work as they age, and yet men survive?

Is the gay always 'typecast'. What was novel about 'Brokeback Mountain' - two straight actors played the love scenes almost violently...proving what? Why did they sit apart and not look at each other on the Oprah show promoting the film? Has this changed - is it changing - are we in a position to change that so that theatre will recognise one's talents, above society's imposed (negative) definition of sexuality? This is just the tip of the iceberg. You've already survived reading the many other issues in earlier chapters. There was no reply.

How can we encourage everyone to tell their own stories today and their truth in theatre as an artform? We create new voices, new performance opportunities and new audience - we are 40% the size of the vibrant Dublin Fringe and literally get no funding. As one whose time has been consumed, at a serious cost to my own creativity, this has annoyed me. I usually do not hide my annoyance or disappointment, especially when those who could support us, instead spend time criticising us for the failures that could easily be addressed, if we had equal access to the resources they control – and they know that. Like an over protective parent, I have taken on the controversies so that the volunteers can enjoy the giving of their time and talents, to the benefit of others and hopefully their own future careers in theatre and advocacy.

Sure we are angry when limits are imposed on us, or our creativity, by a few people's warped notion of sexuality or worse still, their right to own and define the arts. But I refuse not to discuss that or not to provide an opportunity for those whose talents are admired and respected, to have an opportunity to encourage others, young and old, to reject the stereotype, to build new audiences and to assert artistic citizenship. That's what the plays, free events and discussion sessions are about – an artistic debate which liberates the artist to reveal their art for the enlightenment of all.

As a programmer of gay theatre – a rather unique job globally, I am not that interested in 'coming out' stories. I challenge the writer to construct a narrative about what have you come out for - what is your contribution to society - this is much more important? I am intolerant of never ending angst and victimhood which has its origins in the imposed exclusion and isolation of the love of previous LGBT generations. We must make these different times different or the struggle for equality will be worthless. True, things happen to vulnerable people and have cruelly done so in the past and that is relevant to our artistic programming. I am interested in what you have to say in a freer society, when as an adult you can influence and control your destiny, by rejecting constructed shame and unequal status of your citizenship, present or historical. There is a distinct gay culture and lifestyle because of the absence of any societal structure to support our relationships – this should be told 'warts and all' and not in any sentimental way. I am advocating active citizenship through the arts and equality of opportunity, where gay culture will be recognised and will be listened to, on its artistic merit.

Many good people will exclude themselves from our Festival programme because the word gay is in it. I will not imply the word and will state it even at that unfair cost. That's the challenge - to broaden the imposed definition by creating the opportunity for people to have access to our artform in the mainstream. I am delighted our audience is about 50/50 straight and gay. I am delighted men go to the 'women's plays'. I am pleased to expand in a meaningful way that short word 'gay' to tell the stories of men, lesbians, bisexuals and straight people in a new truth that theatre often had censored in the past. I am pleased to link the common causes of discrimination of minorities in the event including transgender people and people of different ability, race, religion, age and status in the stories that complete the cultural map of any pluralist society. I am glad to give a space to the voices of the young and to create an opportunity for them to hear the stories of those who have charted this path to freedom and a better life opportunity, cruelly denied to many previous generations of LGBT people throughout the world. I am in a humble awe of the generosity of those who share even one of those ambitions or see their own ambitions in the work and impact of this modest event.

So there is a job to be done, there are new voices to be heard, new stories to be told, new audiences to entertain and inform, new assertion of our citizenship and our complete identity in theatre as an artform. IDGTF has a great programme and a great team. Some companies are investing in our work for the first time and travelling thousands of miles, others are returning from long distances as this Festival is their one validation in a year of creativity. It is open to everyone – it is not an event for one community, unless you come from the diverse, inclusive community that is this city and more so, this country!

We, as a country have benefitted greatly from the heroism of Casement and Pearse and the art of Bacon, Edwards, Mac Liammoir, Wilde, Gore Booth and Handel, after they passed. That will not happen again. We now live in a time where the artist can be who he or she is, and tell their truth through theatre and the arts, which can acknowledge and value their contribution, complete identity and citizenship. The times have changed and the more we pursue our intercultural dialogue through gay theatre as an artform, the more we liberate art and the diverse society in which it is presented and appreciated. It is a challenge for all LGBT artists to meet.

I have been very proud to present and commend the work of our Irish and International artists in the programmes of the International Dublin Gay Theatre Festival beginning each May Bank Holiday for a fortnight. I sincerely thank all who have contributed so much to this worthy endeavour, including you the readers. I hope the Festival, which has carved an important and valid niche for itself and others, will continue to evolve and tells its truth in the years ahead in Dublin, Ireland. My wish is that my own role will now diminish as others step up to invigorate this event with new ideas and voices, to bring it through its second decade.

To those who support us, and especially from the start ten years ago – please celebrate the fruits of your own vision and contribution this year. To those who would wish us well, but exclude themselves from the programme – join us. To those who don't, open your eyes, life is a lot more colourful and meaningful, than often constructed by the perceived majority or those with the loudest voice. We have always urged people 'not to attend just because it is gay theatre, but to attend because it is good theatre'. It is – it is Irish and International. It is important. Stories as told in these new plays do complete the cultural map of every country, but modern Ireland is a country, unlike so many others, where they will be heard.

The gift was ours to borrow.
It's as if we always knew,
And I won't forget, what I did for love

Lyric from 'A Chorus Line'

Please only think well of those names in this book, as my agreement is not
the prerequisite to be confident they were all doing their best